ASSER International Sports Law Series

For further volumes:
http://www.springer.com/series/8858

Alexander Wild
Editor

CAS and Football: Landmark Cases

T·M·C·ASSER PRESS

Springer

Alexander Wild
Stuttgart
e-mail: wild@falkenstein-partner.de

ISSN 1874-6926
ISBN 978-90-6704-807-1 e-ISBN 978-90-6704-808-8
DOI 10.1007/978-90-6704-808-8

Library of Congress Control Number: 2011941756

Published by T.M.C. ASSER PRESS, The Hague, The Netherlands www.asserpress.nl
Produced and distributed for T.M.C. ASSER PRESS by Springer-Verlag Berlin Heidelberg

Cover design: eStudio Calamar, Berlin/Figueres

Printed on acid-free paper

Springer is part of Springer Science+Business Media (www.springer.com)

Series Information

Books in the *ASSER International Sports Law Series* chart and comment upon the legal and policy developments in European and international sports law. The books contain materials on interstate organisations and the international sports governing bodies, and will serve as comprehensive and relevant reference tools for all those involved in the area on a professional basis.

The Series is developed, edited and published by the ASSER International Sports Law Centre in The Hague. The Centre's mission is to provide a centre of excellence in particular by providing high-quality research, services and products to the sporting world at large (sports ministries, international—intergovernmental—organisations, sports associations and federations, the professional sports industry, etc.) on both a national and an international basis. The Centre is the co-founder and coordinator of the Hague International Sports Law Academy (HISLA), the purpose of which is the organisation of academic conferences and workshops of international excellence which are held in various parts of the world. Apart from the Series, the Centre edits and publishes *The International Sports Law Journal.*

Series Editors

Dr. Robert C. R. Siekmann, Director Asser International Sports Centre
e-mail: r.siekmann@asser.nl

Dr. Janwillem Soek
e-mail: j.soek@asser.nl

M. A. van der Harst LL.M.
e-mail: m.van.der.harst@asser.nl

Editorial Office

ASSER International Sports Law Centre
T.M.C. Asser Instituut
P.O. Box 30461
2500 GL The Hague
The Netherlands
www.sportslaw.nl

Foreword

I am very pleased and honoured to write the foreword to this book.

As Professor Ian Blackshaw, a member of and expert on the Court of Arbitration for Sport (CAS), points out in his Introductory Remarks to this book, the CAS, which is in its 27th year of operations, is establishing itself in the sporting world, as its founders intended to be, as the 'Supreme Court of World Sport'.

Claimed to be the world's favourite sport—and it must be added the world's most lucrative one—football, not surprisingly, is providing the CAS with a lot of cases, especially disputes on international transfers of football players, since football's world governing body, FIFA, joined the CAS in 2002.

It is most fitting, therefore, that a collection of landmark cases has now been made and commented upon by sports law experts in this book, which is both timely and most welcome. I would warmly congratulate the editor, Alexander Wild, and also the publisher, Philip van Tongeren of the T.M.C. Asser Press, on this worthy initiative.

The book is the latest in the Asser International Sports Law Series, of which the editors are Prof. Dr. Robert Siekmann and Dr. Janwillem Soek, and which is a publication of the ASSER International Sports Law Centre, based in the 'legal capital of the world', The Hague, The Netherlands. It is also the first book on this important subject.

As already indicated, this book will fill a gap in the international sports law literature and provide an invaluable resource for all those involved in the legal aspects of the 'beautiful game', particularly extra-judicial dispute resolution, including administrators, regulators, football agents and their legal advisers. The book will also prove very useful to students and researchers in this particular field.

It will certainly find a place on my book shelf and, once again, I would welcome and commend this book to all those concerned with this developing and significant aspect of the activities of the CAS and its continuing—and, I would add, very valuable—contribution to a so-called *Lex Sportiva* in sport in general and in football in particular.

New Delhi, Summer 2011 Amaresh Kumar*

* Advocate, Supreme Court of India, Secretary General, Asian Council of Arbitration for Sport, Honorary Visiting Professor of International Sports Law, ASSER international Sports Law Centre, The Hague, The Netherlands.

Contents

Chapter 1
Ancient Chinese Football

Bram Cohen

The very first sources that refer to kicking against a ball come to us from the Chinese. At the time of the Western Han dynasty (206 BC–24 AD), Liu Xiang wrote his *Analects of Tactics*, in which he described *zu-gu,*[1] the football of the Chinese people. For a long time, it was thought that *zu-gu* (*zu* means 'shooting with the foot'; *gu* means 'ball') was played from around 500 BC on. But archaeologists have not remained idle. Numerous historical writings, inscriptions and remains have been found from the period predating the fifth century BC. These sources show that the Chinese were playing football nearly 5000 years ago.

A part of these writings and inscriptions contain legends that attribute the introduction of football to the mythical Yellow Emperor Huang Di, who ruled around 2690 BC. One legend describes how the Yellow Emperor cut off his own head and ordered his subjects to play football with it. Huang Di introduced his subjects to writing, music, bows and arrows, carts, boats, earthenware and the breeding of silkworms. We might as well add football to that list of accomplishments. In the city of Xi'an in the northwest of China, one can find stone balls, as works of art and as burial artefacts, that are just under 3000 years old.

We know next to nothing about the rules of the very earliest form of Chinese football. What we do know is that football had a certain significance as a cult activity.

During the Zhou Dynasty, which came to power in the eleventh century BC and lasted roughly 700 years, it was no longer just the notables who played football,

---

Bram Cohen—*De Geschiedenis van het Voetbal* [The History of Football], Amsterdam 1996, pp. 5–8.

---

[1] The transcription from the Chinese is arbitrary. *Tsuh-kuh* (the usual English transcription) is transcribed here as *zu-gu*.

B. Cohen (✉)
Amsterdam, The Netherlands

A. Wild (ed.), *CAS and Football: Landmark Cases*,
ASSER International Sports Law Series, DOI: 10.1007/978-90-6704-808-8_1,

唐人蹴鞠图

but also the common people. They must have played the game with considerable fanaticism, because the rules were tightened up to prevent it from degenerating. The players used a ball made from eight pieces of leather that were sewn together. The ball itself was filled with feathers and hair. The air-filled ball was invented later on.

It definitely was not waywardness that inspired the Chinese to play football: during the Han Dynasty (206 BC–220 AD) soldiers were ordered to play football to improve their physical strength and enhance their discipline and military enthusiasm. Such measures were taken in response to the incursions by northern peoples.

The same period saw the development of a football idiom, as well as books written about *zu-gu*. *Jucheng* meant pitch, *jushi* goal, *li* or *chang* the rules of the game, *zhang* the referee and *ping* the linesman. These are all concepts that are familiar enough today, but which we have only known since the end of the nineteenth century. In *Yantielun*, the historian Huan Kuan describes how football was played by soldiers in the streets. The soldiers probably contributed to football's popularity among the common people.

These writings about *zu-gu* show that the rules of the game were brought in line with the Chinese conception of the cosmos. According to this conception, the universe was round and the earth quadrangular, and so the ball needed to be round and the pitch quadrangular. Twelve months meant twelve goals, and as the year had 24 solar signs, each team numbered twelve players.

The Chinese could not get enough of it. Football flourished until the end of the sixth century AD. During the Han Dynasty, the Chinese still regularly played football in honour of the Emperor's birthday. *Zu-gu* became a game—a form of entertainment that many people participated in—but at the same time it was subject to growing athletic professionalism. Winning teams received a silver goblet and valuable fabrics, while the losers could count on *schadenfreude* and sometimes even a good hiding.

But not everyone was happy about football. Officials condemned the game and had nothing good to say about the highly paid (!) players, who in their opinion were nothing more than hooligans. We might as well leave aside whether this was the first time people expressed concern about the loss of a civilised preserve of gentlemen amateurs.

During the Tang Dynasty (618–907 AD), improvements were made to both the ball and the players' gear. *Zu-gu* underwent further popularisation and professionalisation. People did not always stick to the team of twelve any more, occasionally playing with sixteen men to a team.

In the following 300 years, *zu-gu* was professionalised and regulated to such an extent that according to some historians, this was the cause of football's declining popularity among the Chinese around 1200. Teams that could consist of as many as 24 or even 32 players gave demonstrations at the Imperial court. These court players also mingled with the people and showed them their skills. In this period, the air-filled ball was perfected by the introduction of a primitive ball pump.

Incidentally, the players were not all men. The Mongols defeated the Chinese and founded the Yuan Dynasty in 1279, which lasted for close to a century. The Mongol Emperor Shizu encouraged his subjects to play *zu-gu*, and not just the men—women could join in on the game as well!

This highly developed, regulated game gradually disappeared from the scene after the Mongolian defeat and the Chinese return to power. Fewer and fewer people still played the game. The rulers at the time of the Qing Dynasty (1644–1911) might have been able to breathe new life into *zu-gu*, but they preferred a kind of football that was played on ice and that did not involve goals.

The Chinese sometimes had the curious habit of simply quitting with something. They were on the verge of conquering the world when, plagued by internal troubles, they suddenly turned around and went home. The Portuguese, with whom they had come face to face, were left behind in a state of bewilderment. This is more or less what happened to *zu-gu* also. Around 1500, very few Chinese were still playing football. The ball had lost its appeal. It was far more common—later in England and France—for football to be temporarily played less due to political and social factors, only to return in all its splendour later on.

Postscript

There were three kinds of zu-gu (or *CuJu)* in Chinese history: the direct game, the indirect game and the free game. The *direct game* was widely accepted in the Han dynasty. There were 12 players in each team, and there were two goals in the field. They played the game like a battle. The team which scored most was the winner. This kind of play was used for military practice, for example for the training of soldiers. The *indirect game* was popular in the Tang and the Song dynasties. There was only one goal in the field. The players kicked a leather ball through a hole in a piece of silk cloth which was strung between two 30 feet long poles. A remarkable feature is that while they played, the ball should not drop on the ground. The team that scored the most was the winner. This kind of play was usually for diplomatic performances and the entertainment of the royalty. The *free game* was the most popular one and had the longest history. There was no goal in the field, the players kicked the ball freely, and the game's most important factor was the skill of the players; the most attractive one was the winner.

The *direct game* is similar to the basics of modern association football; the *indirect game* is somewhat like the modern training form of 'foot volley' (tennis football—keeping the ball in the air. The *free game* in fact is a free-style and jury type of football, purely showing one's technical skills.

[R.S.]

Chapter 2
Introductory Remarks

Ian Blackshaw

Contents

The Court of Arbitration for Sport, based in Lausanne, Switzerland, was the 'brain child' of the late and long-time former President of the International Olympic Committee, Juan Antonio Samaranch. It was established in 1983 with the object of settling sports disputes "within the family of sport" and began to function in 1984.[1] Since then, the CAS has developed into, what Samaranch—always a visionary—had in mind, a 'Supreme Court of World Sport'.

Over the years, sport has become a global business accounting for more than 3% of world trade; and, in the European Union, sport now represents more than 2% of the combined GNP of the twenty-seven Member States. It is not surprising, therefore, with such a rise in the value of the sports industry and related sports rights, not least sports broadcasting rights,[2] that there has been a phenomenal rise in

Ian Blackshaw—MA LLM Solicitor of the Supreme Court of England; International Sports Lawyer; Honorary Fellow of the TMC Asser International Sports Law Centre. Visiting Professor at several Universities, including Anglia Ruskin and a Founder Member of their International Law Unit; and Member of the CAS.

[1] On the organisation and activities of the CAS, see Blackshaw 2006.
[2] See Blackshaw 2009a.

I. Blackshaw (✉)
The Hague, The Netherlands
e-mail: ian.blackshaw@orange.fr

A. Wild (ed.), *CAS and Football: Landmark Cases*,
ASSER International Sports Law Series, DOI: 10.1007/978-90-6704-808-8_2,

the number of sports disputes. There is often more to play for off than on the field of play! In line with Samaranch's aims, many of these disputes have been submitted to the CAS for settlement—either by arbitration or by mediation[3] under the corresponding express provisions in sports contracts of various kinds, including commercial ones, or regulations of international sports governing bodies or on an *ad hoc*—case by case—basis.[4] The CAS also offers non-binding Advisory Opinions under its Consultation Procedure.[5] A useful procedure in appropriate cases.

Also, it may be noted, *en passant*, that a party may apply to the CAS for the interpretation of an Award issued in an Ordinary or Appeals Arbitration:

> whenever the operative part of the award is unclear, incomplete, ambiguous or whenever its components are self-contradictory or contrary to the reasons, or whenever the award contains clerical mistakes or a miscalculation of figures.[6]

The Panel must rule on the request for interpretation within one month.[7] Again, this is a useful procedure in practice.

Furthermore, during the Summer and Winter Games, the CAS operates a so-called Ad Hoc Division (AHD) to deal expeditiously and without charging any fee with disputes arising during the Games. The CAS AHD has been continuously in operation since the Centennial Summer Games held in Atlanta in 1996 and has worked well, particularly as many sports disputes are time sensitive and subject to tight sporting deadlines.

The CAS is governed by the International Council of Arbitration for Sport (ICAS), whose main function is to safeguard the independence of the CAS and the rights of the parties appearing before it (see below). The ICAS is also responsible for the CAS finances. For a complete list of the functions of ICAS, see Article S56 of the CAS Code of Sports-related Arbitration 2010.

Although CAS arbitrators are not generally obliged to follow earlier decisions and obey the sacred Common Law principle of *stare decisis* (binding legal precedent),[8] in the interests of comity and legal certainty, they usually do so.[9] As a result of this practice, a very useful body of sports law—a so-called *Lex Sportiva*—is steadily being built up.[10]

---

[3] At the time of writing (August 2010), there are some 300 CAS Arbitrators and some 65 CAS Mediators.

[4] On Alternative Dispute Resolution of Sports Disputes in general and, the settlement of them, in particular, through the CAS, see Blackshaw 2009b.

[5] See, for example, Advisory Opinion CAS 2003/C/445, Canadian Olympic Committee, 24 April, 2003, rendered by Ian S. Blackshaw.

[6] Article R63, para 1, CAS Code of Sports-related Arbitration, 2010.

[7] Ibid., para 2.

[8] See *UCI v J.* 7NCB, CAS 97/176 Award of 28 August 1998, 14.

[9] As an exception, which proves the rule, see Dabscheck 2010.

[10] See further on this, Nafziger 2001, 57; Nafziger 2004, 48–61, and Blackshaw 2006. See also Blackshaw 2002.

However, one of the difficulties faced by the CAS in its desire to develop a *Lex Sportiva* and provide some degree of legal certainty and consistency stems from the fact that, generally speaking, CAS proceedings and decisions are a matter of private law and confidential to the parties. CAS by its nature is a private arbitral body. And therein lies the paradox—the need, on the one hand, of the sporting community 'not to wash its dirty sports linen in public'; and, on the other hand, the need of a wider public to know how cases are being decided, including details of the evidence adduced to the CAS, particularly for future guidance and reference. As regards the confidentiality of CAS Ordinary Proceedings, Article R43 of the CAS Code of Sports-related Arbitration 2010 provides as follows:

> Proceedings under these procedural rules are confidential. The parties, the arbitrators and the CAS undertake not to disclose to any third party any facts or other information relating to the dispute or the proceedings.

However, the last sentence of this Article provides the following exceptions to the general rule of confidentiality:

> Awards shall not be made public unless all parties agree or the Division President so decides.

However, as regards the confidentiality of CAS Appeal Proceedings, Article R59 of the CAS Code of Sports-related Arbitration 2010 provides in para 5 as follows:

> The award, a summary and/or a press release setting forth the results of the proceedings shall be made public by the CAS, unless both parties agree that they should remain confidential.

Thus, in CAS Appeal cases, the emphasis is more on publication of the Awards and less on confidentiality, unless both parties agree otherwise, and, therefore, in this particular respect, this provision goes some way towards encouraging the development of a *Lex Sportiva* (see below).

In practice, more CAS Awards are being published,[11] especially on the CAS official web site.[12] In fact, the CAS itself is interested in developing a *Lex Sportiva* as the following extract at page xxx from Volume II of the CAS Digest of Awards makes clear:

> The 'Digest of CAS Awards 1986-1998' recorded the emergence of a lex sportiva through the judicial decisions of the CAS. It is true that one of the interests of this court is to develop a jurisprudence that can be used as a reference by all the actors of world sport, thereby encouraging the harmonisation of the judicial rules and principles applied within the sports world.

Furthermore, as the work of the CAS continues to expand and becomes more widely known and discussed, especially in press reports and articles, the need for

[11] The Secretary General of CAS, Matthieu Reeb, has edited and published three Digests of several CAS cases covering the periods 1986–1998; 1998–2000; and 2001–2003. A further volume in the series is expected shortly.

[12] 'www.tas-cas.org'. The CAS official web site under the title 'Jursiprudence' contains a new section, entitled, 'Archive', which, at the time of writing (August 2010) is still under development. Once this section is fully 'live', it will be interesting to see how comprehensive it is and what it covers.

such publicity also increases, especially in football cases where substantial sums of money are often in contention. In fact, a 'public interest' argument comes into play and needs to be satisfied in appropriate cases.[13] But, in this context, it should be remembered that what interests the public is not necessarily the same as what is in the public interest![14]

The CAS operates generally under Swiss Law having its 'seat' in Lausanne.[15] Awards of CAS can be legally challenged before the Swiss Federal Supreme Court, which is also based in Lausanne. However, the grounds for appeal are limited under the provisions of Article 190(2) of the Swiss Federal Code on the Private International Law of 18 December, 1987.[16] In practice, the right to a fair hearing (ground (d)) is perhaps the most important ground and the CAS bends over backwards in each case to ensure that the parties are given every opportunity of presenting their case and being heard and also receiving a fair hearing.[17] In practice, there have been few legal challenges to CAS awards. In the latest fundamental challenge in 2003 concerning the independence of the CAS, in view of its association with and partial funding by the IOC, the Swiss Federal Supreme Court held that the CAS offered all the guarantees of independence and impartiality to be regarded as a real court of arbitration, even where the IOC — as in that particular case — was a party in its proceedings.[18] The Court further included the following ringing endorsement of the CAS in its Judgment:

> The CAS is growing rapidly and continuing to develop. An important new step in its development was recently taken at the World Conference on Doping in Sport, held

---

[13] See, for example, the Decision in the *Gaia Bassani* case (CAS 2003/O/468), where the author of these Introductory Remarks was the Sole Arbitrator and, because of the particular circumstances of the case and the need for a wider audience to know about the case and its outcome, directed that the Decision be published.

[14] On this point, see the discussion in the English case of *Lion Laboratories Ltd v Evans* [1984] 2 All ER 417.

[15] See the Australian case of *Angela Raguz v. Rebecca Sullivan & Ors*, 2000 NSECA 240; CAS Digest II, p. 783—CAS Awards Sydney 2000, p. 185, in which case it was held that the CAS Award could only be challenged in a Swiss Court under Swiss Law.

[16] The grounds are as follows:

(a) if a sole arbitrator was designated irregularly or the arbitral tribunal was constituted irregularly;
(b) if the arbitral tribunal erroneously held that it had or did not have jurisdiction;
(c) if the arbitral tribunal ruled on matters beyond the claims submitted to it or failed to rule on one of the claims;
(d) if the equality of the parties or their right to be heard in an adversarial proceeding was not respected; and
(e) if the award is incompatible with Swiss public policy.

[17] See the Judgment of 22 March, 2007 in the *ATP Tour Appeal* case brought before the Swiss Federal Supreme Court against a CAS Award of 23 May, 2006 - Reference 4P 172/2006.

[18] See Judgment of 27 May, 2003 of the First Civil Division of the Swiss Federal Tribunal in the case of *A. & B. v International Olympic Committee and International Ski Federation* (4P.267/2002; 4P.268/2002; 4P.269/2002; and 4P.270/2002).

> in Copenhagen at the beginning of March 2003. This Conference adopted the World Anti-Doping Code as the basis for the worldwide fight against doping in sport. Many States, including China Russia and the United States of America, have adopted the Copenhagen Declaration on Anti-Doping in Sport. Under the terms of Art. 13.2.1 of the new Code, the CAS is the appeals body for all doping-related disputes related to international sports events or international-level athletes. This is a tangible sign that States and all parties concerned by the fight against doping have confidence in the CAS. It is hard to imagine that they would have felt able to endorse the judicial powers of the CAS so resoundingly if they had thought it was controlled by the IOC. This new mark of recognition from the international community shows that the CAS is meeting a real need. There appears to be no viable alternative to this institution, which can resolve sports-related disputes quickly and inexpensively. Having gradually built up the trust of the sporting world, this institution which is now widely recognised remains one of the principal mainstays of organised sport.[19]

Awards made by the CAS, like other international arbitral awards, are legally enforceable generally in accordance with the rules of Private International Law, and also specifically under the provisions of the New York Convention on the Recognition and Enforcement of Foreign Arbitral Awards of 10 June, 1958.[20] The CAS is also recognised under the European Convention on the Recognition of the Legal Personality of International Non-Governmental Organizations.

Since FIFA, the world governing body of football, agreed to use the CAS as a final court of appeal for football disputes in 2002, the workload of the CAS has increased dramatically year after year and continues to do so, not least in relation to international transfer disputes coming up for review de novo (a complete review of the facts and the law) by the CAS from the FIFA Dispute Resolution Chamber (DRC).[21] Such appeals must be filed with the CAS within 21 days of the date of notification of the DRC Decision. Indeed, the CAS has established a list of arbitrators who are specialised in football matters.[22]

In this book—the first of its kind—the Editor, Alexander Wild, has assembled a number of high profile football CAS cases with commentaries on them—provided, in many of these cases, by the lawyers involved in them. As such, this not only lends insight into the actual cases themselves, but also adds to the authoritativeness of this work.

One final point, which is particularly important in relation to football disputes, the CAS has wide powers to order so-called 'provisional or conservatory measures' including suspension of sporting sanctions pending the outcome of an appeal to the CAS in which those measures are legally challenged by the party affected by them.[23] This happened on 6 November 2009 in the appeal by Chelsea Football Club to CAS over a transfer ban imposed on the Club by the FIFA DRC

---

19 Ibid. at para 3.3.3.3.

20 The majority of countries around the world have ratified this Convention; in the case of enforcing CAS Awards in those countries that have not ratified the Convention, the legal process of '*exequatur*' must be followed, which involves a full review of the case by the judicial authorities of the country concerned.

21 See De Weger (2009).

22 See www.tas-cas.org and follow the links to CAS Arbitrators.

23 Article R.37, CAS Code of Sports-related Arbitration, 2010.

in the *Gael Kakuta* case, in which the CAS lifted the ban pending the outcome of the appeal. In fact, the dispute was subsequently settled amicably by an agreed payment of compensation by Chelsea to Kakuta's former football club Lens FC and the CAS 'ratified' the settlement agreement reached by the parties.[24]

Football is not only the world's favourite sport but also its most lucrative one and, as this book demonstrates, football disputes provide a rich seam to be worked by sports lawyers, who, together with sports administrators and other interested parties, including sports marketers and corporate sponsors, need to be fully briefed on the subject of 'CAS and Football'.

References

Blackshaw I (2002) Mediating Sports Disputes: National and International Perspectives. TMC Asser Press, The Hague

Blackshaw IS (2009) Sport. TMC Asser Press, Mediation and Arbitration, The Hague

Blackshaw IS, Siekmann RCR, Soek W, eds. (2006) The Court of Arbitration for Sport 1984–2004. TMC Asser Press, The Hague

Blackshaw IS, Cornelius S, Siekmann RCR, eds. (2009) TV Rights and Sport: Legal Aspects. TMC Asser Press, The Hague

Dabscheck B (2010) Being Punitive: The Court of Arbitration for Sport Overturns Webster, ISLJ 2010/3-4

De Weger F (2009) The Jurisprudence of the FIFA Dispute Resolution Chamber. TMC Asser Press, The Hague

Nafziger J (2001) Arbitration of Rights and Obligations in the International Sports Arena, 35(2) Valparaiso University Law Review 57

Nafziger, JAR (2004) International Sports Law, Second Edition (2004), Ardsley, NY, Transnational Publishers, Inc., 48-61

Since 1986, CAS jurisprudence has been published in the volumes of the Digest of CAS Awards, edited by the CAS Secretary General Matthieu Reeb (Recueil des sentences du TAS/Digest of CAS Awards 1986-1998, II—1998-2000; III—2001-2003; Edité par/Edited by Matthieu Reeb,Staempfli Editions SA Berne (1998: I)/Kluwer Law International (1998-2000/2001-2003: II/III), which cover the period 1986–2003.
For the full text of the recent CAS Awards—also including those commented upon in this book—see www.tas-cas.org and the CAS Newsletter (since June 2004).

[24] See www.soccernet.espn.go.com/news/story?id=694773&cc=5739

Chapter 3
Club Ownership

Ivan Cherpillod and Juan de Dios Crespo Pérez

Contents

Prof. Dr. Ivan Cherpillod, Attorney-at-law, BMP Associés Lausanne, Switzerland. The commentary reflects the author's personal view.
Juan de Dios Crespo Pérez, LL.M., Attorney-at-law, Ruiz Huerta & Crespo Sports Lawyers, Valencia, Spain

I. Cherpillod (✉)
Lausanne, Switzerland
e-mail: ivan.cherpillod@bmp.ch

J. de Dios Crespo Pérez
Valencia, Spain
e-mail: jddcrespo@ruizcrespo.com

A. Wild (ed.), *CAS and Football: Landmark Cases*,
ASSER International Sports Law Series, DOI: 10.1007/978-90-6704-808-8_3,

3.1 CAS 98/200 AEK Athens and Slavia Prague v. UEFA

Ivan Cherpillod

In the AEK Athens and Slavia Prague v. UEFA Award, the CAS had to rule on the consequences of the qualification of two or more teams—under common control—for the same UEFA tournament. Following the participation of three clubs under one owner in the 1997/1998 UEFA CUP season, UEFA introduced the "Integrity of the UEFA Club Competitions—Independence of Clubs" rule for the 1998/1999 UEFA Cup season. Under its provisions, the owner of several clubs was (and still is) only allowed to play one club out of several in the tournament. UEFA ruled this way when AEK Athens and Slavia Prague, both owned by ENIC plc, qualified for the UEFA Cup 1998/1999. The CAS confirmed the validity of the UEFA rule and established a jurisprudence that can be regarded as fundamental to the integrity of the game. The author's analysis deals in detail with European Law, especially European Community competition law, Swiss civil and competition law and the general principles of law.

3.1.1 Background

ENIC plc is an English company which had invested in several European football clubs. In 1997, it acquired controlling interests in AEK, Slavia and Vicenza. In the 1997/98 European football season, these three clubs took part in the UEFA Cup Winners' Cup and all qualified for the quarter final. Thus, three out of eight clubs left in the same competition belonged to a single owner.

ENIC and UEFA met together to discuss the issue of multi-club ownership in football. ENIC proposed a "code of ethics" but this was not considered as a viable solution by UEFA. After internal consultation, UEFA preferred a rule which had the effect to prevent clubs under common control to play in the same competition.

A few days after having sent the UEFA Cup regulations for the season 1998/1999 to its member associations (regulations which at that time did not contain any limitation regarding multi-ownership), UEFA adopted the Contested Rule. It provides that "in the case of two or more clubs which are under common control, only one may participate in the same UEFA club competition".[1] Further, to determine which of two—or more—commonly owned clubs should be admitted, UEFA decided that the club with the highest "club coefficient" (i.e. a coefficient based on the club's results of the previous 5 years) would be admitted (and if the club coefficients were the same, the club with the highest national association coefficient based on the previous results of all the teams of the national association would be admitted; and in case of equal national association coefficients, lots would be drawn).

In application of the Contested Rule and these additional criteria, UEFA informed AEK Athens that it was not admitted to the UEFA Cup (Slavia Prague had the highest club coefficient). Thus, AEK had to be replaced by the club which had ranked immediately below AEK in the Hellenic championship.

AEK and Slavia Prague proposed to submit the case to CAS, and UEFA agreed.

3.1.2 CAS Decisions

The Claimants AEK and Slavia first sought an interim order petitioning their admission to the 1998/1999 UEFA Cup. This interim order has been granted by the President of the CAS Ordinary Division, who considered that the Contested Rule had been enacted too late, i.e. shortly before the start of the 1998/99 season and

---

[1] More precisely, the rule establishes that:

(1) no club participating in a UEFA club competition may, either directly or indirectly:

  (a) hold or deal in the securities or shares of any other club, or
  (b) be a member of any other club, or
  (c) be involved in any capacity whatsoever in the management, administration and/or sporting performance of any other club, or
  (d) have any power whatsoever in the management, administration and/or sporting performance of any other club.

(2) No person may at the same time, either directly or indirectly, be involved in any capacity whatsoever in the management, administration and/or sporting performance of more than one club participating in the same UEFA competition.

(3) In the case of two or more clubs which are under common control, only one may participate in the same UEFA club competition. In this connection, an individual or legal entity has control of a club where he/she/it:

  (a) holds a majority of the shareholders' voting rights, or
  (b) has the right to appoint or remove a majority of the members of the administrative, management or supervisory body, or
  (c) is a shareholder and alone controls a majority of the shareholders' voting rights pursuant to an agreement entered into with other shareholders of the club in question.

(4) The Committee of the UEFA Club Competitions will take a final decision with regard to the admission of clubs to these competitions. It furthermore reserves the right to act vis-à-vis clubs which cease to meet the above criteria in the course of an ungoing competition.

after the Cup Regulations had been sent—*nota bene*—without any restriction regarding multi-ownership. Therefore, CAS admitted that the Claimants could legitimately expect that no restriction was going to be adopted for that season. In CAS' view, the late adoption of the Contested Rule amounted to a violation of the rules of good faith and procedural fairness. However, this decision was only made for the duration of the 1998/1999 season, without prejudice as to the validity of the Contested Rule.

In its final award of August 20, 1999, CAS confirmed the validity of the Contested Rule but decided that it could not be implemented until the end of the 1999/2000 football season—on the ground that commonly controlled clubs and their owners should have some time to determine their course of action.

3.1.3 Applicable Law

As per Article R45 of the CAS Code, the dispute had to be decided "according to the rules of law chosen by the parties or, in the absence of such a choice, according to Swiss law".

The Claimants argued that the Contested Rule violated Swiss civil law: violation of the UEFA Statutes because it allegedly created different categories of members; breach of the principle of equal treatment (alleged discrimination between clubs which were under common control and other clubs); disregard of the Claimants' right to be heard; unjustified violation of the Claimants' personality; violation of EC competition law and Swiss competition law (restriction of competition; abuse of a dominant position), violation of EC provisions on freedom of establishment and free movement of capital, and general principles of law.

The parties agreed that Swiss law applied and that CAS should apply EC competition law and Swiss competition law if the dispute fell within the scope of these laws.

The Panel went a little further and considered that EC competition law had to be taken into account even if the parties had not agreed on its applicability. It held that Article 19 of the Swiss Act on Private International Law applied here. According to that provision, a foreign mandatory rule must be also "taken into consideration", even if the law applicable to the merits is different, provided that three conditions are met: (a) the foreign mandatory rule is a so-called *loi d'application immédiate* (rules which have to be applied irrespective of the law applicable to the merits of the case); (b) there is a close connection between the subject matter of the dispute and the territory where the mandatory rule is in force; (c) it is necessary to take that rule into account to protect overriding interests (which must be legitimate from a Swiss law point of view).

CAS considered that these conditions were met: the rules of law of competition are typical examples of mandatory rules; most of the strongest football clubs taking part in UEFA competitions are located in the EC (and this was true for AEK, but not for Slavia Prague at that time); and the underlying values of the

Swiss Federal Act on Cartels and of European law of competition are the same, which means that the rules of EC law on competition are compatible with the values supported by the Swiss legal system.

However, it is far from being certain that EC law on competition could have been applied by CAS in the absence of agreement between the parties on this point. First, if the conditions set forth by Article 19 of the Swiss Act on Private International Law are met, this does not lead to direct application of the foreign mandatory rules: the court is only invited to "take into account" these rules, which is different; in particular, it is conceivable that they may be applied only in part.[2] Second, as suggested by the German text of this provision, it may be the case that the legitimate and overriding interests which may trigger the application of the foreign mandatory rules are only those of *a party*[3] (e.g. if one of the parties cannot fulfill its obligations without incurring the risk of being severely sanctioned for having breached such foreign mandatory rules[4]).

Be it as it may, it is certain that the rules of European law of competition were applicable to UEFA insofar as the Contested Rule would have been restrictive of competition on the European market: in particular, these rules could be applied to UEFA by the European authorities—and as a matter of fact the European Commission has rendered a decision on the compatibility of the Contested Rule with EC law on competition in furtherance of a complaint which had been lodged by ENIC plc.[5]

Further, it must be reminded that an arbitral tribunal with seat in Switzerland cannot decline its jurisdiction to apply the rules of foreign (especially EC) competition law if either party pleads the nullity of its (e.g. contractual) obligation on the ground that it contravenes such rules.[6] However, whether they are applicable or not is a different question.

3.1.4 Merits

3.1.4.1 Protection of the "Integrity of the Game"

Both parties agreed that it was necessary to protect the integrity of the game.

However, the Claimants argued that match-fixing was rather unlikely, especially if the common owner is a corporation listed on the stock exchange. They

---

[2] See Dutoit 2005, Article 19 N 5.

[3] Several authors in the Swiss legal literature consider however, in accordance with the French text of Article 19, that it is also possible to justify the application of foreign mandatory rules by general interests: see e.g. Dutoit 2005, Article 19 N 1. This point has been left open in the Swiss Federal Supreme Court decision ATF 130 III 620.

[4] Cf. Vischer 2004, Article 19 N 23.

[5] See Sect. 3.1.5.

[6] Swiss Federal Supreme Court decision 118 II 193.

suggested that a code of ethics or some rules governing the transfer of players would be sufficient to preserve the integrity of the game.

The Panel did not follow this view and pointed out that "integrity, in football, is crucially related to the *authenticity of results*, and has a critical core which is that, *in the public's perception,* both single matches and entire championships must be a true test of the best possible athletic, technical, coaching and management skills of the opposing sides".[7] In other words, the main issue regarding the "integrity of the game" was whether multi-ownership within the same football competition could be perceived by the public as affecting the authenticity of sporting results or, put in a different way, whether the public could perceive a conflict of interest which might alter the competitive process when two commonly owned clubs play in the same sporting event.

The Panel answered positively to this question. In its Award, it held that "even assuming that multi-club owners, directors or executives always act in compliance with the law and do not try to directly fix any match, there are situations when the economic interests of the multi-club owner or parent company are at odds with sporting needs in terms of public perception of the authenticity of results".[8] In particular, fans might doubt whether transfers of players between commonly owned clubs would occur in the sole interest of their club rather than in the interest of the other club. Further, club executives are in a position to make choices which may either positively or negatively influence performance of players.[9] In addition, if unrelated third clubs end up in a qualification group together with two commonly owned clubs, it may be the case that the teams need a draw to the detriment of the third club; in such a case, the situation of the conflict of interest is quite obvious.

Against this background, the Panel held that a problem of conflict of interest exists in multi-club ownership situations. As it had been stated before the European Parliament by Mr. Karel Van Miert, who was EC Commissioner for competition policy at that time, "clearly, if clubs with the same owner can take part in the same competitions, whether national or international, doubts may arise as to whether the outcome is really undecided in advance".[10]

However, this conclusion was not sufficient to admit the validity of the Contested Rule: it just meant that "ownership of multiple clubs competing in the same competition represents a justified concern for a sports regulator and organizer".[11]

---

[7] CAS Award, at para 25.

[8] CAS Award, at para 45.

[9] On this point, see CAS Award, at para 39 and following.

[10] Answers given by Mr. Van Miert on behalf of the Commission to parliamentary questions nos. E-3980/97, 0538/98, P-2361/98.

[11] CAS Award, at para 48.

3.1.4.2 Swiss Civil Law

Compliance with UEFA Statutes

The Claimants first argued that the Contested Rule created different categories of UEFA members. They considered that they should be treated as "indirect members" of UEFA, because they are members of their respective national association which, in turn, is a UEFA member. In furtherance of this argument, they claimed that UEFA breached its own Statutes because the creation of different categories of members would have required a modification of the UEFA Statutes, which was in the power of the UEFA Congress—not of the Executive Committee, which had adopted the Contested Rule.

The Panel left open the question to know if the clubs could be considered "indirect members" of UEFA. It held that the Contested Rule did not create different categories of member clubs but merely established conditions of participation in UEFA competitions, something which was in the power of the Executive Committee.[12]

Right to Submit Arguments Before Adoption of the Contested Rule?

The Claimants also argued that they should have been granted the possibility to present their arguments to UEFA before adoption of the Contested Rule. This argument was again based on the assumption that the clubs were "indirect members" of UEFA.

The Panel considered that a right to a legal hearing existed only "in the event of administrative measures or penalties adopted by a sports-governing body with regard to a limited and identified number of designees".[13] Further, if the Claimants' argument had to be followed, this would have meant that UEFA should consult with tens (or even hundreds) of thousands of clubs before passing a resolution which could affect such "indirect" members. The Panel concluded therefore that it could be advisable for a regulator or legislator to hear the views of those who would be potentially affected by a new regulation, but it could not be a legal requirement.

Rules of Procedural Fairness (as Regards the Entry into Force of the Contested Rule)

The Panel agreed with the opinion expressed by the President of CAS Ordinary Division in its interim order that UEFA violated the principle of procedural

[12] Award, at para 52 and following.

[13] CAS Award, at para 58.

fairness by adopting the Contested Rule too late and after the Cup Regulations for the 1998/1999 season had been issued without any restriction regarding multiple ownership (thus creating a legitimate expectation that no such restriction would be enacted for that season). Therefore, the Panel ratified the CAS Procedural Order which had temporarily stayed the application of the Contested Rule for that season.

However, as pointed out by the Panel, this violation of the principle of procedural fairness was of a transitory nature and, as a result, could not render the Contested Rule unlawful on its merits with respect to all future football seasons.[14]

Principle of Equal Treatment

The Claimants also argued that the Contested Rule violated the principle of equal treatment by creating different categories of members. This argument, which was also based on the assumption that clubs were indirect members of UEFA, had already been discussed.[15]

Personality of the Clubs

The Claimants further invoked Article 28 of the Civil Code, which provides for protection of personality in broad terms: any breach of the rules protecting personality "is unlawful unless it is justified by law, by the consent of the victim, or by an overriding public or private interest".[16]

The Panel expressed doubts as to the applicability of this provision in the present case. These doubts might have been unjustified: in the field of high-level sports, it has been decided that this protection includes a right to sports activity and, for professional sports, a right to develop an economic activity.[17] However, the Panel considered that in any event, the public's perception of a conflict of interest potentially affecting the authenticity of results would constitute an "overriding interest" in the meaning of Article 28 CC which justified the Contested Rule.

3.1.4.3 European Community Competition Law

The Claimants complained that the Contested Rule violated Articles 81 and 82 of the EC Treaty: in their opinion, this Rule was a decision by an association of undertakings, or an agreement between undertakings, which affected competition

---

14 Award, at para 60 and following.

15 See section "Compliance with UEFA Statutes".

16 Translation by the author.

17 Federal Supreme Court decision ATF 134 III 193.

in the football market, and in various ancillary football services markets, "by preventing or restricting investments by multi-club owners in European clubs, by changing the nature, intensity and patterns of competition between commonly controlled clubs and the others, and by enhancing the economic imbalance between football clubs".[18] As regards the application of Article 82, the Claimants argued that UEFA (being the only body empowered to organize European competitions) dominates the European professional football market and the ancillary football services markets and abused of its dominant position by restricting competition in an unnecessary, disproportionate, and discriminating manner.

Sporting Exception?

UEFA first responded that the Contested Rule was not caught by competition law because it was a rule of a merely sporting character (to protect the integrity of the game). This view could be supported by the jurisprudence of the European Court of Justice, which stated in the *Walrave* and *Donà* cases that "the practice of sport is subject to Community law only in so far as it constitutes an economic activity within the meaning of Article 2 of the Treaty".[19]

The Panel agreed that a sporting exception exists, "in the sense that some sporting rules or practices are somewhat capable of, as the Court puts it, «restricting the scope» of EC provisions".[20] In his view and in the light of the Court's jurisprudence, a sporting rule would not be caught by EC law if (*a*) it concerns a question of sporting interest having nothing to do with economic activity, (*b*) it is justified on non-economic grounds, (*c*) it is related to the particular nature or context of certain competitions, and (*d*) it remains limited to its proper objective.[21]

CAS however considered that the Contested Rule, by dealing with the question of ownership of clubs taking part in UEFA competitions, addressed the economic status of clubs which are involved in economic activities. Therefore, the Contested Rule could not be viewed as having nothing to do with economic activities, and it could not be covered by this "sporting exception".[22]

---

[18] CAS Award, at para 77.

[19] Case 36/74, *Walrave*, in *E.C.R.* 1974, 1405, para 4; case 13/76, *Donà*, in *E.C.R.* 1976, 1333, para 12. See also case C-415/93, *Bosman*, in *E.C.R.* 1995, I-4921, para 76: "the provisions of Community law concerning freedom of movement of persons and of provision of services do not preclude rules or practices justified on non-economic grounds which relate to the particular nature and context of certain matches. It stressed, however, that such a restriction on the scope of the provisions in question must remain limited to its proper objective. It cannot, therefore, be relied upon to exclude the whole of the sporting activity from the scope of the Treaty".

[20] CAS Award, at para 82.

[21] CAS Award, ibid.

[22] Further, the Panel expressed doubts as to the possibility to operate a distinction between sporting questions and economic issues: see the examples discussed in para 84 of the Award.

Is UEFA an "Undertaking"?

Then the Award addressed the question whether UEFA could be viewed as an undertaking or as an association of undertakings in the meaning of Articles 81 and 82. The Panel agreed that "a good part of UEFA's activities is of a purely sporting nature, particularly when it adopts measures as a mere regulator of sporting matters".[23] However, UEFA is also involved in economic activities (e.g. contracts relating to television rights). As regards these activities, UEFA is an undertaking in the meaning of competition law, and the same applies as regards its members (national federations). Therefore, the Panel concluded "that UEFA, with respect to the economic activities in which it is engaged and in which national federations are engaged, is at the same time an undertaking and an association of undertakings".[24]

The Award also examined whether UEFA could be viewed as an "association of associations of undertakings" (or if it could be considered merely as a regulator above the clubs rather than some kind of trade association of clubs engaged in economic activities). In the Bosman case, Advocate General Lenz considered that UEFA was an association of associations of undertakings, acting as an instrument of professional clubs' cooperation, notwithstanding the fact that many amateur clubs are also members of the national federations.[25] But the Panel emphasized the difference between a league of professional clubs and a national football federation: the latter represents all their member clubs, including many amateur clubs, while the former should be viewed as a proper trade association (it being reminded that national leagues are not direct members of UEFA and that the most important of them had constituted their own independent association). As said by the Panel, "within UEFA, representatives of national federations should be regarded less as delegates of the clubs engaged in economic activities than as delegates of amateur or grassroots clubs".[26] However, in the absence of concrete evidence in this respect and despite the doubts it had expressed, the Panel decided—for the purpose of the competition law analysis but without excluding the possibility that UEFA might not be an association of "club undertakings" through which clubs coordinate their economic behavior—that UEFA should be considered as "an association of 'club undertakings' whose decisions and rules concerning club competitions constitute a medium of horizontal cooperation between the competing clubs"[27] thus clearly falling under the scope of Article 81 para 1.

[23] CAS Award, at para 87.

[24] CAS Award, ibid.

[25] Opinion delivered on 20 September 1995, case C-415/93, *Bosman*, in *E.C.R.* 1995, I-4921, para 256.

[26] CAS Award, at para 92.

[27] CAS Award, at para 94.

Market Definition

As regards the market definition, the Claimants suggested the existence of a "European football market" which would comprise the supply of all football matches played in Europe and a variety of related "ancillary football services markets" (market for capital investment in football clubs, players market, media rights market, sponsorship, advertising, and merchandising market). The Panel rejected this definition: "the notion of a general European football market is too ample, and the other related markets are too heterogeneous to be included therein. Given that the definition of a market should be determined primarily by interchangeability (or substitutability) from the consumers' viewpoint, it is implausible to regard all European football matches as interchangeable. (...) Furthermore, if the products of the European football market are the European matches, most of the various other markets mentioned by the Claimants are certainly related in some way or another to the supply of such football matches, but they cannot be 'comprised' within that market".[28]

Rather, the Panel considered that there are several "football markets" in which professional football clubs operate, which are clearly segmented in both their product and geographic dimensions. As regards the market more directly related to, and potentially affected by, the Contested Rule, it has been defined by CAS as the "market for ownership interests in football clubs capable of taking part in UEFA competitions".[29] In the opinion of the Panel, the Contested Rule was "only indirectly related, if at all, to the various other markets suggested by the Claimants, such as the market for players, the sponsorship market, the merchandising market, the media rights market and the market for gate revenues".[30] The effects on these markets had therefore to be considered only on a subsidiary basis to the said principal relevant market, concerning ownership interests in European professional football clubs.

As to *geographic market* definition, the Panel concluded quite logically that the relevant geographic market extended to whole Europe (more precisely to the territories of the European federations affiliated to UEFA).

Compatibility with Article 81

In the absence of evidence that the true object of the Contested Rule was an anti-competitive one, the Panel examined if its *effect* could appreciably restrict competition by preventing or restricting investment by multiple owners in European

---

[28] CAS Award, at para 98.

[29] CAS Award, at para 101, with reference to some US antitrust cases: *NASL v. NFL*, 505 F.Supp. 659 (S.D.N.Y. 1980), *reversed* 670 F.2d 1249 (2d Cir. 1982); *Sullivan v. NFL*, 34 F.3d 91 (1st Cir. 1994); *Piazza v. MLB*, 831 F.Supp. 420 (1993).

[30] CAS Award, ibid.

clubs. In accordance with the EC case-law,[31] CAS tried to define how the market for ownership interests would have evolved in the absence of the Contested Rule.

Assuming that multi-club control could be expected to expand, in particular if single club owners would feel a necessity to improve their position by acquiring additional clubs, the Panel found that such an expansion would lead to a decrease in the number of club owners, and thus in the number of undertakings on the market; club ownership could concentrate into fewer hands, it being reminded that new entrants on the market would have been hindered by a sporting barrier (in the European sporting system, any new club has to go through the pyramidal structure of national championships for several years before attaining a top professional level, so that entry into the market could be achieved only by acquiring already existing clubs). In a scenario which CAS qualified as being too extreme, this process of concentration could lead to an oligopoly with undesirable effects on competition (e.g. price increase for tickets or pay television subscriptions). However, this showed that in the absence of the Contested Rule, "the number of undertakings on the market would sooner or later decline while the effects on prices, although scarcely noticeable in the short term, would in due course tend to show an increase".[32] In conclusion, the Panel held that, "in the absence of the Contested Rule, competition on the relevant market and on other football markets would initially probably remain unaffected and, when affected, it would be restricted. In the light of this *a contrario* test, the Panel finds that the actual effect of the Contested Rule is to place some limitation on mergers between European high-level football clubs, and thus to increase the number of undertakings on the relevant market and on other football markets; accordingly, the Contested Rule preserves or even enhances economic competition between club owners and economic and sporting competition between clubs".[33]

As a consequence, CAS held that either the Contested Rule had no effects on the relevant market or, if it had, it would "exert a beneficial influence upon competition, insofar as it tends to prevent a potential increase in prices for ownership interests in professional football clubs (and to prevent potential price increases in other football markets as well)".[34] The Award states that "the Contested Rule, by discouraging merger and acquisition transactions between existing owners of clubs aspiring to participate in UEFA competitions, and conversely by encouraging investments in such football clubs by the many potential newcomers, appears to have the effect of preserving competition between club owners and between football clubs rather than appreciably restricting competition on the relevant market or on other football markets".[35] The Panel referred to the situation in

---

31 Cf. e.g. case 42/84, *Remia*, in E.C.R. 1985, 2545, para 18.

32 CAS Award, at para 117.

33 CAS Award, at para 118.

34 CAS Award, at para 119.

35 CAS Award, ibid.

England, where—despite the fact that the Premier League had enacted a rule which was even stricter[36]—clubs could successfully attract capital investment.

The Claimants also argued that the Contested Rule favoured the rich and strong clubs over the weak and poor ones, and thus impaired the pattern of economic competition. However, on the basis of its previous findings, the Panel considered that polarization of market power between bigger and smaller clubs would continue or even increase in the absence of the Contested Rule. The provision of "incentives for actual or potential club owners to invest their resources in only one high-level club, as the Contested Rule tends to do, is conducive to an economic and sporting balance, rather than an imbalance, between football clubs".[37] Hence, the Contested Rule has pro-competitive effects.

Further, the Contested Rule could not be viewed as being capable of affecting the quality of the sporting product offered to consumers: the quality of the entertainment provided to European football fans could not be significantly impaired by the Contested Rule, which provides that the excluded club has to be replaced by the club which, in the same national championship, ranked immediately below the excluded club.[38]

Proportionality (Less Restrictive Alternatives?)

Even if the Panel was convinced that the Contested Rule did not appreciably restrict competition, it examined if it could be viewed as being disproportionate. The Claimants contended that the objective of protecting the integrity of European football competitions could be attained by less restrictive means, such as a code of ethics and criminal penalties to prevent match-fixing. However, as it had been pointed out before,[39] the "integrity question" raises the issue whether consumers could perceive a possible conflict of interests, capable of affecting the authenticity of results, when commonly controlled clubs participate in the same competition. In this respect, "rules bound to protect public confidence in the authenticity of results appear to be of the utmost importance",[40] CAS said.

With regard to any possible "less restrictive alternative", the Panel observed that the Contested Rule proscribes only the participation in the same UEFA competition of commonly controlled clubs: commonly controlled clubs may participate in different UEFA competitions. Further, the Contested Rule does not

---

[36] It does not allow any person or corporate entity, except with the prior written consent of the Board (which had never been granted so far), to "directly or indirectly hold or acquire any interest in more than 10 per cent of the issued share capital of a Club while he or any associate is a director of, or directly or indirectly holds any interest in the share capital of, any other Club": Award, at para 120.

[37] CAS Award, at para 122.

[38] CAS Award, at para 123.

[39] See Sect. 3.1.4.1.

[40] CAS Award, at para 129.

prevent the acquisition of shares—up to 49% of the voting rights—in a large number of clubs participating in the same competition. Moreover, the Panel held that the Contested Rule could not be substituted by a posteriori sanctions such as disciplinary or criminal sanctions applying to match-fixing: such sanctions could not alter the public's perception of a conflict of interests in case of two commonly owned clubs participating in the same UEFA competition.

The Claimants had also proposed, as an alternative, that UEFA should conduct a "fit and proper test" to determine if a person or legal entity could become the owner of a club. However, this could not represent a viable alternative (difficulty to find out objective requirements, administrative and legal costs—risk of being sued for economic and moral damages after publicly declaring someone as being not a fit and proper person). Further, a rule requiring intrusive ethical examination of clubs' owners, directors, and executives could hardly be characterized as a "less restrictive" alternative.[41]

The Claimants also pointed out that some other rules preventing the participation of commonly owned clubs in the same competition allowed for the possibility to obtain derogation from the respective sports-governing body. However, the Panel noted that no such approval had ever been granted in practice; further, denial of derogation would lead to expensive litigation, while an authorization could always lead to suspicion from the part of the public, for the reasons already described.

Other possible solutions proposed by the Claimants have been considered as being inappropriate. In particular, a requirement that multi-club owners divest their ownership interests in all but one of the owned clubs solely for the period of the UEFA competition, through the establishment of an independent trust to which control of commonly owned clubs could be transferred for the duration of UEFA competitions or through the appointment of an independent nominee who would exercise the owner's voting rights in its sole discretion, has been seen as being "not only complex to administer but also quite intrusive upon the clubs' structure and management; in any event, the true problem would be that the interim suspension of control or voting rights does not modify the substantial ownership of a club, and thus does not exclude the underlying continuance of a conflict of interest".[42] Lastly, regulations restricting bonuses and transfers of players would have addressed only some aspects of the conflict of interest but the problems related to the allocation of resources by the multi-club owner among its clubs would still exist (as seen before, club executives are in a position to make choices which may either positively or negatively influence performance of players) and such regulations would not have taken into account the interest of third clubs (unrelated third clubs ending up in a qualification group together with two commonly owned clubs).[43]

---

41 CAS Award, at para 133.

42 CAS Award, at para 135.

43 CAS Award, at para 33 and following, 43 and 135.

In conclusion, the Panel held that the Contested Rule did not violate Article 81 of the EC Treaty: it "is an essential feature for the organization of a professional football competition and is not more extensive than necessary to serve the fundamental goal of preventing conflicts of interest which would be publicly perceived as affecting the authenticity, and thus the uncertainty, of results in UEFA competitions".[44]

Abuse of a Dominant Position?

The Panel admitted that UEFA could exert a dominant market power in the market for the organization of pan-European football matches and competitions. However, the Claimants were not actually or potentially competing with UEFA on that market. In the present case, the relevant product market was the market for ownership interests in football clubs capable of taking part in UEFA competitions. With respect to that market, UEFA is a mere regulator, and national federations are not present on that market either. Thus, there is no dominant position of UEFA on the relevant market.

As to a possible abuse on a neighboring market, the Panel analyzed the EC case-law as requiring that the dominant undertakings had to be active on both the market of dominance and the neighboring non-dominated market—which was not the case here.[45]

Anyway, with respect to Article 82 of the EC Treaty, the Claimants relied on essentially the same arguments as for Article 81, and the Panel had already rejected them (no restriction of competition, proportionality, absence of discrimination). CAS thus denied the existence of any abuse of a dominant position.

3.1.4.4 Swiss Competition Law

The Claimants also relied on the provisions of Swiss law of competition (Articles 5 and 7 of the Federal Act on Cartels). However, the arguments were the same as those discussed in application of European law of competition, and thus were rejected under Swiss law as well.[46]

---

[44] CAS Award, at para 136.

[45] CAS Award, at para 143.

[46] The existence of a sporting exception had not been discussed under Swiss law of competition: the only exemption from the law on cartels which had been admitted under Swiss law related to the "rules of the game" (mainly those applying on the pitch), which are not subject to the law on cartels. The Contested Rule could not be assimilated to a "rule of the game", and the parties concurred in this respect. Whether a (much broader) "sporting exception" existed under Swiss law remained undecided: the Panel had already decided that the existence of any "sporting exception" could not have the effect that the Contested Rule would be exempted from the application of the law of competition (Award, at para 84).

The Panel however noted that "the envisaged oligopoly scenario is much more likely within a small market such as Switzerland, where there are not many teams aspiring to participate in UEFA competitions; indeed, there are only twelve clubs in the Swiss first division. Therefore, the described pro-competitive effect of the Contested Rule is even amplified within the Swiss market".[47] Against this background, CAS concluded that the Contested Rule could not be viewed as being restrictive of competition on the Swiss market.

3.1.4.5 European Community Law on the Right of Establishment and on Free Movement of Capital

In case the Contested Rule could be seen as restricting the freedom of establishment or the free movement of capital, the Panel observed that it did not institute any discrimination based on a person's (or corporation's) nationality. Thus, the Contested Rule could be admissible insofar as it pursued legitimate interests with proportionate means—issues which had already been addressed by the Panel.

3.1.4.6 General Principles of Law

The Claimants also relied on the "general principles of law" and argued again that the Contested Rule was the expression of some abusive behavior. As CAS had already considered that the Contested Rule was justified to protect the authenticity of the game, this argument has been rejected. The Award however contains some interesting developments which must be reminded here:

> The Panel is of the opinion that all sporting institutions, and in particular all international federations, must abide by general principles of law. Due to the transnational nature of sporting competitions, the effects of the conduct and deeds of international federations are felt in a sporting community throughout various countries. Therefore, the substantive and procedural rules to be respected by international federations cannot be reduced only to its own statutes and regulations and to the laws of the country where the federation is incorporated or of the country where its headquarters are. Sports law has developed and consolidated along the years, particularly through the arbitral settlement of disputes, a set of unwritten legal principles—a sort of lex mercatoria for sports or, so to speak, a lex ludica—to which national and international sports federations must conform, regardless of the presence of such principles within their own statutes and regulations or within any applicable national law, provided that they do not conflict with any national "public policy" ("ordre public") provision applicable to a given case. Certainly, general principles of law drawn from a comparative or common denominator reading of various domestic legal systems and, in particular, the prohibition of arbitrary or unreasonable rules and measures can be deemed to be part of such lex ludica.[48]

---

[47] CAS Award, at para 149.

[48] CAS Award, at para 156.

3.1.5 Epilogue: Decision Rendered by the European Commission

In February 2000, ENIC plc filed a complaint against UEFA with the European Commission and reiterated the arguments based on EC law of competition which AEK and Slavia Prague had brought before CAS. The European Commission rejected this complaint in a decision which may be summarized as follows.[49]

First, the Commission declared that professional football clubs were undertakings in the meaning of Article 81 para 1 of the Treaty. Thus, national federations can be viewed as associations of undertakings, and the Commission considered UEFA as an association of associations of undertakings, notwithstanding the fact that a large number of amateur clubs are also members of the national federations.[50] In addition, UEFA is also an undertaking for certain activities such as the organization of European club competitions, said the Commission.

The Commission confirmed that the object of the Contested Rule was not to distort competition: its main purpose is to "ensure the uncertainty of the outcome and to guarantee that the consumer has the perception that the games played represent honest sporting competition between the participants, as consumers may suspect that teams with a common owner will not genuinely compete".[51]

As to the effect of the rule, the Commission held that "without the UEFA rule, the proper functioning of the market where the clubs develop their economic activities would be under threat, since the public's perception that the underlying sporting competition is fair and honest is an essential precondition to keep its interest and marketability. (…) For instance, should two clubs under joint control or ownership meet at a certain stage of the competition, the public's perception of the authenticity of the result would be jeopardised".[52] Like CAS, the Commission also noted that the Contested Rule could not be viewed as preventing investment in football clubs insofar as it is limited to prohibiting more than one club with the same ownership from participating in the same UEFA competition. Further, the Contested Rule does not prevent investors from acquiring an interest in clubs: below the level of majority control, clubs remain free to play in the same UEFA competition. The Commission also mentioned that even stricter rules had been adopted in some Member States, so that the Contested Rule seemed to "constitute a prolongation of the national rules and their natural corollary".[53] The Commission also agreed like CAS that a code of conduct could not constitute a workable alternative. As to a system "which would allow the football regulator to analyze a specific common-owned club's participation on a case by case basis only, [it] would not enable clubs (or spectators) to know in advance whether or not they

---

[49] Case COMP/37 806 ENIC/UEFA.

[50] It is reminded that CAS expressed some doubts on this point: see section Is UEFA an "Undertaking".

[51] Decision, at para 28.

[52] Decision, at para 32.

[53] Decision, at para 35.

would be likely or able to participate in a UEFA competition and would not be a workable alternative to the UEFA rule either".[54]

The Commission therefore concluded that the Contested Rule was "inherent to the very existence of credible UEFA competitions" and did not go "beyond what is necessary to ensure its legitimate aim of protecting the uncertainty of the results and giving the public the right perception as to the integrity of the UEFA competitions with a view to ensure their proper functioning".[55] Therefore, it could not be viewed as a restriction of competition.

As to a possible application of Article 82 of the Treaty, the Commission also concluded that the Contested Rule was neither discriminatory nor disproportionate, in the absence of any less restrictive alternative.

3.1.6 Conclusions

By its in-depth analysis of the market issues, this CAS Award is undoubtedly one of the landmark cases in this field. CAS' views as regards law of competition have been largely followed by the European Commission—which is quite illustrative of the quality of this Award.

As always, some questions remain open. In particular, it must be noted that "control" is defined by the Contested Rule as the acquisition of a majority of the voting rights—while it is quite clear that *de facto* "control" may be achieved with much less voting rights, at least in certain instances. In this respect, it is reminded that some national rules are much stricter. Therefore, it may be the case that a stricter rule should be needed. However, as long as the public does not perceive the acquisition of a lower interest in (two or more) clubs as a situation which would lead to conflicts of interests as those described by CAS in the present case, there is perhaps no need for a stricter rule. Further, the threshold applied by the Contested Rule allows for investment in several football clubs up to 49% of the voting rights and may hence be viewed as permitting some flexibility so as not to discourage investment in football clubs.

3.2 CAS 2007/0/1361 Real Federación Española de Fútbol v. Liga Nacional de Fútbol Profesional

Juan de Dios Crespo Pérez

Is it "illegal" or "contrary to sporting principles" to buy a club and change its name and domicile? The author investigates this issue from the perspective of Spanish Law. Its basis

[54] Decision, at para 36.

[55] Decision, at para 47.

is the Real Federación Española de Fútbol (RFEF) v/Liga Nacional de Fútbol Profesional Award. He considers legal aspects and fears inherent in RFEF and FIFA that two teams might compete against each other in the same league, but using the same resources and shareholders. He ultimately concurs with the CAS, that the purchase and then changing the name and domicile were acceptable.

3.2.1 Preamble

This case was clearly about power and money and not only about the specificity of sport. The Spanish FA ("RFEF") did not accept that a club of the Second Division (Ciudad de Murcia SAD) changed his name (Granada 74 SAD) and his domicile even though its shares were bought by a company (CD Granada 92 SDU) which had the right to do so, according to Spanish Companies Law.

The problem seemed to be that the buying company was owned by the same person who was also the President (not the owner has it was not a company) of a fourth division club (CD Granada 74).

We have just to remind that the Second Division is a professional one, depending of the Spanish League (Liga de Fútbol Profesional or "LFP") and the Fourth Division was not professional and depend of the RFEF.

The question was that RFEF did not accept such a legal buying and the use of the Spanish Law to then change the name and domicile of the club as being "illegal" and "contrary to sport" as it was a "hidden promotion" of a club from a category to another. Let us say that the fourth division club remained in its category and was not in any way "promoted" to second division and that the new club named Granada 74 SAD had other players and coaches. The only link was that a President of an amateur club was also the owner of a professional one with similar names: Granada 74 SAD and Club Deportivo Granada 74.

What was strange is that RFEF and LFP had agreed to sign a "Regulation for Franchises" which permit the buying of a place in First or Second Division by another club. Thus, RFEF admits that a club can "buy" a place which was not the case here. The issue of this case could be that if there is a selling and buying of a place through the so-called "Regulation for Franchises", the RFEF is entitled to a certain amount of money and with the mere acquisition of shares of a Sporting Company (SAD) there is no chance that the RFEF receives a single penny. We are not assuming that this is what happened but the fact is that those Regulations exist.

3.2.2 Facts

On the 1st of August 2007 the Liga Nacional de Fútbol Profesional (LFP) sent a circular letter around containing all the prospective clubs to be registered for the 2007/2008 season. One of the clubs included in the list was Granada 74 SAD with the mention that the club had previously been known as Ciudad de Murcia SAD.

The LFP had granted provisional membership and league status to Granada 74 SAD for a position in the Spanish second football division. However problems arose when the RFEF had to also approve this provisional membership.

The RFEF inquired about the validity of the transfer of Ciudad de Murcia SAD in location and name to Granada with their superiors; FIFA. FIFA were uncomfortable with this move and subsequent league position because it looked like the owners of another club Club Polideportivo Granada 74 (CP Granada 74) were attempting to buy their other team a place in a higher division, or effectively "purchase promotion".

FIFA informed the RFEF that they should not sanction the league membership of Granada 74 SAD. When the RFEF told the LFP this they said that if the LFP did not comply with this league admission denial the RFEF would not sanction any referees to take charge of any of the club's matches, and they would not accept any of the club of player licenses.

The owners of Granada 74 SAD had to act, and they had to act quickly. The Spanish league matches were due to start in a matter of weeks. Therefore despite their superior position under Spanish Law they took a case straight to the Court of Arbitration for Sport with the LFP as their representatives against the Spanish Football Association (FA). The case between the Spanish League and Association addressed many interesting topics, especially the "specific nature of sport".

However before we discuss the trial and the case developments, it is probably best that we get some more background information about the Granada 74 case.

3.2.3 Background

In the first weeks of August 2007 the Owners of Ciudad de Murcia SAD decided to sell shares of the company—Sociedad Anónima Deportiva (SAD[56]). A number of prospective bidders arose, including the owners a company named Ciudad Deportiva Granada 92 SLU. The owner of this company, Mr. Carlos Marsá, already was the President of a non-league football club in the Spanish fourth division called Club Polideportivo Granada 74.

According to the legislation regarding the development of Sociedades Anónimas a company is entitled to sell its shares to other parties, rename the company, and change the address of domicile of the company. The legislation regarding SAD's extended this right to football clubs. As a result, the group Ciudad Deportiva Granada 92 had the right, and had the desire to move Ciudad de Murcia SAD to the city Granada in Spain, and change the name of the club to Granada 74 SAD. A name very similar to the one of the club which they already owned, Club Polideportivo Granada 74, but with no legal links.

[56] This was a way of changing a club into a sporting company and was granted/required by reason of Spanish Law 1084/1991.

Therefore, it appeared to the RFEF and FIFA that Club Polideportivo Granada 74 were purchasing a club, and consequently a league position, in a division two tiers higher than the division they were currently in. However, eventually the CAS found that although because of their similar names and same location the two, in fact, remained separate clubs and no violation of any rules had occurred.

3.2.4 *Significant Participation*

One of the few restrictions on moves of this nature is a mechanism known under Spanish law as "significant participation" or "*participaciones significativas*".

The significant participation prohibition is one when company owns more than 5% of the shares in two separate sporting enterprises which share the same competitive market territory.

The RFEF and FIFA believed that this purchase could amount to significant participation because of the potential for these two football clubs to exist in the same league.[57] The two football organization bodies were concerned that the purity of the Spanish competition could be attacked by the prospective of same division multi-ownership.

3.2.5 *The "August Heat"*

The RFEF tried to solve the case by insisting on the illegality of the selling of shares and the change of name and domicile and asked FIFA to help it. The LFP and the club Granada 74 SAD were decided to go to any ordinary Court in order to protect their rights.

The RFEF made a request for a CAS ordinary proceeding in a matter of urgency with a short deadline for the claim and the answer, as well as for a hearing. This was submitted to the LFP on the 21st of August and was done in order to have the potential league membership of Granada 74 SAD reviewed for the 2007/2008 season. After an intense day of brainstorming about the need or not to go to CAS to deal with this case, the LFP accepted the decision to go to the CAS in the interest of time, with the league set to start only days after the request to have the case heard. This sacrificed their strong stance if strictly adhering to Spanish law and trying the case in Spanish Courts. A couple of days were needed for the statements to be made by both parties and then let the room to the hearing.

[57] In fact, had these clubs not signed a "sponsorship agreement", a contract which will be discussed later in the article, it would have been popular for the two clubs, with the same ownership, to have existed in the same division within 1 year that is, if Granada 74 SAD was relegated, and CP Granada 74 promoted to the Spanish third division in 2007/2008 season.

The hearing took place on the 24th of August and with the League having to start quite immediately, and thus giving the Panel very little time to make their monumental decision. The RFEF was of course present but FIFA sent a couple of heavyweights to supplement its theory.[58]

3.2.6 Main Arguments and Sole Arbitrator Response

The main arguments of the claimants was the damage caused to the integrity of the league and promotion system, the attack on the fundamental principles of sport and fair play, and the potential for gross distortion of competition. The RFEF and FIFA were essentially saying two things about the purchase of the shares of Ciudad de Murcia SAD by the owners of Granada 74 SAD.

This said purchase effectively amounted to a team purchasing promotion and jumping up two leagues as a result of financial clout, and a small name change.

The potential for abuse of the competition was too great, and that the existence of two clubs under the same ownership in the same league was dangerous, and unfair to the other participants.

3.2.7 Preservation of Competitive Practice

UEFA and FIFA sought to preserve this idea of competitive practice and enshrined these morally sound ideas in legislation in Articles 2.1e and 2.1 of their respective statutes.

UEFA Statutes 2.1e

> … shall be to prevent all methods or practices which might jeopardize the regularity of matches or competitions or give rise to the abuse of football.

FIFA Statutes 2.1

> to prevent all methods or practices which might jeopardize the integrity of matches or competitions or give rise to the abuse of football.

The RFEF and FIFA had to heavily rely on their arguments regarding the "prevention of practices which could jeopardize the integrity of football", because there was no mention in the regulations of UEFA or FIFA about what would happen in the case of a change of name, address, or owners of a club, and how the situation should be handled so as not to adversely affect the competition.

58 Mr Jerôme Champagne and Mr. Marco Villiger, Heads of International Affairs and Legal of FIFA, respectively.

The first argument was not about the buying of the shares by another corporation but the affect of these owners buying the shares on the competition.[59]

Rui Botica Santos, the sole arbitrator for this dispute, could not see how this purchase of shares equaled a promotion because the "former club" or CP Granada 74 continued to exist.[60] He also could not see how the acquiring of said shares could lead to any competitive distortion due to the two division gap between the club′s and the improbability of them having to play each other.[61]

The arbitrator also took note of the slightly hypocritical nature of the submissions of the RFEF about how buying shares in another club, effectively buying their position in the league, might adversely affect the competition. He took note of the fact that the RFEF and LFP *already* had an agreement in place which would allow one club to sell its right to compete in the first division to another club or a sporting corporation already based in Spain.[62]

The sole arbitrator failed to see the difference, with regard to "purchasing promotion" between the owners of CP Granada 74 purchasing a new club in a different division, and CP Granada 74 purchasing the position of Ciudad de Murcia SAD in the second division.[63]

3.2.8 Change of Ownership, Name, and Domicile

Another task the RFEF tried to accomplish was to draw a line between the Granada 74 SAD/Ciudad de Murcia SAD case and the Wimbledon/MK Dons case. By using FIFA as an expert witness they attempted to show how the case facts were

---

59 This being the leading submission seems strange, it would be normal practice to allege first that the shares were acquired illegitimately and then state that even if they were acquired legitimately that holding said shares could amount to competitive abuse. However the counsel for the claimants entered their submissions in reverse order. It likely made little impact on the outcome of the case, and is more a stylistic note.

60 Found at para 57 of the Decision.

61 In fact, it was proven later that due to the existence of a "sponsorship agreement" it was impossible for these clubs to play each other in official competitive matches.

62 However as part of this agreement the RFEF would receive 1% of the amount of any money spent in order to purchase said position in the league. Due to the nature of the purchase, a company buying Ciudad de Murcia SAD shares rather than CP Granada 74 buying Ciudad de Murciás spot in the second division, the Spanish FA were set to lose out on some money. These underlying tones were never discussed at the court, but they were certainly something to think about.

63 It should be noted that this agreement has since been dispensed of. Which is probably excellent news for the "preservation of the integrity football" especially with the increasing presence of extremely wealth private ownership coupled with financial difficulty in the world, as well as the world of football. The ability to "buy your place in the league" would no longer be a euphemism for overspending, but a literal reality.

different and that no precedent regarding change of ownership, name, and domicile could carry from the English case to the Spanish one.

However, the arbitrator saw little or no legal distinction between the two situations. While the owners of Granada 74 SAD already owned another club with the same domicile and a similar name, it did not change the fact that the core issues remained the same. It was a case of change of ownership, name, and domicile.

His decision was made easier because of the ability of Granada 74 SAD to demonstrate that, by in large, the internal structure existing at the club would remain the same. Most of the players, staff, and administration continued to work with the club, and even the former owner stayed on to work as Sporting director.

3.2.9 The Relationship Between the Clubs in Granada

It was true that Granada 74 SAD and CP Granada 74 had a special relationship and even a contract called a "Sponsorship Agreement". The Sponsorship Agreement expressly stated that the two clubs would be affiliated, a point which was raised by council of the RFEF.

However, this actually favored the case of Granada 74 SAD because these types of agreements are common within Spain, and there has been no problem with the existence of these Sponsorship Agreements in the past.[64]

In fact, these contractual relationships make it *impossible* for these affiliated clubs to play each other in competitive matches. For example, only one of the two teams can enter the Copa del Rey[65] and if they are destined to play in the same division the "lower" of the two clubs shall be demoted, or in rare cases they will be denied promotion to the same league as their counterpart.[66]

3.2.10 Jeopardizing Match Integrity

In light of the existence of this agreement, the final argument of the RFEF, which was based on Article 18.2 of the FIFA Statutes,[67] was completely quashed

[64] Sevilla CF SAD and Sevilla Atlético, Villarreal CF SAD and Villarreal B, and Real Madrid and Madrid B are three perfect examples of already existing "Sponsorship Agreements".

[65] The National Cup of the Spanish FA.

[66] They also have the opportunity to renounce their Sponsorship Agreement, but this is an option which has not been explored yet as most teams who have Sponsorship Agreements do so for training purposes and want to continue the affiliation rather than dispose of it. However, as this option and its legal consequences have not yet been discussed, we will leave the issue to rest for the moment.

[67] Article 18.2 of the FIFA Statutes – "in any case, the member shall ensure that neither a natural, nor a legal person (including holding companies and subsidiaries) exercises control over more than one club whenever the integrity of any match or competition could be jeopardized".

because, as previously stated, it was impossible for these clubs to meet each other in the competition.

Furthermore, at the time of the decision, CP Granada 74 was not part of the league and therefore not obliged to follow the obligations set out according to Article 18.2 of the FIFA Statutes.

3.2.11 Conclusion

When looking at this decision from a National perspective, in other words, if dealt with properly applying Spanish law in front of a Spanish court, there would be little or no doubt of the outcome of the case.[68]

Any uncertainty as to the outcome of this case only reveals itself when looked in the light of the specificity of sport.[69]

The main problem that the RFEF and FIFA had with this scenario was the prospect of two teams competing against each other perhaps in the same league, but using the same resources and shareholders. They were afraid[70] of the potential competitive strain this multi-ownership could place on the league.

This issue was completely resolved when the existence and the objective of the "Sponsorship Agreement" became known to the sole arbitrator, and the nature of the takeover was verified.

The Clubs were not merging and they were both keeping a huge amount percentage of their former staff as employees at both clubs. They were not "pooling their resources", nor were they promoted players and staff from CP Granada 74 to Granada 74 SAD.

This decision is highly sport specific in this respect as one of the main aspects of this case which allows this change of ownership deal to pass is an agreement between two organizations, which is essentially detrimental for one of the parties. One of the parties promises to stay in the league below the other at all times, sacrificing money and sporting success as a result, in order to not adversely affect the other organizations who are participating in the same marketplace.

---

[68] The RFEF had attempted to prove that Granada 74 SAD had not properly inscribed or registered their company and therefore had no right to legal personality, or to exist. However it was proved that it was not the inscription of Granada 74 SAD that should be examined by the inscription of Ciudad de Murcia SAD. The purchase of the shares, the change of name, and the transfer of domicile did not affect the inscription of the company (paras 108–111 of the Decision).

Furthermore, Article 15 of the Real Decreto 1564/1999 Ley de Sociedades Anónimas dealt with situations of this nature. It stated that the lack of inscription of a company would not negate the validity of the undertakinǵs actions but just transfer liability from the entity to the founders and directors of the company (including a period of up to 3 months after inscription as well).

[69] In the sense that sporting bodies understood it.

[70] With good reason due to the amount of extreme in football these days.

This is an aspect of sport like very few other businesses in the world. The necessity for the existence of competition in order for a club/company to success. Without the other participants the level of interest in the competition will decrease and the company will suffer.[71]

Finally, we must also say that LFP raised the point, at the hearing, that FIFA seemed to be afraid of that Spanish situation but failed to say anything when the English club Wimbledon FC, a long (1889) established Londoner football association which moved at the end of season 2003/2004 to the town of Milton Keynes and renamed itself as Milton Keynes Dons, after having been bought by investors. Wimbledon FC simply disappeared and FIFA answer at the hearing was that Milton Keynes is kind of a London suburb.

But, not only English regulations allow those moves, and Australian, Chilean, Mexican, or USA rules also permit a club to change his name and domicile, a matter that has happened quite a few times and, again, nobody has said nothing.

The actions of the Ciudad Deportiva Granada 92, CP Granada 74, and Granada 74 SAD did not distort the competitive marketplace, and did not amount to one buying their position in the league,[72] for rather reason the CAS, and its sole arbitrator, Rui Botica Santos, make a difficult, but ultimately correct decision.

References

Dutoit B (2005) Droit international privé suisse, 4th edn. Schulthess, Basel
Vischer F (2004) Zürcher Kommentar zum IPRG, 2nd edn. Schulthess, Zurich

[71] In order to explain by means of example, it is impossible to imagine a situation where Adidas and Reebok agreeing to operate on two different levels of performance so as not to distort the marketplace for Nike and Puma.

[72] Even though this practice was acceptable at the time of the decision.

Chapter 4
Contractual Stability: Breach of Contract

Juan de Dios Crespo Pérez, Gianpaolo Monteneri, Wil van Megen and Peter A. Limbert

Contents

Juan de Dios Crespo Pérez—LL.M., Attorney-at-law, Ruiz Huerta and Crespo Sports Lawyers.
Gianpaolo Monteneri—Attorney-at-law, Monteneri sports law.
Wil van Megen—FIFPRO Legal Department.
Peter A. Limbert—Associate, Attorney-at-law, Squire, Sanders and Dempsey (UK) LLP.

J. de Dios Crespo Pérez (✉)
Valencia, Spain
e-mail: jddcrespo@ruizcrespo.com

G. Monteneri
Zürich, Switzerland
e-mail: gianpaolo@monteneri.com

W. van Megen
Hoofddorp, Netherlands
e-mail: wil@fifpro.org

P. A. Limbert
London, England
e-mail: peter.limbert@ssd.com

A. Wild (ed.), *CAS and Football: Landmark Cases*,
ASSER International Sports Law Series, DOI: 10.1007/978-90-6704-808-8_4,

4.1 CAS 2003/O/482 Ariel Ortega v. Fenerbahçe and Fédération Internationale de Football Association

Juan de Dios Crespo Pérez

The Ortega Award is a vivid demonstration of the consequences of a player's credulousness and ignorance. It marks the first case of a unilateral breach of contract by a player after the 2001 Fenerbahçe and Fédération Internationale de Football Association (FIFA)

Regulations for the Status and Transfer of Players (FIFA Regulations) were amended. Ortega had breached his contract during the protected period. Largely because of allegedly late salary payments and an ostensible failure to provide for adequate medical service, Ortega decided to quit Fenerbahçe Istanbul. Unaware of Article 32 of the Turkish Football Association Regulations and the 2002 FIFA Regulations, Ortega ultimately ended up paying US $11 million to Fenerbahçe Istanbul. The Court of Arbitration for Sport (CAS) also imposed a four-month suspension on Ortega from the date of the award. The author explains the background and its context.

4.1.1 Preamble

The "escape from Istanbul" could be the title of a movie but unfortunately it was only the behaviour that the football player Arnaldo Ariel Ortega did, in trying to end his contract with the Turkish club Fenerbahçe Spor Kulübü, that had just began some months before.

This case was the first one of a breach of contract by a footballer brought before the CAS after the FIFA Regulations for the Status and Transfer of Player was amended on 2001 (in force the 5th of July 2001), after a "gentlemen's agreement" between FIFA and the European Commission.

The Articles 21 and 22 (now revamped as the famous Article 17 of Webster and Matuzalem) were too new for been known and when Ortega decided to leave he had just a few words with somebody in his native Argentina and he was told that he could leave without any problem and would pay quite nothing as an indemnity. This was what he had in mind when he quit Fenerbahçe.

This advice changed Ortega's life and he had to suffer afterwards during a long time to put his career again into a normal way and made him a leading case of a new line of proceedings of football matters held before the CAS.

4.1.2 Facts

On the 23rd of May 2002, Fenerbahçe Spor Kulübü, hereinafter "Fenerbahçe" or "the Club", and Club Atlético River Plate, hereinafter "River Plate", agreed to sum of US $7,500,000 for the transfer of the football player Ariel Ortega, or "the Player".

On the 8th of June 2002, Mr. Ortega signed a global contract with the Club, containing provisions regarding image rights for US $2,000,000 per season, and on the 24th of June 2002, Mr. Ortega signed a contract to play football with Fenerbahçe for 4 years for a salary of US $1,000,000 per season.

During the winter break in the 2002–2003 season, Mr. Ortega returned to Argentina to receive treatment for an injury from his personal physiotherapist. However, the Club was not entirely comfortable about this departure and was concerned that the athlete may not return to Turkey to resume playing.

Afterwards, Mr. Ortega flew to Amsterdam, for a friendly match between Argentina and Holland on the 12th of February. After the match, Mr. Ortega returned to Argentina instead of making the short trip back to Turkey. He claimed he had the consent of the Club's President to be present at the birth of his third child, however, this assertion was denied by Fenerbahçe.

On the 18th of February 2003 the Club faxed a complaint to the representatives of Mr. Ortega. As a result of said complaint the Club and River Plate began negotiations discussing the possible transfer of Mr. Ortega back to Argentina.

These negotiations were broken down in early March, and on the 3rd of March 2003 the Club sent Mr. Ortega a fax requesting his immediate return. Having heard no response, the Club submitted a claim against the Player in front of FIFA on the 11th of April 2003.

On the 6th June 2003 the FIFA DRC ordered, *inter alia*, that Mr. Ariel Arnaldo Ortega pay Fenerbahçe US $11,000,000 as compensation for breach of his employment contract with the Club and decided that the Player had a sporting sanction of fourth month.

Following the decision against him Mr. Ortega asked to stay, suspend and set aside the order of the decision.[1]

On the 19th of September 2003 the CAS held a hearing and the parties made their various submissions.

4.1.3 Main Submissions and CAS Decision

The Parties agreed on the CAS as the place in which to hold their trial. This was permitted both by FIFA and the CAS.[2] Furthermore, the FIFA DRC decision stated that:

> This decision may be appealed before the CAS within 20 days of the receiving notification of this decision by contacting the court directly in writing and by following the directions issued by the CAS, copy of which we enclose hereto.

This was before FIFA approved its new Statutes that enter into force on the 1st of January 2004 and thus all the parties that would like to appeal a FIFA body decision had to accept the CAS jurisdiction. Some clubs[3] did not accept it and thus the case was not held before the Court of Arbitration but before the Ordinary Courts of Zurich (the place where FIFA had its address).

---

[1] On the 19th of August 2003 the CAS granted the stay of the execution of the decision.

[2] FIFA had accepted the jurisdiction of the CAS in Circular letter no. 827 from the 11th of November 2002. Article R72 of the CAS code provided that whenever the parties had agreed to refer a sports-related dispute to the CAS the CAS could hear the dispute.

[3] Sint-Truiden, from Belgium in 2003 for instance.

By the way, this was the only way to discuss FIFA decision at that time and various cases brought by clubs[4] were held before such Courts in the previous years.

But, in this case, Ortega thought that the CAS would be a better jurisdiction than the Swiss Courts and thus accepted to appeal it there.

Despite the contract operating in the jurisdiction of Turkey, and subsequently being subject to Turkish law, neither Party requested the dispute be heard according to Turkish law. Therefore the dispute was decided in accordance with FIFA Regulations and complimentarily Swiss law.[5]

4.1.3.1 Breach of Contract

Both Parties claimed that the contract had been breached by the other party at the hearing.

Mr. Ortega asserted that three terms of his contract had been breached by the Club:

- The payment of his salary,[6]
- The payment to Mr. Iacoppi,[7]
- The failure of the Club to provide adequate medical service.[8]

The Club asserted the contract had been breached by Mr. Ortega by:

> Failure to report to the Club and refusing to play according to the terms of his employment contract after the 12th of February 2003.[9]

With regard to payment of the salary of Mr. Ortega the CAS found that the Club had paid the Player for the months of September, October and November, and in March 2003 they made the payments for December and January.

The Club submitted, and the CAS accepted that the payment had not been made into the Player's bank account because they did not know where the Player was for a large part of December and January. Furthermore, the Player did not file a formal

---

[4] Rayo Vallecano de Madrid, Olimpia de Asunción, Sint-Truiden, Atlético Madrid or Alavés were some of them.

[5] Article R58 of the CAS code provides that the Panel shall decide the dispute according to the rules of law chosen by the parties or, in absence of such a choice, according to the law of the country in which the federation, association or sports body which has issued the challenged decision is domicile. In this case, according to Swiss law, as FIFA's domicile is in Zurich.

[6] Mr. Ortega's salary was US $1,000,000 per season for 4 years to be paid in 10 equal instalments which commenced from the 10th of September 2002.

[7] Mr. Iacoppi had an undefined role as a friend, mentor and advisor to Ariel Ortega and was entitled to a monthly payment of US $6,000 from the club.

[8] It was presumed by the CAS that the medical treatment and physical welfare of the player were obligations which had to be assumed by the Club.

[9] It was presumed by the CAS that the most basic of obligations of a professional football player is to play football for the club to which he is contract when they request him to do so.

against the Club for the payment of these outstanding salaries.[10] This failure to demand his salary weakened the Player's position in the case.

The CAS found that the failure of the Club to make the payment of the salary owed to the Player for December and January until March could not, in itself, constitute a breach of contract and entitle the Player to treat the contract as terminated.

The CAS found that although Mr. Iacoppi had only been paid the first instalment of US $6,000 this was not enough to discharge Mr. Ortega from the contractual obligations he owed to the Club.

With regard to the Club's alleged failure to provide adequate medical service the CAS found that these claims were grossly exaggerated. They noted that Player had suffered a strained groin in December and when the Club doctor's could not treat the Player effectively they allowed him to return to Argentina to seek the advice of his personal physiotherapist.[11]

The CAS panel also refused to acknowledge the Player's submission that he had gone back to Argentina, following the February 12th friendly match with Holland, with the consent of the Club President. The evidence provided by the Player failed to prove anything to support this claim, and the Club President gave first hand evidence that he had given no such permission to the Player.[12]

With regard to the behaviour, actions and submissions of the Player the Panel stated:

> We are bound to say that Mr. Ortega did not solicit, or certainly did not receive, proper advice as to the risk he ran in adopting his chosen course of action.... Mr. Ortega was determined for reasons which could not in law be held responsible, to move on from the Club as soon as possible—trying to negotiate an exit which would not involve him in potentially onerous liabilities.[13]

4.1.3.2 Suspension

The CAS panel considered whether or not the FIFA DRC had the competence and the power to give Mr. Ortega a playing sanction. They drew upon the FIFA regulations to evaluate whether or not said ban could be given to the Player for his

---

[10] It is strange that the Player did not file a complaint against the Club because Article 32 of the Turkish Football Association Regulations provides a specific mechanism for early termination of contract for a player who has not been paid his salary by his club. "The Player may issue a notice of termination within 15 days if the Player has not been paid by the Club as per the agreement...".

[11] Furthermore they found that the upset stomach the Player suffered in February 2003 was ultimately treated, albeit overseas, by the Club doctor's advice to give the Player certain pills.

[12] It was noted with the huge amount of foreigners on the books at Fenerbahçe it would be impossible to grant leave to every Player who had a wedding or a birth to attend.

[13] Para 29 of the Decision.

unilateral breach of contract. They looked at Articles 21, 22, 23 and 42 of the FIFA Regulations and Status for Transfer of Players, 2002 edition.[14]

The CAS panel decided to suspend the Player for four months from the date of the award pursuant to Article 23(a) of the FIFA Regulations for Status and Transfer of Players 2002, hereinafter "the Regulations".

Article 23(a) of said Regulations states:

> If the breach occurs at the end of the first or the second year of contract, the sanction shall be a restriction of four months on his eligibility to participate in any official football matches as from the beginning of the new season of the new club's national championship.

The CAS decided to construe the phrase "at the end of" as including the period up to the end of the first year. Therefore they decided FIFA were entitled to impose a suspension order against the Player.

The representatives of the Player attempted to contest this suspension order stating that the breach with "no just cause" had occurred in "exceptional circumstances[15]". They declared that Mr. Ortega's wife's pregnancy was an exceptional circumstance and was reasonable grounds for the breach of contract.

The Panel replied that Mr. Ortega's wife had delivered the baby without complications on the 13th of March and Mr. Ortega had ample time to return to the club following said delivery.

Furthermore, the representatives of Mr. Ortega alleged that due to FIFA's involvement in the case the Player was effectively suspended from as early as March 2003 and therefore had already served his suspension.

The Panel again disagreed saying that Ortega had only been officially suspended as of the 6th of June 2003 and could have played for whichever club he so chose after he had left Fenerbahçe earlier in the season.

4.1.3.3 Final Sum Awarded to Fenerbahçe

Ariel Ortega addressed the CAS and stated that if the award given by the DRC remained, it would mark the end of his playing career, as he would not be able to pay the amount for which he was deemed liable.

The CAS immediately admitted that the US $200,000 owed to Ortega by the Club would have to set off the final figure.

---

[14] Most of this information can now be found under Article 17 of the Regulations on Status and Transfer of Players 2009 edition.

[15] As per Article 23 of the Regulations. But those exceptional circumstances were accepted in the Mexès case and then were eliminated from the new Regulations in 2005, due to their lack of preciseness.

The CAS noted that Ortega had broken his contract within the protected period, in the first season nonetheless, and it would have a detrimental impact on the performance and the planning of the Turkish club.[16]

Furthermore, the CAS noted that Fenerbahçe had paid US $7,500,000 for the services of the Player, and were losing the Playing without having been able to use their "asset" to any effect. Additionally, Fenerbahçe had paid US $750,000 to the Argentinean Football Federation for the mandatory 15% participation fee. Fenerbahçe had also paid "Image Promotion Company" US $1,500,000 in order to obtain the image rights of the Player.

Finally the CAS noted that the Player would be receiving US $1,000,000 for playing salary, and US $2,000,000 for his image rights and had 3 years and 3 months remaining on his playing contract.

But CAS refuses the claim from the Turkish club about the "sporting loss" they have suffered. This loss has been accepted by CAS in the Matuzalem case, as a part of the "specificity of sport".

Taking into account all of these factors the CAS awarded Fenerbahçe with the final reimbursement amount of US $11,000,000.

4.1.4 Commentary

By and large this case was an easy one for the CAS to decide. The Player was clearly unsatisfied with life at his new club in Turkey. He wanted to return home to Argentina but did not have the legal tools to do so without having to compensate Fenerbahçe.

Although the Club did not pay him as contractually agreed for the months of December and January, the Player did not submit a formal complaint to the Club, the Turkish FA, FIFA or any number of governing/judicial bodies.

4.1.4.1 Article 23 Interpretation

However, one of the more interesting and controversial aspects of this CAS decision was the interpretation the CAS took to the old Article 23 of the Regulations.

These Regulations were obviously poorly drafted at the time, and when read word for word and interpreted literally they do not give FIFA the ability to impose a playing sanction on Ariel Ortega. Article 23(a) says the breach must occur at the

[16] The Player was intended to be an integral part of the team and having left immediately after the transfer window, for no compensation, he would affect how the team would perform on the field.

end of the first or second year; however, Mr. Ortega breached his contract in February, well before the end of the first year of the contract.

While it is obvious that the drafters of the FIFA Regulations intended to maintain contractual stability, and discourage a cavalier attitude towards contract; it cannot be said that the drafters had enshrined the maintenance of contractual stability in statute in this scenario and without the highly interpretative nature of the article by the CAS, Ortega would not have got a playing suspension.

4.1.4.2 Non-Payment Under Turkish FA Regulations

It is strange to consider that the outcome of this case may have completely changed had Ortega relied on Domestic regulations and complained about the non-payment of his salary to the Turkish FA. Mr. Ortega had the opportunity to make a formal claim for salaries that were owed to him by Fenerbahçe.

Mr. Ortega never availed of this opportunity most likely because of ignorance of the existence of a provision which would allow him to terminate his contract if he was not paid by his employer.

The CAS mentioned at para 21 of their decision that the Player could have relied on Turkish Football Association Regulations in order to terminate his contract. Articles 32 and 33[17] of the Turkish Football Association regulations define under which circumstances and by which means a player may inform his club of early termination of contract as a result of non-payment of salary.

Ortega had the opportunity to give notice of early termination of contract if he had not been paid within 15 days of the due date of salary. He would have had to issue a notice of termination of the contract to the Turkish Football Association and Fenerbahçe would have had 7 days to make payment of the said outstanding salaries.

Despite the fact that Ortega was in Argentina and not training with the Club, if he had issued the notice of termination, and Fenerbahçe failed to make the payment of the salaries before this trial his case might have been decided differently.

However, it is unlikely that he knew of the existence of these regulations[18] but this is not strange if he had received the same advice as for his early termination of contract.

As a result one of the first "unilateral breach of contract" cases was borne.[19]

---

[17] Article 32, as previously mentioned, sets out when the Player may issue a notice of termination. Article 33 sets out of the methodology of issuing said notice of termination.

[18] This could have been because of poor representation and legal advice, or because of the different language that the regulations were written in.

[19] The CAS discussed this missed opportunity at para 21 of the Decision.

4.1.5 Additional Commentary

It should also be noted that while the CAS noted in their award that Mr. Ortega had spoken about how an award of equivalent level to the one given against him by the FIFA DRC would end his career, they nonetheless confirmed the award of US $11,000,000.

While it had no legal relevance, it is stylistically strange that the CAS arbitrators would mention the pleas of Mr. Ortega perhaps garnering him some public sympathy but condemn him to pay the same amount.

Finally, while the decision of the case is sound, the final award is without calculations, which leaves the academic or interested reader searching for some sort of test with which to develop the jurisprudence for what were to become "Article 17 unilateral breach of contract cases". However this was the early days of said cases and the award, although lacking mathematical explanation, was legally sound.

And just for the public knowledge of how things have finished with Ortega, let us say that the very same night before the hearing was held, the parties agreed to an indemnity to be paid by several individuals and companies involved in the case for an amount of 4.5 million USD. This agreement was accepted by all of the parties but finally one of the paying individuals decided not to follow and then the settlement fall down. It was really a pity as the result of the case was not so evident in favour of Ortega. The funny thing is that Ortega reached finally an agreement with Fenerbahçe in August 2004 for the very same amount of US $4.5 million in order to play with the Argentinean club Newell's Old Boys and end his non-playing situation.

Thus, he lost eight months from the CAS decision plus what the time he had not played previously as not a club was wanting to contract him subject to pay the huge indemnity decided by FIFA, for finally settling for the same amount he could have paid much before.

4.2 CAS 2004/A/708 Philippe Mexès v. Fédération Internationale de Football Association (FIFA); CAS 2004/A/709 AS Roma v. FIFA; CAS 2004/A/713 AJ Auxerre v. AS Roma and Philippe Mexès; CAS 2005/A/902 and 903 P. Mexès and AS Roma v. AJ Auxerre and AJ Auxerre v. P. Mexès and AS Roma; CAS 2005/A/916 AS Roma v. FIFA

Juan de Dios Crespo Pérez

In the Mexès Award the CAS considered the legal coherence between the contract extension and the protected period under the 2001 FIFA Regulations for the Status and Transfer of Players (FIFA Regulations). Contrary to the 2005 Regulations, the 2001

Regulations did not explicitly state the renewal of the protected period by the renewal of the contract. Based on the ratio legis, the Panel concurred on the renewal of the protected period and thus on Mexès' breach of contract during the protected period. Other interesting issues which arose were sanctioning the player leniently as well as calculating the compensation. In his analysis the author sets these legal problems against the issues of the FC Pyunik cases and the Webster Award. The analysis also considers the AS Roma sporting sanctions: reduction of the transfer ban from two registration periods to one.

4.2.1 Preamble

Philippe Mexès had a very good relationship with the then Auxerre coach, the famous and renowned Guy Roux, who usually treated his players like his sons but when a father gives you his word you normally understand that he is going to comply with.

And this is what happened when Mexès thought that Roux had given him the possibility to be transferred to a club of his choice at the end of season 2003–2004. But a word is not a written contract and Roux denied the chance to his "son" to leave Auxerre so easily and he asked for a huge transfer fee.

This was sensed by Mexès like a treachery and then the Mexès saga began…which will involve not only the player and Auxerre but also AS Roma, his future club in a case that was to transform the FIFA Regulations of 2001 into the revamped 2005 which are quite the same as today. So the saga was not just another case but really a leading one.

4.2.2 Introduction

Before engaging in an analysis of the AJ Auxerre, hereinafter "Auxerre", Philip Mexes, hereinafter "Mexes" or "the Player" and AS Roma, hereinafter "Roma", cases it is best to clarify that there were three cases with the same facts but different party interests all heard together on the 11th of March 2005.

1. Philippe Mexès and AS Roma v. Fédération Internationale de Football Association (FIFA) and AJ Auxerre (and vice versa) for the sporting sanction of FIFA against the player. (TAS 2004/A/708/709/713).
2. AJ Auxerre c. AS Roma and Philippe Mexès (and vice versa) for the indemnity to be paid to Auxerre (TAS 2005/902 and 903).
3. AS Roma v. FIFA for the sporting sanction of FIFA against that club (TAS 2005/A/916).

Each of the three cases had to deal with Philippe Mexès prematurely terminating his employment contract with Auxerre in France, and subsequently signing a playing contract with Roma in Italy.

4.2.3 Facts

Philippe Mexès, born on the 30th of March 1982 in Toulouse, France, had been with the French club Auxerre from the age of 15. On the 13th of May 1998 Philippe Mexès signed a youth contract with Auxerre for 5 years. On the 20th of June 2000, Philippe Mexès replaced this youth contract by signing a professional football player's contract for a period of 5 years.

On the 15th of December 2002 Auxerre and Mexès agreed to extend the contract by one year, thus concluding at the end of the 2005–2006 season, the Player's salary was improved and the Club agreed to pay the Player a transfer bonus if he moved to another club. This was crucial to the dispute between the Parties, and will be discussed thoroughly later on in this commentary.

During the course of the employment contract, the Player asked the Club what transfer fee they would demand, if the contract was amicably terminated before its expiration date. The Club did not respond to the Player with a figure and just reminded him that he was under contract with the Club until the 30th of June 2006 and they would expect him to satisfy said contractual obligations.

On the 24th of May 2004 Roma informed Auxerre that they were interested in signing the player and they intended to make an offer for the Player's services. On the 4th of June 2004, Roma made an offer of €4,500,000 to Auxerre for the Player.

Auxerre told Roma that this offer was way below their valuation of the Player and therefore would not agree to the transfer for this amount of compensation. They added that the Player would remain under contract with the Club until the 30th of June 2006.

On the 11th of June 2004, Philippe Mexès made an appeal to FIFA requesting to be released from his contract on the basis of Article 42[20] of the Regulations on the Status and Transfer of Players, hereinafter "RSTP", 2001 edition. Less than 24 h later, Roma and Mexès signed a 4 year long contract from the 2004/2005 season to the 2007/2008 season.

Despite formal demands issued by the Club on the 21st of June 2004 and 1st of July 2004, the Player refused to attend training sessions with AJ Auxerre.

4.2.4 FIFA Dispute Resolution Chamber Decisions

On July 8th 2004 Auxerre filed a complaint to the FIFA DRC, requesting that their Panel hear a dispute regarding a breach of contract and inducement to breach contract by Mexès and Roma, respectively.

[20] Dispute Resolution Chamber will have to determine whether one of the parties has committed a unilateral breach of contract without just cause.

On the 31st of August 2004 the DRC rendered a decision regarding the validity of Mexès' contract with Roma, and any sporting sanctions which might apply to the player and the Club.

They determined that the Player would not be eligible to play for Roma for 6 weeks after the commencement of the Italian Championship on the 12th of September 2004. The DRC also determined that the alleged inducement for the Player to breach his contract would be ruled upon at separate disciplinary proceedings, and that any sanction given as a result of said inducement would be awarded after the other disciplinary proceeding. None of the parties were happy with the sporting sanction to the player and then appealed to the CAS (first Mexès case).

On the 13th of May 2005, the FIFA DRC decided that Mexès would have to pay Auxerre €8,000,000 for breach of contract. The FIFA DRC considered the objective criteria which were set out in Article 22.1 of the RSTP 2001 edition.

They took note of the higher salary Mexès would be receiving at Roma, and that Mexès had received 7 years of training, from the age of 15–22, at a Club with an excellent reputation for training players.[21] They stated that the remaining value of the Player's contract with Auxerre was €2,403,614. The DRC stated that they based their decision on the special circumstances of the case and objective criteria. Furthermore, Roma were found to be jointly and severally liable for the compensation payable to Auxerre because the DRC decided that they induced the Player to breach his contract.

Each of the Parties was unhappy with their decision. Auxerre believed the valuation of the Player to be closing to €18,000,000,[22] while the Club and Player were both unhappy with the amount of compensation they would have to pay and the length of the sporting sanctions they would receive.

On the 3rd of September 2004, Mr. Mexès and Roma each submitted an appeal against the decision of the FIFA DRC to the CAS in Lausanne, Switzerland, in accordance with Article 60.1 of the RSTP 2001 edition.(Second Mexès case).

Meanwhile, the case against AS Roma for inducing the breach of contract of the player continues and was finally decided by the DRC on the 23rd of June 2005, and sanctioned the Italian club with a prohibition of acquiring any new players during two transfer windows. This decision was appealed by AS Roma before the CAS. (Third Mexès case).

---

[21] One should assume that the DRC made mention of this in order to demonstrate that Mexès would not have the opportunity to play at such a high level and earn so much money, but for the fantastic training he received while playing at AJ Auxerre.

[22] Their valuation was supported by the assertion by Gazetta Dello Sport on the 31st of August 2004, where they publish the value of about 500 players, that Philippe Mexès worth €17,000,000.

4.2.5 Commentaries

4.2.5.1 CAS Decision First Mexes Case (Sporting Sanction to the Player):

Stay of Decision

Before the CAS held its final hearing on the dispute, they had to hold a preliminary hearing to decide whether or not to stay the decision of the FIFA DRC, effectively postponing any bans until after final judgment had been passed.

The Parties, following the lines of the CAS jurisprudence that the stay of the decision should be granted because:

There was a *chance of success on appeal*, that is to say, that the chance of having the decision overturned on appeal could not be discounted.[23,24]

On the *balance of interests* of the Parties. Which means that Auxerre and FIFA would not be suffering any significant damage.

The premature execution of the decision would be the Parties at the risk of suffering *irreparable harm*. In other words, if the Player and Club were set to receive suspensions from playing and registering players, but were later found to be innocent they would receive suspensions for offenses which they were not guilty of.

In light of the magnitude of the irreparable harm and the proximity in time of the final hearing, the CAS Panel elected to grant the petition for the stay of decision.

Final Award: Contract Extension and Protected Period

The CAS had to rule upon was whether or not Player had in fact breached his contract within the "Protected Period[25]". This was necessary in order to determine if sporting sanctions should apply to the parties, and what level of compensation would be awarded to the aggrieved party.

The CAS felt that due to the prolongation of the playing contract, and the extension of the playing contract, Philip Mexès and Auxerre had effectively reset the timer on the Protected Period and subsequently brought the timing of the breach of contract within the 3-year safe zone and consequently obliged the CAS to impose sporting sanctions on the Player and his new Club.

---

[23] Jurisprudence on this issue of "chance of success on appeal" was established in CAS 2003/O/482 Ariel *Ortega* v *Fenerbahçe* SK and FIFA.

[24] The representatives of the Player in their submissions stated in their Stay of Decision order that the "chances of success… are *prima facie* reasonable in the sense that they cannot be discounted."

[25] Defined in the Regulations.

However, some creativity was required by the CAS in this instance because the 2001 Regulations did not specifically state that the renewal of a contract would result in the renewal of the Protected Period. The Panel had to find the *ratio legis* for the rules which policed the legal relationship between the two parties.

The Panel thought that it was appropriate to consider the intention of FIFA for its own 2001 Regulations by examining the new version of the FIFA Regulations, and what they stated with regard to the extension of the term of a professional player contract and triggering a new stability period.[26] Therefore the DRC determined that the Player's signature of an extension agreement to their previous playing contract would restart the Protected Period even though this was not indicated in the 2001 Regulations and had to be changed in the 2005 ones.

Final Award: Suspension

The Regulations state that the player shall be banned from playing for 4 months, and the new club shall receive a ban from registering players for 2 transfer windows. However, these suspension times enshrined in the Regulations of FIFA were ignored by the CAS and other sanctions were imposed.

With regard to the Player's suspension Auxerre had no interest in the length of the playing ban imposed against Mexès as he was no longer part of the team. In the absence of any legitimate submissions stating why the sanction should be increased, and according to the principle of n*e ultra petita*, the CAS could not impose a playing ban of longer time than the one award which was given by the FIFA DRC, which was six weeks, according to the "exceptional circumstances of the case" that was stated in Article 23 of the 2001 FIFA Regulations.

Once again, those "exceptional circumstances" that had permitted the reduction of the usual sanction, had been taken off in the new Regulations of 2005.

Ignoring FIFA regulations

FC Pyunik Cases

Upon reading the CAS award of this dispute, one often wonders how Philip Mexès breaches his contract unilaterally within the Protected Period[27] and escapes with a 6-week playing ban, when the relevant Status clearly stated that Mexès should have received a 4-month playing ban.

However, this is not the first time that this happened. In the *FC Pyunik* cases,[28] which were also regarding unilateral termination of contract, the Player's Carl

---

[26] http://www.thefreelibrary.com/Publication+of+CAS+awards:+(per+March+2006).-a0169017238

[27] As a result of the CAS's interpretation that a renewal of contract shall be seen as a new contract, thus triggering the commencement of a new protected period.

[28] CAS 2007/A/1358 FC Pyunik Yerevan v. Carl Lombe, AFC Rapid Bucaresti and FIFA, CAS 2007/A/1358 FC Pyunik Yerevan v. Edel Apoula Edima Bete, AFC Rapid Bucaresti and FIFA.

Lombe and Edel Apoula Edima Bete both escaped sporting sanctions despite the FIFA Regulations indicating that their actions merited suspension.

Within their submissions and during the trial the Appellants, FC Pyunik Yerevan, stated that both of the respondents, the players and Rapid Bucharest,[29] should be condemned to sporting sanctions of six months[30] playing ban and two transfer registration period ban, respectively. They submitted effervescently, in capital text; at para 73.2 of the Carl Lombe decision[31] that:

> That both respondents have to be condemned to sporting sanctions of 6 months and of two transfer windows without inscriptions of players on the national and international level. AS FIFA FAILED TO SANCTION THEN ACCORDING TO THE FIFA REGULATIONS FOR THE STATUS AND TRANSFER OF PLAYERS.

FIFA had originally stated in their DRC decision, with regard to Article 17.3 and the stipulated sanction to apply to parties in breach of contract, that:

> [Article 17.3] assigns the competent deciding body the power, but by no means the obligation, to impose a sporting sanction on a player found to be in breach of contract during the protected period.

The CAS later confirmed FIFA's decision not to sanction the parties stating at para 118 of the Carl Lombe decision[32]:

> In view of the specific circumstances of the case, including the age of the Player at the time he signed the Employment Contract[33] and the controversy surrounding his registration from the Appellant, the DRC decided not to impose any sporting sanctions, which would have had a considerable impact on the Player and were considered to be excessive and inappropriate.

However, it does not appear that neither the FIFA DRC nor the CAS should have interpreted application of the clause as optional. The relevant provision, 17.3 of the Regulations, is clear in its wording when it states that "In addition to the obligation to pay compensation, sporting sanctions *shall* also be imposed."

The CAS admits in para 119 of the Carl Lombe decision that if the intention of the FIFA Regulations was to give the competent body the power to impose a sporting sanction, it would have employed the word "may" and not "shall".

There was nothing ambiguous about the wording of the article in either the Mexès or FC Pyunik cases. However, in each of the cases the DRCs decided to

---

[29] The club that the players joined after having breached their contract with Pyunik.

[30] Pyunik felt that a six, rather than four, month sanction should apply because they believed the breach of contract to have been made with aggravated circumstances.

[31] See n. 28 above.

[32] See n. 28 above.

[33] The Players, Lombe and Edima Bete were minors at the time of signing the playing contract with FC Pyunik.

make a decision in the interest of the "Spirit of the Regulation", which was then confirmed by the CAS.[34]

While one can understand the sympathetic nature of the Pyunik cases it is hard to understand why Mexès, a player who requested a transfer and then took matters into his own hands when he was not given one, was treated leniently when it came to the handing out of a sporting sanction.

It is the opinion of the writer that in certain situations the DRC or the CAS need to be lenient on the athlete because of unfortunate circumstances, mistreatment of one of the parties, the age of the player or any number of criteria.

However, it would be more legally sound and certain if FIFA were to redraft their Regulations to give the *power* to the DRC to impose a ban on the player and the club, rather than the obligation. Each time a player breaches his contract and the DRC or CAS does not feel that a ban is appropriate they are given the difficult task of straying away from unambiguous regulations, and essentially improperly interpreting the text in order to give a fair decision.

Mid-Season Breach

The FIFA regulations not addressing the scenario where a contract is extended rather than a whole new contract drafted with regard to the Protected Period. The CAS considered that the new Protected Period should take effect from when the contract extension comes into force. Ergo, they stressed that FIFA should clarify how the Protected Period should apply when a contractual extension comes into effect during the season.

However, it is my opinion that such clarification is now not necessary as the FIFA Regulations define the Protected Period[35] as "a period of three entire seasons or three/two years, whichever comes first, following the entry into force of a contract…" Therefore, FIFA has stipulated that if the breach of contract occurs mid-season but less than three years or seasons to the day after the signing of an extension of contract, then the Player will be deemed to have committed the breach within the protected period.

CAS Decision Second Mexès Case (Player and Roma Indemnity to Pay to Auxerre):

Final Award: Compensation

In its decision on the 13th of May 2005 the CAS felt one of the main issues to be considered is that the DRC had not properly communicated what their motivation

---

[34] In the case of Mexès this was because AJ Auxerre did not request the Player receive a longer playing ban. The maxim of *Ultra petita* was therefore applicable for the rights of the athlete.

[35] #7 in the Definitions Section of the FIFA Regulations on the Status and Transfer of Player 2009.

or method of calculation was in their decision obliging Roma to pay Auxerre €8,000,000 compensation.

Therefore, they believed it to be one of their primary mandates to calculate the amount of compensation due to be paid, if any, and state how they had reached this decision.

The CAS reviewed the facts concerning the potential transfer of the Player to another club from Auxerre.

The Panel first took into account the "investment" made by Auxerre on the player. Mexes had initially signed a five-year contract from 2000 to 2005, but then, on December 2002, he signed an extension until the end of the 2005–2006 season. This extension was made retroactive to 2002, so the extension was effectively a new four year contract from 2002 to 2006.

The Panel concluded that the difference between the old salary and the new salary that was effectively paid from the date when the extension was signed, in the summer of 2002, until the date in which the contract was terminated, in the summer of 2004. They also accounted for the bonus paid to Mexes for signing the extension, and the fee paid to the agent for the extension agreement. Therefore the effective costs incurred by Auxerre came to a total of €2,289,644.

The Panel then took into account the future earnings for the transfer of the player that Auxerre lost due to the breach. This is when they took into account Roma's offer of €4,500,000, as this was the only existing offer for the player.

This offer was the only official one and moreover was made by the future club of the player who signs a contract quite immediately after having ended his relationship with Auxerre. The offer in Mexès case is really an important issue and has been the example for the following breach of contract proceedings like the Webster one.

Comparison of Webster Offer

Later on in the case commentaries we shall analyse the Andrew Webster case[36] however, for the purposes of the Mexès case it is important to consider why the CAS interpreted the offers received from a third club.

The answers are two. One is timing. The fact that Hearts received the offer for Webster's services after the Player had broke his contract with the Club means that Hearts are not suffering any damage because the Player and the Club no longer have any contractual ties. The Club is not entitled to accept any offer; therefore it is money which they never could have earned.

However, in the Mexès case, these offers were received while the Player was still under contract with the Club and still was an asset of the Club. Therefore, the Panel was of the opinion that these offers were legitimate losses for the Club.

The pattern of these offers, and perhaps even the renewal of the contract with a clause providing for the Player to receive a certain proportion of any transfer offer

[36] CAS 2007/A/1298 and 1299 and 1300.

received, demonstrates that the Club had the intention, or at least, other clubs had the motivation to buy this player. In contrast, no offers were received for Webster in the time leading up to his breach; therefore it did not appear as if the Club would be able to earn any money from the Player, but for his breach of contract.

However, it is my belief that if the Panel thought Hearts were not entitled to any money because the offer was received after Webster had breached his contract and therefore the Club never could have accepted this offer. It would also appear that the refusal of an offer to purchase the Player by a third party should also not carry with it financial value because in this case Auxerre also could never have accepted this offer having previously turned it down.

One can only assume that it is because Auxerre had already received offers for the Player and thus there was the indication that the Club would continue to receive offers in the future, that the CAS took the view that Auxerre might suffer potential loss because of the breach of contract of Mexès. Whereas, there was no indication that Hearts would suffer potential loss because Hearts had not received an offer for the Player until after he had terminated his contractual ties with the club.

The second answer is who made the offer. In this case, AS Roma was not only offering a transfer fee just a week before a contract is signed between the club and Mexès.

Forfeiting Transfer Fee

One point which is often ignored but interesting to note when reviewing this case is that Philip Mexès signed a contract extension which had a clause inserted to allow him to collect a certain percentage[37] of the transfer fee received by Auxerre for his playing services. However, because the Player unilaterally terminated his contract no transfer fee was received by Auxerre from Roma, so Philip Mexès would have forfeited any right to this percentage that he may have once had.

Valuation of the player

One of the most interesting parts of this case, and something which Auxerre were certainly unsatisfied with was the CAS's valuation of the Player, perhaps the Club's most prized asset. Auxerre in their submission to FIFA compared Mexès to several other professionals who had been acquired or transfer by Roma, and they compared Mexès to other professionals who had been acquired by different Club's in several positions.

Auxerre made note of several transaction involving AS ROMA, submitting the following information:

[37] The percentage of the transfer he was entitled to would increase the longer he spent with the Club.

- Walter Samuel, a 31 year old Uruguayan, had transferred from Roma to Real Madrid for 25 million euros, and played "exactly the same position as the player Mexès" who was only 22 years of age, and arguably just as talented.
- Emerson, a Brazilian defensive midfielder, had transferred from Roma to Juventus approximately 26 million euros[38]; and
- Ferrari, an Italian defensive minded player, had transferred from Parma to Roma for 16 million euros, and was not rated as highly as Mexès.

They also submitted the following information about comparable transfers:

- Ricardo Carvalho, a Portuguese centre-back, had transferred from Porto to Chelsea for 30 million euros, and this was after they had engaged in failed negotiations for Mexès.
- Gabriel Heinze, an Argentinean centre-back or full-back, had transferred from French team PSG to Manchester United for 11.5 million euros.
- Wayne Rooney, a young English forward, had transferred from Everton to Manchester United for 37.5 million euros.
- Finally Djibril Cisse, a young French forward, had transferred from Auxerre to Liverpool for about 20 million euros.

While not all of the information that Auxerre submitted with regard to other transfers was relevant to the dispute[39] it was clear that Auxerre had established that, in the current market, Mexès was a very valuable asset, and were Auxerre to transfer the Player he would command a fee comparable to the other footballers mentioned in their submission.

The Panel decided that Auxerre did not prove its commercial and sporting damages. It also determined that Auxerre had obstructed Mexes' possibilities to obtain a transfer by refusing to enter into any negotiations whatsoever.[40] At the same time, the Panel also determined that Roma's offer did not reflect the true value of the player, and that the offer's sole objective was to lead to the termination of Mexes contract with Auxerre.

In the end, the indemnity was fixed at €7,000,000, as a result of the sum of the costs incurred by Auxerre, €2,289,644, and Roma's offer, €4,500,000, plus the other criteria taken into account by the Panel, although no specification of why

[38] If the exchange of the Player Matteo Brighi was accounted for.

[39] Comparing a French centre-back of 22 years of age, to an English forward of 19 years of age is somewhat difficult. Furthermore, not every team is equally proficient in the transfer market. Some teams have a history of paying over market price for a Player in order to obtain the player they believe is necessary to win, and to prevent their direct competition from acquiring the talent. Real Madrid, Manchester United and Chelsea are three perfect examples of clubs who engage in this practice.

[40] It was submitted that Portsmouth FC in England had offered €7,000,000 for the Player's service, and this offer was also refused by Auxerre. Furthermore, it was brought to the attention of the CAS that both Manchester United and Chelsea FC had contract with Auxerre and engaged in a series of negotiations to by the Player. However, Auxerre were very reluctant to negotiate and made it difficult for the player to secure a transfer elsewhere.

they rounded the indemnity to exactly €7,000,000,[41] reducing the FIFA DRC amount by 1 million euros.

CAS Decision Third Mexès Case (Roma Sporting Sanction):

The CAS determined that Roma would receive a transfer ban of only 1 more registration period and thus reduced the ban from the previous two that the DRC had decided.

Roma had stated at the trial that because they had received notice from FIFA on the 30th of June 2005 and that during June some players have already signed a contract with the club.

Then Roma filed an appeal as well as a request for the stay of the execution. Such a stay was not granted by the President of the TAS Appeal proceedings initially on his decision dated 25th July 2005 but a second request was made to the Panel itself on the 2nd August 2005, with new facts such as a claim by the players that have signed with the club and that cannot be registered because of the ban.

The Panel decided that due to those new facts, the stay should be granted and gave it on the 8th of July 2005. Thus, Roma was not only entitled to register the previous players that have already signed a contract but also the possible news ones up to the end of that transfer window (i.e. 31st of August).

Once it was clear that Roma made the offer for a transfer and they signed quite immediately afterwards a contract with Mexès, the induction to the breach was evident and a sanction had to be taken by CAS.

The fight was on whether the sanction had to be reduce to one only as July 2005 had not been a free month due to the decision of not granting the stay to Rome. CAS accepted Roma's position that July and the eight days of August should be accepted as having been already punished, even though players have been contracted before that date (June) and after (rest of August).

Roma expressed the view, and the CAS agreed[42] that this should constitute having already served half of their transfer registration ban, and they should only be prevented from signing players for one more transfer window.

This was a splendid decision for Roma, as it had really only one ban being the only case where a reduction on two transfer windows was given.

---

[41] However, perhaps it is appropriate to draw attention to the Portsmouth bid which was turned down by Auxerre and recognise that the two figures are identical; €7,000,000.

[42] The CAS took the view that imposing a ban of two transfer window periods on Roma when they had not acted during the previous transfer window allegedly anticipating a ban was contrary to the "Spirit of the Regulations", therefore they did not take a literal interpretation of the Regulations.

4.3 CAS 2006/A/1100 Tareq Eltaib v. Club Gaziantepspor

Gianpaolo Monteneri

The Tareq Eltaib Award may be regarded as a guideline for determining ‘just cause’, as well as for calculating compensation. In this case, player Tareq Eltaib terminated his contract with Club Gaziantepspor for alleged late and non-payments of his remuneration. The Panel laid out what the player is expected to do for a valid termination of his contract where remuneration payment is delayed or is not forthcoming. The principle of good faith means the player must notify his club of his frustration with a clear warning. In the Panel’s opinion the player’s silence is to be seen as acceptance of the Club’s conduct. Under these provisions, the CAS stated that Tareq Eltaib had breached his contract without just cause during the protected period. The author explains the guidelines in light of this case.

4.3.1 Preamble

(1) One of the most joyful moments for a football club and its fans is the signing of a new player for the club. The new player is meant to give to the club the vitality and strength it needs, so as to be competitive in the new season. The signature is usually widely broadcasted in the local media and based on the pictures offered to the public, the relationship between the player and the club is supposed to last forever. The reality, however, sometimes develops in a completely different way than the expectations of the parties and the agreements concluded between the clubs and the players are not performed in a proper way. Often the misunderstandings and failure to conform to the contractually agreed terms lead the parties to the breach or even the early termination of such agreements.

(2) In the same way, regrettably, it has become fashionable that clubs and players use minor infringements of their agreements as a ground for an exit of the employment relationship and subsequent claims for compensations of alleged damages. However, some termination of contract could have been avoided had the parties clearly comprehended their contractual capabilities prior to committing any of such actions. But since football is first of all passion and emotion, now and again rational thinking and balanced handling are neglected in a crisis situation between a player and club, with usually devastating effects for all parties involved.

(3) The public opinion, in particular the own fans, play an important role in the handling and decision-making process of a club but also of a player, creating pressure and expectation on them. But what appears to be reasonable from the point of view of an average person or fan cannot be often appreciated in the same manner in the light of applicable legal frame of State law or sports body regulations and reserves often surprises when the relevant decision is notified to the parties concerned.

(4) Fact is that employment-related disputes are increasing (both in number and in the value of the dispute), which is on one side explicable with the complete globalisation of football (more and more players are ready to leave their home countries and go to play abroad, even to the most unusual football destination) and on the other side with the increase of revenue generated by the leagues and clubs which is based primarily on television and commercial rights.

(5) The reasons for the disputes have always a simple common denominator: *remuneration*! For a player it is either a default in payment on the side of the club or a better financial offer coming from a third club. For a club it is the default in paying the salary of a player on time, which can be based either on a provisional cash flow problem or on the intention to part from the player since he has become uninteresting from a sporting perspective. The parties then use their tailor-made strategies so as to be released from their respective engagements.

(6) Whenever an employment-related dispute between a club and player occurs, the aggrieved party seeks recourse to the competent State or sports courts. In the event of a dispute which has an international dimension the parties have a tendency to start legal procedure before the FIFA Dispute Resolution Chamber ("DRC")[43] with the possibility to appeal the decision of this body to the Court of Arbitration to Sport ("the CAS"). The main reason for this choice is the fact of having an independent international body investigating and deciding on the matter with the possibility to have the decision taken respected and enforced through disciplinary measures in case of non-compliance.

(7) The first question to which these sports courts have to give an answer while analysing a dispute who is right and who had therefore *just cause*, i.e. a valid reason for the termination of an agreement?

(8) As far as the definition of the term "just cause" is concerned, the legislator (both at State and sports law level) has always preferred not to give a comprehensive definition but has left its assessment to the circumstances of the case, trusting in the correct evaluation of the judges. This had as an end result that the decisions about "just cause" depend solely on the appreciation of the concrete circumstances of a case by the judge(s) in question and may thus find slight divergences in understanding, interpretation and application depending on the person who is deciding and the legal background he is coming from.

(9) This article will provide the reader with the review and analysis of an award rendered by the CAS few years ago in respect of a dispute between the Libyan player, Tareq Eltaib ("the Player") and a Turkish Club Gaziantepspor ("the Club"), which has become a bench mark in establishing general guidelines for the evaluation of "just cause" as well as for determining the due conduct for the termination of an employment contract.

---

[43] For more details on the procedure before the FIFA Dispute Resolution Chamber please refer to the Regulations on the Status and Transfer of Players as well as on the Rules governing the procedures of the Players' Status Committee and the Dispute Resolution Chamber.

4.3.2 Facts of the Case

(10) The entire factual underlying of this case is rather hackneyed. The Player and the Club entered into an employment agreement for three seasons (from 2004/05 to 2006/07). However, in the middle of the second season, on 14 March 2006, the Player suddenly submits to the DRC a letter, claiming for his release from the employment relationship with the Club due to the repeated delays of payments under the agreement and non-payment of two monthly salaries, namely those of December 2005 and January 2006.

(11) In the same time the Club directed to the DRC its own claim relating to the unexcused absence of the Player. Thereof, the Club requested the DRC to order the Player to immediately return to the Club. The Club further maintained that it fulfiled its financial obligations towards the Player.

(12) The DRC, as the first instance deciding body, after due consideration of the positions submitted by both parties, issued an order to the Player to immediately resume duty with the Club ("the challenged Decision"). The decision taken by the DRC has for sure a big *Solomonic* component, as this body had clearly identified that the Player had left the Club without just cause and instead of straight away establishing that the Player breached and terminated the employment contract without just cause, with all the disciplinary and financial consequences of such decision, it offered to the Player the possibility to repair to his mistake and resume duty with the Club, particularly considering that the latter was more than happy to welcome him back, since he was a key player of the squad.

(13) The Player had however a different agenda and for sure no intention to go back (probably because he started to receive financially and sportive interesting offers) and instead appealed against the decision of the DRC requesting as provisional measure the stay of execution of the challenged Decision allowing him thus to enter into a contract with a new clubs pending the outcome of the appeal procedure.

4.3.2.1 Overview of the Submissions of the Player

(14) The Player requested the Panel to annul the challenged Decision asserting that he terminated the employment contract with just cause due to the repeated violations committed by the Club. In this respect, the Player also asked to recognise him as a free agent and to condemn the Club to the payment of compensation for the damage he had allegedly suffered.

(15) In addition, in order to explain the Player's reluctance to return to the Club and to resume with his obligations under the employment contract, the Player's submissions referred to an articles published in a Turkish newspaper, where the attempt to smear the Player's integrity was expressed by a high Club's representative.

4.3.2.2 Overview of the Submissions of the Club

(16) The Club in its turn rejected any assertion or assumption related to the just cause of the Player for termination of the employment contract and reasserted its interest in respecting what had been contractually stipulated with the Player. The Club alleged that it has always acted in perfect compliance with the provisions of the employment contract and never produced any valid reason for such illicit conduct of the Player.

(17) As regards to the consequences of the Player's behaviour, the Club requested the Panel to condemn the Player to the payment of compensation as well as to impose the sporting sanctions on him as consequence of the breach of the employment contract. Additionally, the Panel was called for holding the new club of the Player jointly and severally liable with the compensation for the payment of the compensation.

4.3.3 Questions Posed Before the CAS

(18) Prior to commencing with the legal analysis of the Panel's considerations of the case in question, it is essential to determine the main issues that are at stake and will need a closer scrutiny.

(19) The two central questions that have to be addressed are the following: figure: first, whether the Player and/or the Club committed a breach of the employment contract, and second, in the event any of the parties committed a contractual breach, to define the consequences thereof.

(20) The Panel was hence asked to establish the existence or non-existence of "just cause" in the sense of the FIFA Regulations on the Status and Transfer of Player ("the Regulations"), which would permit the Player either to be released from its contractual obligations or to be found liable for the breach of the contract and sanctioned accordingly.

4.3.4 Legal Analysis of the Case

(21) Within the entire discussion made by the Panel with respect to the grounds of termination of the employment contract, one can follow the general line of adherence to the *principle of contractual stability* established in Chap. IV of the Regulations. The Regulations want to ensure that, in the event a club and a player choose to enter into a contractual relationship, this contract will be honoured by both parties and that unilateral termination of contract is therefore only admissible whenever there is a valid reason for it, a just cause.

4.3.4.1 "Just Cause" for the Termination of an Employment Agreement

(22) Article 13 of the Regulations provides that in principle a contract between a professional player and a club can only be terminated solely on expiry of the term or on mutual agreement of the parties. Obviously, the said principle is called to caseharden globally the system of contractual relations and its stability in football.

(23) However, Articles 14 and 15 of the Regulations establish two exceptions from the general rule announced above. Thus, a contract can be terminated by either party without consequences of any kind (either payment of compensation or imposition of sporting sanctions) in the case of just cause.

(24) Beside the general just cause, the Regulations distinguish the so-called *sporting just cause*, described in more detail in Article 15 thereof, which is though not related to the "classical" just cause and will therefore not be considered at this stage in detail.

(25) However, if in respect of sporting just cause the FIFA legislator gives at least its general outline on its definition and general application, nothing is provided for the definition of a "just cause". Consequently, in each particular event the surrounding circumstances need to be considered separately and objectively, on case-by-case manner.

(26) A behaviour which is in violation of the terms of an employment contract can still not justify the termination of the contract for just cause. However, should the violation persist for longer time or should many violations be added all together over a certain period of time, or should the violation be a severe one, then it is most probable that the breach of the contract reaches a dimension that the party suffering the breach is entitled to unilaterally terminate the contract for just cause.

(27) In the case in question the Panel addressed the issues of the "just cause", however, being faced to the absence of clear guidance on the applicable law, as the contract did not provide for such a clause, the Panel, in application of the Code of Sport-related Arbitration established that in such circumstances one must fall back on Swiss law. Pursuant to this, an employment contract which has been concluded for a fixed term can only be terminated prior to the expiry of the term of the contract if there are valid reasons for the parties or if the parties reach a mutual agreement.

(28) In this respect, the CAS Panel cited Article 337 of the Swiss Code of Obligations which reads as follows:

> A valid reason is considered to be, in particular, any circumstances under which, if existing, the terminating party can in good faith not be expected to continue the employment relationship.

(29) According to Swiss case law, whether there is "just cause" for termination of a contract depends on the overall circumstances of the case; the existence of a valid reason has to be admitted when the essential conditions, of an objective or personal nature, under which the contract was concluded are no

longer present. In other words, as the Panel concluded, "it may be deemed as a case of application of the *clausula rebus sic stantibus*".

(30) Swiss law provides that only a breach which is of a certain severity justifies termination of a contract without prior warning. This is however an exception to the rule that finds application only in few selected cases where the stance of the defaulting party is extremely reproachable and the violation of massive gravity.

(31) In all other cases, the party that intends to terminate the employment relationship has to notify the other party about the violation of the contractual engagement and if this party does not rectify the violation within a short timeframe, the correct handling party is entitled to unilaterally terminate the contract.

(32) In principle, the breach is considered to be of a certain severity and justifies the premature termination of the employment contract when there are objective criteria which do not reasonably permit to expect the continuation of the employment relationship between the parties such as a serious breach of confidence.[44]

(33) The Panel took into account that in the case in question the Player was naming mainly two reasons for justification of his early termination of the employment contract. On the one hand, the Player referred to the alleged non-payment of contractually agreed amounts, and on the other hand, he affirmed that the publication of articles in the Turkish newspapers made it unreasonable to resume his employee's duties.

(34) First, the Panel noted that the newspaper publications mentioned by the Player were published only *after* the termination of employment contract indeed took place. In this respect the Panel noted:

> (…) the citations referred may not constitute a valid reason for the Appellant to terminate the Contract, as the newspaper articles were published only after the letter of termination and therefore at a time when the Appellant had left his place of residence and (…) thereby expressed that he no longer wished to resume his work with the Respondent.

(35) Consequently, the circumstances which occurred *after* the declaration of termination shall not be taken into account while determining whether there was or not a valid reason to terminate contract.

(36) Furthermore, the Panel considered the alleged delays in payments provided under the employment contract. Actually, none of the parties to the dispute argued that certain payments were in delay. The only thing disputed between the parties is how late the payments were effectively made.

(37) In the final analysis this question can be left unanswered. In the Panel's opinion, the fact that payments owed under the employment contract were made late does not constitute in general a valid reason for termination of the contract, particularly considering that the Player had accepted in the past the delayed payments of his salary without opposing or complaining to the Club

---

[44] Wyler 2002, p. 364. See also: Tercier 2003, p. 496.

about the delays. The Player should have clearly notified the Club about his frustration about the delays and the fact that he would not tolerate them any longer. But the Player has clearly failed to do so and has *de facto* accepted that the Club was making the payments with a certain delay.

(38) In any event, it is to consider that many clubs are not always in the position to pay the players' salary on the due date and light delays are usually accepted and acceptable as long as they do not represent a financial hardship for the player concerned.

4.3.4.2 Necessity to Give Warning

(39) Having considered the arguments exposed by the Player, in particular the fact that the Player left the Club for the continuous breach of the employment relationship and delays in fulfilling its financial commitments, the Panel made a fundamental conclusion related to the early termination of a contract:

> A prerequisite for terminating because of late payment is that the player should have given a warning. This follows from the principle of good faith; for the breach of duty is—objectively—from the outset not so grave that it would have been unreasonable to expect the Appellant to continue the employment.

(40) Thus, before the Player has terminated the employment contract, it should have been not only advisable but compulsory to let the Club know, firstly, that he is complaining that the Club's conduct is not in accordance with the contract and, secondly, that he is not prepared to accept such breaches of contract in future. But the Player did not send any warning to the Club.

(41) Moreover, the Panel established that:

> If the Appellant did not at the time consider the belated payments to be a "significant" breach, then this fact cannot on its own later constitute a valid reason for termination of a Contract. Instead, the player's silence must be considered to be acceptance of the Club's conduct, which would make it appear to be in bad faith to justify termination of the contract by reference to the belated payments.

(42) The party who terminates the contract and who blames the other party must act without delay; if he does not act immediately he is deemed to have renounced to the right of termination.

(43) The Player claimed that the Club was not only unpunctual in payments, but also that the Club did not pay the salaries for the last two months of employment. Nevertheless, even with respect to this argument of the Player, the Panel noted that it is important to understand whether the salary has already been in arrears for a considerable amount of time or whether the arrears amount to a considerable amount. What is also of relevance is whether the debtor simply refuses to make payment and if there are circumstances that could easily be resolved through a warning notice.

(44) The Panel thus concluded that at the time of termination, the Player had no reason to assume that a warning notice would not change the Club's conduct, particularly considering that the Player was a key player of the Club and that the disappearance and thus breach of the Player occurred in an extremely delicate phase of the championship while the Club was competing for not being relegated to the second division.

(45) Consequently, it would in good faith have been reasonable to expect the Player first to warn the Club prior to terminating the contract. However, a warning addressed to the Club may have given to the latter the chance to possibly rectify an alleged illicit situation and the Player did maybe not want to go through the risk to have to remain with the Club in case of full compliance with the terms of the contract on the side of the Club.

(46) In essence, the Panel therefore decided that the Club had not committed a breach of contract and consequently the Player had no just cause for the termination of the employment contract.

(47) The award does not give any elucidation with respect to the procedure, the form, the contents, etc. regarding the warning of the early termination. In this respect, it is advisable to observe the mandatory formal requirement existing under the national labour law under which the employment contract is concluded, which is in the majority of the cases the law of the country where the Club is domiciled, unless the party have agreed in the contract to put the same under the application of another law.

(48) The party who declares the contract terminated must have previously fixed an additional period of time of *reasonable length* for performance by the other party. In such a case, the party who declares the contract terminated must normally send two communications to the other party, the first one putting the counterparty officially under default and the second one terminating the contractual relationship if the defaulting party has still not complied with it.

(49) The termination of a contract is made by unilateral declaration of the party faithful to the contract to the other party; it does in general not require a specific form, unless it is compulsorily imposed by law, but it has to be notified within reasonable time. It is generally made in writing but theoretically it could be even made orally.[45]

---

[45] Although there is in general no form requirement for notice giving, one main problem is that oral/telephonic notices are difficult to prove. The burden of evidence of notice giving is clearly on the party giving notice, and if this cannot be proven, the judge will not allow this party to rely on the notice, and this will result in the loss of a remedy. For notices of major importance like the termination of an employment contract written form is therefore indispensable. Moreover, so as to have sufficient evidence in case of dispute it is advised to send notices via registered mail, courier, plaintiff or any other form that guarantees to prove safe receipt by the counterparty. Where national law imposes a qualified notification of notices, these shall be complied with for the notice to be valid.

(50) While there may not be any specific requirements as to form or content, the aggrieved party's declaration must at least make it clear that the other party no longer can count on the former's performance in respect of the contract concerned.

(51) That is to say, the notice must express with sufficient clarity that the party will not be bound by the contract any longer and considers the contract terminated. A high standard of clarity of the notice is necessary, i.e. the unequivocal terms that the party wanting to terminate the contract believes that the contract is terminated that is to say, it must be evident to a reasonable person that the notice in question must clearly express the aggrieved party's wish to terminate the contract as a remedy in consequence of a particular breach.

4.3.4.3 Employment Freedom of the Player

(52) One further issue referred to by the Panel in the case in question was the Player's argument about his employment freedom. The Player refused to return to the Club following the challenged Decision asserting that he could choose to sign for a new club. The Panel in this respect concluded that:

> A player cannot be compelled to remain in the employment of a particular employer. If a player terminates his employment contract without valid reason, then the latter is not withstanding the possibility of sporting sanctions—obliged to compensate for damages, if any, but is not obliged to remain with the employer or to render his services against his will.

(53) According to the CAS jurisprudence in principle a person should not be compelled to remain in an employment relationship of a particular employer, if he does not wish so. An employee who breaches an employment contract by wrongful and premature withdrawal from it may be liable in damages or even imposed sanction according to the Regulations, but is not subject to an injunction to remain with his employer. This position is under Swiss law (Article 337d of the Swiss Code of Obligations) and under CAS jurisprudence.[46] Should the Player be compelled to remain as an employee of the Club he would "suffer irreparable harm, be it because he would have to renounce to other job opportunities or simply because he would be forced to work for an employer against his own will".[47]

(54) The general position of the CAS regarding employment freedom of a player as an employee is in compliance with the relevant international standards.

---

[46] Preliminary Decision of 17 August 2004 in the matter CAS 2004/A/678 Apollon Kalamarias F.C. v/FIFA and Oliveira Morais; Preliminary Decision of 30 August 2004, in the matter FC Barcelona v/Manchester United F.C.

[47] CAS 2006/A/1100, Order rendered by the President of the Appeals Arbitration Division of the Court of Arbitration for Sport, dated 6 July 2006.

The freedom of employment is recognised by the numerous conventions of the International Labor Organization as well as by the international human rights acts.

(55) The fact of not being compelled to remain with the Club despite the existence of a valid employment contract may not be understood from a practical point of view, considering the remuneration the player is receiving or the acquisition costs incurred by the Club so as to guarantee the services of the player from his former club.

(56) Moreover, this is a situation that has been used (but also abused) many times by players, that simply refuse to resume duty with the club and disappear, putting the club before an accomplished fact. There is in most of the situations already the complicity of a new club interested in hiring the services of the player.

(57) The club risking to lose the player is put before a dilemma: on the one side, insist on the performance of the contract and establish its termination by fault of the player, who did not come back, or on the other side accept the requests of the player and allow his transfer to rather favourable conditions for the new club and the player.

(58) It is extremely difficult for a club to hold a player who intents to leave, irrespective of the existing employment contract. Accepting the transfer of the player avoids to the club having to enter into a legal battle that may lasts for years and that may give only partial satisfaction to the aggrieved club and keeping a player in the squad that is not motivated causes sportive damage, both on the pitch as well as in lockers as such player may have a negative impact on the other. The right balance for the welfare of the club (under due consideration of the situation of the player) has to be found in each case.

4.3.4.4 Calculation of the Compensation Due to the Club

(59) Since the DRC while passing the challenged Decision did not make any thorough investigation of the facts and did not make any conclusions on the amount of compensation due, but instead decided on the Player having to return to the Club, the Panel preferred to refer the case back to the DRC so that this body could calculate the compensation due to the Club.

(60) The Panel however gave some guidelines on the method of calculating the compensation, so as to assist the DRC in this respect.

(61) Thus, the Panel, pointed out that the amount of compensation must particularly be guided by the effective loss suffered by the Club. The particular importance is attached in this case to the "law of the country concerned", and in the present case this is Swiss law. Article 337d para 1 of the Swiss Code of Obligations grants an employer the right to receive compensations for the damage due to the termination of the contract by the employee if the latter, without valid reason, does not appear at the working place, or if he leaves it

without notice. The amount of compensation equals to one quarter of the wage of one month.

(62) The Club is however entitled to claim compensation for additional damages that goes beyond that in Article 337d para 1 of the Swiss Code of Obligations. If the existence or the exact amount of damages cannot be established, the judge shall assess them in his discretion, having regard to the ordinary course of events and measures taken by the damaged party in equity and on the basis of the ordinary course of the events.

(63) Since the moment the present award was rendered, many subsequent awards have dealt with the calculation of the damage following a termination of an employment contract and the case law at CAS level is continuously developing, completing in this way the general guidelines given in this case.

4.4 CAS 2007/A/1298 Wigan Athletic FC v. Heart of Midlothian; CAS 2007/A/1299 Heart of Midlothian v. Webster and Wigan Athletic FC; CAS 2007/A/1300 Webster v. Heart of Midlothian

Juan de Dios Crespo Pérez

The Webster Award deals with the breach of contract by a player outside the protected period. During this term Webster was offered a contract extension. Because he refused, in effect Webster was banned from the first eleven (by sitting on the bench) despite his high potential and all his efforts. So in May 2006 Webster decided to terminate his contract due to end on 30 June 2007. Webster could leave for a compensation of £150,000 plus interest. The Webster Award has often been styled the new 'Bosman'. Because of the lenient compensation, clubs were afraid of future compensation barely reaching a quarter of the possible transfer sums. These fears arose through the CAS' remaining value approach in calculating compensation. However, the Matuzalem decision demonstrated that these fears did not materialise. The author sheds light on the circumstances of this decision, as well as on the Panel's considerations and differences in CAS' compensation calculation.

4.4.1 Preamble

As the lawyer of Andrew Webster, I have probably talked and wrote about the "Webster case" more than a hundred times and it is somehow difficult to summarise such a *long and winding road* in some minutes or pages. The case was known as a new revolution in football when I had never had that idea. Article 17 of the FIFA Regulations for the Status and Transfer of Players is so uneasy to interpret for anyone in football, even the most experienced lawyer, that I must say that Webster is just *another brick on the wall* of the construction of the relationship between clubs and footballers.

We shall see other bricks and some layer between them coming in the future and this case was just the beginning of the story but at least it was known as the first one where a player correctly and regulatory used his right to end his contract after the FIFA "protected period".

4.4.2 Facts

Remember just a few of the facts of the case. On 30 March 2007 18 year old Andy Webster signed for Heart of Midlothian LC (Hearts) from Arbroath club, two Scottish clubs, for a transfer fee of 75,000 GBP.

Webster signed a contract due to run from the 31st of March, 2001 to the 30th of June, 2005. On July 1st, 2003 Andy Webster signed a contractual extension with Hearts until the 30th of June, 2007.

Andy Webster's progression as a player was steady and strong. He had become one of the most important players at Hearts as a leader in their defence, and a Scottish international. Hearts were keen to tie down Mr. Webster to a longer contract with improved terms in order to secure the long-term future of one of their prize players.

However, Andy Webster rejected this contractual offer until 2009, in fact he rejected several subsequent offers, giving the impression that Andy Webster was ready to move on to a bigger club, despite his success with his long-term Scottish club.

During this period of contractual negotiations Mr. Webster was seemingly frozen out of the first team and forced to watch many of his team's matches from the sidelines. Hearts went even through the Scottish Cup to its final and Andy was not in the starting team when he had been of its best components. For a Scot not to be in his final was surely a big disappointment and the beginning of the end of the relationship.

The relations between him and the club continued to simmer until eventually they reached their boiling point. One of the club's major shareholders made negative and critical remarks regarding Andy Webster to the media.

Mr. Webster decided he had enough of what he perceived to be unfair treatment and approached the Scottish Professional Footballer's Association (SPFA) seeking counsel and recourse against his club for the statements of their most important shareholder.

They advised Mr. Webster that the best action would be to lodge a claim in writing requesting to terminate his contract with just cause according to Article 18 of his employment contract. However, with the prospect of missing the entire 2006–2007 season because of a ongoing court procedure Mr. Webster opted to take an alternate rough and unilaterally terminate his contract without just cause making his case falling under the scope of Article 17 of the FIFA Regulations for the Status and Transfer of Players.

After having notified Hearts of his intention to breach his contract, and leaving the club without their official consent Andy Webster signed a three year contract with English club Wigan Athletic FC (Wigan). When the English FA asked the Scottish FA association for the International Transfer Certificate (ITC) of the Player the Scottish FA told the English FA that they would not issue the ITC because the Player was still under contract with Hearts.

On the 31st of August, having approached FIFA with their grievance regarding the issuance of the Player's ITC, Wigan was granted the provisional registration by the Single Judge of the Player's Status Committee.

4.4.3 Claim

Hearts submitted claim against both Andy Webster and Wigan to the FIFA Dispute Resolution Chamber (DRC). They claimed for GBP 5,027,311 compensation and a two-month long playing ban from all official competitions against the Player; and a payment of compensation from Wigan and a one registration period long ban from registering any new players against the Club.

The DRC had to consider what criteria should be considered when evaluating a unilateral termination case. The criteria for cases of this nature were found in Article 17.1 of the Regulations on Status and Transfer of Players 2005 (RSTP in force then) which states:

> In all cases, the party in breach shall pay compensation, Subject to the provisions of Article 20 and annex 4 in relation to Training Compensation, and unless otherwise provided for in the contract, compensation for breach shall be calculated with due consideration for the law of the country concerned, the specificity of sport, and any other objective criteria. These criteria shall include, in particular, the remuneration and other benefits due to the player under the existing of contract and/or the new contract, the time remaining on the existing contract up to a maximum of five years, the fees and expenses paid or incurred by the Former Club (amortised over the term of the contract) and whether the contractual breach falls within a Protected Period.

Later in the commentary section of this article will be critique regarding the above article and its deficiency's however for now we will discuss how the DRC in the Webster dispute interpreted this article in light of particular facts of this case.

Following the decision of the European Court of Justice in the *Bosman*[48] case, it has been established that a Player is free to sign an employment contract with another club of his choice anywhere within the EU, and cannot be denied his Article 39 right to work freely.

Therefore there is no question that Andy Webster was entitled to breach his contract and move from Hearts to Wigan. He could have left without reason, it just so happens in this case he was unhappy with the behaviour and the comments of

[48] *Union Royale Belge des Sociétés de Football Association ASBL and others v. Jean-Marc Bosman; Case C-415/93, ECR I-4921.*

the members of the club hierarchy and wanted to continue the development of himself as a Player at another, perhaps bigger, club.

However, FIFA have established a set of various rules and regulations to deter playing from doing this, including playing suspensions based on when the contract was breached, and the aforementioned Article 17 principles of compensation in the interest of the "Maintenance of Contractual Stability.[49]"

The previously referred to "Protected Period" is a provision which is designed to discourage "contract jumping".[50] The protected period enshrined in para 7 of the Definitions of the Regulations states that the protected period is defined as:

> A period of three entire Seasons or three years, whichever comes first, following the entry into force of a contract, is such contract concluded prior to the 28th birthday of the Professional, or a period of two entire Seasons or years, whichever comes first, following the entry into force of a contract, if such contract was concluded after the 28th birthday of the Professional.

Andy Webster had signed a new contract with Hearts on the 1st of July 2003, and was 24 years old when he breached his contract in July 2006. Three full seasons, and years had elapsed by the time Mr. Webster had breached his contract, however it was unclear if he had properly complied with all the time regulations involving notification of intention to breach one's contract.

Anyway, FIFA is not always so clear about the sanctions for breaching a contract within the "protected period" and sometimes the clear obligation that is established in its Regulations[51] for a sporting sanctions to whom has breached his contract during that period is not followed by the DRC and even CAS has join the same understanding,[52] which is something really strange and contrary to both the exact wording of the article and the aim of the change agreed between FIFA and the EU Commission: the protection of the integrity of sport.

Furthermore, it was unclear which criteria the FIFA DRC would consider because of the absence of a "buy-out" clause,[53] it was only clear that their decision would be made "in light of the applicable national law.[54]" Due to a lack of jurisprudence, different interpretations of the reading of the Regulations, or legal savvy, the parties also had completely differing views on an acceptable

---

49 Chapter IV of the FIFA Regulations on the Status and Transfer of Players, 2005 edition.

50 Soek 2009.

51 Article 17.3 "*In addition to the obligation to pay compensation, SPORTING SANCTIONS SHALL ALSO BE IMPOSED on any player found to be in breach of contract during the protected period.*"

52 CAS 2007/1358 and 1359 FCPyunik Yerevan vs Carl Lombe, Apoula Bete, Rapid Bucuresti and FIFA.

53 Penalty clauses are adjudged to be illegal according to Scottish Law. However Article 17.3 of the FIFA regulations allows for the insertion of contractually agreed unilateral termination compensation clauses. By the way CAS has already ruled in a case in which the unilateral termination amount was considered to be an abusive figure (CAS 2006/A/1082 and 1104 Real Valladolid vs. Barreto).

54 Article 17.1 of the Regulations.

amount of compensation. Webster and Hearts believing the compensation payment amount should be €200,000 and €5,027,311, respectively.

4.4.4 FIFA DRC Decision

On the 4th of April 2007, the FIFA DRC determined that Webster had unilaterally breached his contract, an assertion which was not contested, outside the "Protected Period." The DRC decided that the residual value of the contract was GBP 199,976. The DRC also noted that Andy Webster was due to earn GBP 10,000 per week with Wigan.

Then the FIFA DRC started to discuss criteria related to the "specificity of sport", which might impact on the final amount due to be awarded to Hearts. They mentioned that Hearts should have paid transfer compensation to Arbroath club, which was a consideration which should not have factored in their claim against Webster for breach of contract legally,[55] but showed the club in a bad light in the realm of sport. The DRC also stated that Webster had served 5 years at Hearts, during which time the club had played a significant part in the Player's development and growth in profile as a footballer.

They stated that limiting the amount of compensation due to Hearts to the residual value of the contract would "undermine the principle of the 'maintenance of contractual stability'", and it would inadequately compensate the injured party.

The DRC decided that the final amount that Webster had to pay Hearts was GBP 625,000. This amount was based on the residual value of the playing contract with Hearts in Webster's 1st year with Wigan, and multiplying this amount by a co-efficient of 1.5.[56] Finally, as per the Regulations,[57] Wigan was found to be jointly and severally liable for the compensation amount for assumed induced breach of contract. None of the 3 parties were satisfied with the decision and they all appealed the decision to the CAS.[58]

4.4.5 CAS Decision

One of the most obvious and important point of contention was made by Wigan during the CAS hearing. They stated that the DRC had contravened Article

---

[55] It is the responsibility of Arbroath club to claim against Hearts if they have not been paid the training compensation which they are entitled. Although Hearts have an obligation to pay this amount, it has nothing to do with how much they should be compensated from Webster as a result of breach of contract.

[56] The method of calculation for the figure of 1.5 as a co-efficient remains questionable at best, and there is no indication, statutory, jurisprudential or otherwise, whether this figure came from.

[57] Article 17.2 of the 2005 Regulations.

[58] As per Article 63 of the FIFA Statutes.

13.4f)[59] of the Rules Governing the Procedures of the Players' Status Committee and the DRC by failing to give adequate explanation for the reasons of the decision they made against Webster and Wigan. The CAS agreed with Wigan stating that the FIFA DRC had failed to give a proper account of the manner in which they calculated the sum of GBP 625,000 awarded against Webster and Wigan.

> [I]n the final analysis it is impossible to understand from reading the decision what weight was giving to what criteria determining the quantum (GBP 625,000).

The CAS Panel dismissed the decision of the DRC and decided to make their judgement on the matter, based on R57 of the CAS code.[60] They stated that because of the absence of a clause in the contract which would specify the amount of compensation that would be paid in the event of a breach of contract; it was the duty of the case to determine the level of compensation, on the basis of article 17 of the Regulations.[61]

The Panel decided that they would not consider compensating Hearts for the training of the Player because this was not one of the criteria discussed in Article 17. Perhaps it was their view that the consideration one reviews in exchange for successfully training a Player is the sporting benefit gained by having a talented player in one's squad rather than having a Player who is incapable of contributing to the overall team performance. In other words, you train a player in order to help your team play well on the field, not to sell him later on.[62]

In order to determine the appropriate level of compensation according to Article 17 of the Regulations, the CAS needed to take into account three criteria.

1. The national law of the country concerned.
2. The specificity of sport.
3. Any other objective criteria.

The CAS did not accept Hearts request to have the amount of compensation calculated according to the rules and principles of Scottish law regarding damage for breach of contract (*restitutio in integrum*). They said that Article 17 only required that the adjudicating body make their award for damages with *due consideration* for the law of the country concerned. In other words, it is not necessary to calculate the amount in accordance with the national law, but rather to contemplate whether the award will infringe the principles of the national law concerned.

---

[59] Article 13.4f)—Written decisions shall contain… f) the reasons for the findings.

[60] Article R57—The Panel shall have full power to review the facts and the law. It may issue a new decision which replaces the decision challenged… .

[61] One would assume that *some* compensation was to be paid because of the first sentence of Article 17 of the Regulations. "In all cases, the party in breach shall pay compensation."

[62] However, these days with the increased role business has to play in Sport and the current global financial climate. Some clubs make their living just by training and selling quality footballers.

The CAS then considered how they should evaluate "specificity of sport" when determining compensation. They took the view that the specificity of sport was about balancing the need for contractual stability with the need to ensure the free movement of players.[63]

The Panel took the view that the "protected period" was a measure which existed in order to preserve contractual stability. They believed it existed in order to give players and clubs bans and suspensions if they unilaterally terminated the contract within a certain number of years since the commencement of the contract.

Furthermore, they stated that even if the protected period has expired the level of compensation for the unilateral breach of contract should not act as punishment nor enrichment for said breach. The Panel said the following about compensation:

> [It] should be calculated on the basis of criteria that tend to ensure clubs and players are put on an equal footing in terms of the compensation they can claim or required to pay.[64]

One of the most important things to be drawn from this decision was when the Panel stated that:

> It is in the interest of the football world that the criteria applicable in a given type of situation… be as predictable as possible.[65]

In order for contracting parties to know what the potential damages are when they are about to enter into an employment contract with another it is important that the CAS, or whomever the adjudicating body in the future is, sets out a sound precedent which can be referenced and followed by contracting parties and judges alike.

For this reason the CAS refused to consider Heart's GBP 4,000,000 valuation of Webster. They stated to consider this as part of the damages would both enrich the club and punish the Player which was not the goal of Article 17, nor the objective of the CAS. It had not been mentioned in the contract between the two parties as an amount to be considered in the event of breach of contract, and the CAS stated that even if it had there would be no moral or judicial justification for the existence of such a clause; the merits of said clause would have to be examined.[66]

The CAS also refused to considered the GBP 75,000 request from Hearts for the amount that they paid to Arbroath club and sated that this matter should have been resolved during the contract with Webster and was not a matter for discussion.[67]

---

[63] Para 132 of the Decision.

[64] Para 138 of the Decision.

[65] Also para 138 of the Decision.

[66] Para 139 of the Decision.

[67] Para 140 of the Decision—When you review their request to cover the purchase cost of almost GBP 100,000 for the Player together with their request for GBP 4 million; the Club appears to be claiming GBP 3.9 million for the training of the Player, a Player with which they have played a huge amount of games and also benefited from said training. Furthermore, they said that attaching the transfer cost to a Player after he had unilaterally breached his contract would be the realm of Sport back to the "pre-Bosman days where freedom of movement was unduly hindered by transfer fees."

The CAS also said that the remuneration and consideration to be received by the Player under the terms of his new contract was no subject to review because it was not focusing on the content of the employment contract which had been breached, and could be seen as punitive in nature.

4.4.5.1 Compensation Awarded to Hearts

The CAS stated that they believed the most suitable criterion to consider in accordance with article would be the remaining salary due to the Player. They said that just as a Player is entitled to receive the remainder of his salary if his contract is unilaterally terminated by his employer, the club should be entitled to claim a similar amount of money against the Player. In this that amount was GBP 150,000.[68] The Panel stated that the criteria of Article 17.1 of the Regulations were not necessarily cumulative and they couldnot find any other reason to award with more damages than the value of the outstanding salaries of the Player.[69]

The Panel also said that the GBP 150,000 should carry with it the rate of 5% annual interest rate from the date of the breach. They stated that because neither of the parties contested this rate of interest imposed by the FIFA DRC that they saw no reason to change it.

4.4.5.2 Several and Joint Liability of Wigan

In accordance with Article 17.2 of the Regulations, the CAS determined that Wigan shall be jointly and severally liable for the payment of the compensation paid to Hearts. Wigan contended that they should not be held liable because they had no part to play in Webster's decision to unilaterally terminate his contract and leave Hearts.

While Wigan protested their innocence and in this instance there was no reason for the Panel to doubt otherwise, however, the wording of Article 17.2 was not conditional on fault and Wigan did not present any real evidence to demonstrate that Article 17.2 should be interpreted in any other than the literal sense.

4.4.6 Commentary

4.4.6.1 Expanding on the Specificity of Sport or Equity

The decision made by the CAS in the Webster case is by all means a legally sound decision. The CAS has taken into account all three criteria which should be

[68] Para 153 of the Decision.

[69] Para 154 of the Decision.

reviewed when awarding compensation because of an Article 17 breach of contract.

1. The award is made with due consideration for national law.
2. The award takes into account the specificity of sport.
3. The award considers objective criteria; in this case the future salaries owed to the Player.

However, there is a stark contrast between this case and other Article 17 breach of contract by the Player cases: the amount of money awarded to the Club at the end of the proceeding.

In recent years we have seen Mexes[70] (previously to Webster) condemned to pay €7,000,000, Matuzalem[71] condemned to pay €12,000,000 and Mutu[72] (both *post-Webster* awards) condemned to pay €17,000,000,[73] whereas in the Webster case we saw Andy Webster[74] given a GBP 150,000 sanction. These cases are not only distinctly different because of the vast discrepancies in the levels of compensation awarded. This could be explained simply by examining the difference in quality, and subsequently pay, and acquisition costs of the Players. The main difference between the three cases and Webster is the approach of the CAS to the award with regard to the "specificity of sport".

While the CAS does not specifically state that one of the criteria that was considered when they awarded damages against Andy Webster in favour of Hearts was the Club's treatment of the Player. It is clear that the Arbitration Panel were hesitant to grant a big award in favour of a club who had so badly mistreated one of their most promising players. Thus, it seems that the "just cause" that Andy Webster initially used to end his contract and then replaced by Article 17, was into the arbitrator's mind.

As I said, Andy Webster had played a large part in Hearts' run in the Scottish Cup competition and he was denied a place on the playing field in the final, which they won on penalties, because of the contractual dispute he was having with the club. He was bad mouthed in front of the press by his employers, and he was mistreated within the club. They asked him to sign a new contract, and when he said no because he believed his playing career was destined for bigger and better things and also because of the treatment he has received during the previous month, Hearts representatives tried to, in a way, force him into renewing his deal.

Without saying so, the CAS took the human element of sport into consideration and evaluated the behaviour of each of the parties when making their final award. Webster, a Scottish international, had probably, with no disrespect intended,

---

70 TAS 2005/A/902.

71 CAS 2008/A/1519.

72 CAS 2008/A/1644.

73 The three figures are proximate and not intended to be read as the actual amounts awarded by the CAS, but as round numbers to emphasis the difference in amounts awarded to the parties.

74 CAS 2008/A/1644.

grown too big for a club of Hearts' stature. Rather than handing in a transfer request and demanding a move, Webster was passive in his behaviour and just chose *not to resign* with Hearts. He was treated badly as a result, and when one party has acted maliciously towards another they do not deserve to be rewarded for said bad behaviour. This can be called criteria within the realm of specificity of sport, but not overtly mentioned at trial, or simply equity, but it certainly had a part to play in the decision-making of the CAS.

4.4.6.2 The FIFA Regulations; Article 17

> In all cases, the party in breach shall pay compensation, Subject to the provisions of Article 20 and annex 4 in relation to Training Compensation, and unless otherwise provided for in the contract, compensation for breach shall be calculated with due consideration for the law of the country concerned, the specificity of sport, and any other objective criteria. These criteria shall include, in particular, the remuneration and other benefits due to the player under the existing of contract and/or the new contract, the time remaining on the existing contract up to a maximum of five years, the fees and expenses paid or incurred by the Former Club (amortised over the term of the contract) and whether the contractual breach falls within a Protected Period.

Article 17 is really well intentioned. It is designed to protect something which is surely essential to the preservation of world football; "The Maintenance of Contractual Stability." The common idea of the EU Commission and FIFA to "maintain the contractual stability" is something to follow in order to avoid the possible lack of fair play within a competition. Competitors need to know that few changes are going to be done without an agreement between the parties involved and that a club could prepare its team and the consequent championship in which it participates without sudden shocks of players leaving just before the beginning of the season.

But, in case that such shock happen, the players and the inducting clubs shall have a sporting sanction if the breach is done during the so-called "protected period" and always an indemnity to pay within or outside that period.

And, it was also drafted in order to give clubs and players an idea of how much compensation they may have to pay to each other in the event of unilateral termination of a contract without an indemnification clause. But that idea is not clear in any case and it will be different from case to case.

While some of the criteria which are discussed carry with them merit such as the due consideration for national law, and the specificity of sport. The article is sometimes poorly worded and often misinterpreted.

First and foremost, there is a line which states:

> [C]ompensation for breach shall be calculated with due consideration for the law of the country concerned, the specificity of sport, and any other objective criteria.

This sentence is poorly written, and although it may seem nit-picky it does not make grammatical or logical sense. The "problem" word is *other* when referring to "other objective criteria." The reason why this word cannot be there is because the word other implies that both the national law of the country concerned and the specificity of sport are already objective criteria. We can see from case law and the fantastic amount of academic commentary about the "specificity of sport" that it is not a well defined category and cannot be seen as objective criterion.

Secondly, and most importantly with regard to the Webster decision, the line which reads "the remuneration and other benefits due to the player under the existing of contract", is continuously misinterpreted by the courts, and only recently have they changed their mind with regard to the interpretation of the intentions of the drafters.[75]

This sentence was surely included in Article 17 in order to provide indication to what amount of money should be given to *the player* if his club unilaterally breached the contract. In other words, if the club cancels the contract without just cause, they must pay the player the remainder of the wages he was due to receive during the contract.

However, in this decision both FIFA and the CAS believed that this amount of money should be considered as a means to determine the compensation owed to a club when the player unilaterally terminated the contract. This is wrong. The club is effectively getting "double compensation" in this scenario. When the player breaches his contract and leaves the club, the employer no longer has to pay their employee. Therefore the club is already being "awarded" this compensation. The remaining value of the contract no longer must be paid to the player; the club can keep this money.

The CAS say that they do not wish to consider the amount of money spent training the Player because there is no provision made for such a consideration in Article 17. This is also incorrect. Article 17 says that "other objective criteria" should be considered this idea leaves a lot of room for judicial interpretation. It also says that an example of said objective criteria could be "the fees and expenses paid or incurred by the former club." It is clear that this could be and perhaps should be interpreted as the money spent on training the player during his time at the club.

While it is true that different clubs spend different amounts on training players, it could also be said that the clubs with higher quality training facilities who spend more money on the development of their players, give their players a higher probability of success in the world of professional football, and perhaps even develop better players. Therefore, when the clubs choose to sell these players they should be except to recoup higher figures for the sale of their assets.

Webster, by breaching his contract, could have denied Hearts such an opportunity, which means that the money which they had spent developing his talents and skills was lost. Although they were able to benefit from said training because

---

[75] They choose not to consider the outstanding salaries of the player as damage caused to the club in the Mutu decision because they recognise that these are salaries which Chelsea will not have to pay the player anyway.

of the performances of Mr. Webster on the football pitch while a member of the club. But the main issue is that a football player is also an employee and when someone decides to end prematurely his contract, he would not be asked to pay any "compensation" for leaving his job. Football and sport in general have that "specificity" that has created Article 17, which is that a competition is something more than just a business or a mere employer–employee contractual scheme.

So, in one side there is the freedom for employees/footballers and in another one there are the "sporting aspects" of a contractual relationship, which is not related only to the relationship between those two parties, but have to share it with other competitors (clubs) and a competition (League).

And, there is still a business aspect of football which should have some room to be recognised, which is the transfer value and the sale of a talent like Webster, a talent which had been brooded by the club for several years, would have generated a lot of revenue, and perhaps this is why the Webster award was so misunderstood as the way to end contracts without having to pay anything else but the remaining of the contract. Of course this appears to be a mistake as soon another sputnik was to be seen in the sky: Matuzalem. But this is another story…

Finally, this case was compared to Bosman. It was said that it might have a similar "liberating effect" on the rights of players, and their freedom to move between clubs whenever they wanted to. It was frequently stated that players would have the ability to buy-out their contracts, without playing suspension, if they waited until the protected period of their contract had expired and they paid the remaining salaries owed to the club.

This information was incorrect, for two reasons. First because, in countries where indemnification clauses are legal, and contracts where said clauses are inserted the opportunity to have an Article 17 case heard is virtually nonexistent; and second because, the decision in the Webster case was very facts specific and had a lot to do with the behaviour of the parties.

It will be seen later in the Matuzalem[76] case why said jurisprudence did not last and the "Webster buy-out" theory did not manifest itself in the world of sports law.

4.5 CAS 2008/A/1519 FC Shakhtar Donetsk (Ukraine) v. Mr. Matuzalem Francelino da Silva and Real Zaragoza SAD and FIFA

Juan de Dios Crespo Pérez

The Matuzalem Award is about breach of contract outside the protected period without just cause. The Panel ordered Matuzalem to pay FC Shakhtar Donetsk compensation of

---

[76] CAS 2008/A/1519—FC Shakhtar Donetsk (Ukraine) v/Mr. Matuzalem Francelino da Silva (Brazil) and Real Zaragoza SAD (Spain) and FIFA.

€11,858,934 plus interest. In calculating the compensation the Panel considered the non-amortised transfer sum and the sports-related damages. However, it did not accept the contractual buy-out clause as the basis for calculating compensation. Contrary to the Webster ruling, with the Matuzalem Award the CAS approached the positive interest in calculating compensation. Against this background the author notes that My first thought was that Article 17 of the FIFA Regulations for the Status and Transfer of Players is like the 1001 Nights of the legendary Arabian tales: 'all different and marvellous'.

4.5.1 Preamble

After the revolutionary road that the Webster's case seemed to have opened in 2008, only a year after appeared a new award that hit the news and became the latest of the legal sports law gossip.

In that particular moment, as the lawyer of the winning side, the Ukrainian club Shakhtar Donetsk, I received a lot of felicitations and calls regarding the final decision of one of the (again) leading cases from the CAS.

One of them, from a journalist, focused his questions not on the legal points or on the issues where that award could drive the football world but merely on how I feel to have won against myself.

I was really happy, as any lawyer is when winning such a relevant dispute but that precise thought has not crossed my mind. However, I commenced to wonder about that remark and I immediately reminded that my first thought was that Article 17 of the FIFA Regulations for the Status and Transfer of Players is like the 1001 Nights of the legendary Arabic tales, "all different and marvelous". So, the contractual stability and the possibility to terminate a professional contract by a footballer *ante tempus* was not to be decided on a single angle but on a case-by-case basis and each proceedings will end with a different award, depending on several factors and multiple criteria.

4.5.2 Facts

On the 27th of November 2007, The FIFA Dispute Resolution Chamber awarded FC Shakhtar Donetsk, the sum of 6,800,000 € to be paid by Matuzalem Francelino da Silva, hereinafter "Matuzalem" or "the Player", and for the first time explained how and why the final sum of a compensation has been reached. As it is well known, FIFA deciding bodies were not specially prepared to give their thoughts about how an amount for indemnity is reached when a contract has been breached.

Matuzalem arrived at Shakhtar Donetsk from Brescia Calcio Spa, hereinafter "Brescia", in the summer of 2004 for a fee of €8,000,000. In two seasons the player had developed into the team's most talented player and was appointed as the captain.

On the July 2 2007, Matuzalem terminated his playing contract with his Ukrainian club, Shakhtar Donetsk. He had served three years of a five-year playing contract worth approximately €1,200,000 each year. When Matuzalem terminated his contract, his club was two weeks from the commencement of their UEFA Champion's League qualification rounds. Matuzalem signed a playing contract with Real Zaragoza for three seasons with an annual remuneration of approximately €1,000,000 not including bonuses on 19 July.

On July 17 2008, the Player was transferred to SS Lazio Spa, "Lazio", after the clubs and the Player agreed to a loan agreement. Included in the loan agreement was an option to purchase the Player's registration rights for €13,000,000 or €14,000,000 plus VAT.[77]

Matuzalem signed a three-year playing contract with Lazio, the final two years of which would become active should Lazio choose to exercise their purchase option. The annual salary for the first season of this contract was €895,000 and €3,220,900 for the second and third seasons.

Matuzalem decided to terminate his contract with Shakhtar prematurely and unilaterally using the possibility given by Article 17 of the FIFA Regulations. The Club informed him that he could only extinguish his contract and join a new club if he paid the €25,000,000 buy-out clause stipulated in Article 3.3 of the Player's contract.

It is likely that the Player had received advice that he would be able to terminate his contract prematurely and he would only have to pay his former Club the amount that was owed to him as future contractual salaries.

He also would not receive any sporting sanctions as the "Protected Period[78]" of his contract had expired. This would have been strict compliance to the jurisprudence set by the CAS in the *Webster*[79] decision.

4.5.3 Main Submissions and CAS Decision[80]

4.5.3.1 Parties' Submissions

Both parties appealed the FIFA DRC decision issued on the 12th of November 2007 to the CAS. The CAS decided that they were competent to hear the dispute in

---

[77] 14 million euros if Lazio qualified for the Champions League.

[78] A period of time, determined by FIFA, at which, depending on the age of the Player when he signs the contract, the Player may unilaterally breach his contract without receiving a playing suspension.

[79] CAS 2007/A/1298 Wigan Athletic FC v/Heart of Midlothian; CAS 2007/A/1299 Heart of Midlothian v/Webster and Wigan Athletic FC; CAS 2007/A/1300 Webster v/Heart of Midlothian.

[80] CAS 2008/A/1519-1520 Shakhtar Donetsk v/Matuzalem and Real Zaragoza.

accordance with CAS[81] and FIFA Statutes,[82] the order of the procedure of the two parties[83] and the decision given by the FIFA DRC.

Shakhtar Donetsk made several requests to the Panel. They requested that:

- The FIFA DRC decision be annulled and that the CAS issue a decision stating that the €25,000,000 clause was an indemnification clause, and not a transfer clause,[84] and that they award the Club €25,000,000.
- The CAS award compensation to the Club as per all the objective criteria contained within Article 17 of the CAS Regulations.[85]
- The CAS force Matuzalem to pay 5% annual interest on the amount awarded from the date the Player broke his contract, the 2nd of July 2007.

Matuzalem and Real Zaragoza filed a joint answer and appeal to the Panel with some of the following requests for relief[86]:

- To reject the appeal lodged by the Club.
- To set aside the challenged DRC decision.
- To establish that the amount of compensation due by the Player is €2,363,760 or €3,200,000.

Both parties also requested that the legal expenses and costs of the arbitration procedure were paid by the other party.

4.5.3.2 The Main Issues and the Decision

The Panel noted that the main issues to be considered when deciding this dispute were the following:

A) Was Shakhtar Donetsk entitled to any compensation?
B) If so, how much?
C) Are there any reasons to adjust the award given by the FIFA DRC?
D) Is Real Zaragoza jointly and severally liable for the payment of said compensation?

---

81 Article R47 and R57 of the CAS code.

82 Article 60ff. of the FIFA Statutes.

83 Para 47 of the Decision.

84 If this clause was met it would give any club the right to negotiate a playing contract with Matuzalem.

85 Point 28 of the Decision the Club requested (in Euro):

- 4,788,431 for non-amortised expenses
- 2,400,000 for the remuneration of the player
- 5,000,000 for the *lucrum cessans* – They mentioned the USD 7,000,000 offer made for Matuzalem by U.S. Cittâ di Palermo Spa and stated the minimum amount that should be considered for *lucrum cessans* is the value of an offer made by another club
- No less than 5,000,000 for sports-related damage.

86 Para 30 of the Decision.

Point (A)

The Panel duly noted that neither the Player nor his representatives ever argued the existence of just cause or sporting just cause for the breach of the contract. Therefore Matuzalem was essentially admitting that he had rescinded the contract unilaterally and without just cause.

According to the first sentence of Article 17.1 of the Regulations on the Status and Transfer of Players, hereinafter "the Regulations" or "the FIFA Regulations", "in all cases, the party in breach shall pay compensation."

Therefore it was pretty clear that given the unilateral and premature nature of the termination of contract and because of the absence of any just cause or sporting just cause.[87]

Point (B)

Clause 3.3 of the employment contract between the parties which stated that:

> During the validity of the Contract, the Club undertakes—in case the club receives a transfer offer in amount of €25,000,000 or [more] the club undertakes to arrange the transfer within the agreed period.

The CAS came to the conclusion that this clause could not be interpreted as an indemnification clause and therefore they would have to calculate damages in light of Article 17. They noted that the calculation should be made with "due consideration[88]" for:

- The law of the country concerned
- The specificity of sport
- Any other objective criteria including:
  - The remuneration and other benefits due to the player under the existing and/ or new contract.
  - The amortised fees and expenses paid or incurred by the Former Club.
  - Whether the breach occurred within the protected period.[89]

The Panel considered the aforementioned elements in mixed order in the following manner:

---

[87] Which allow parties to breach their employment contracts according to Articles 14 and 15 of the Regulations, respectively.

[88] As per Article 17 of the Regulations.

[89] Para 76 of the Decision.

The Remuneration Element

The Panel deemed that very important non-exclusive criteria mentioned in Article 17 para 1 of the FIFA Regulations is the remuneration and other benefits due to a player under the existing and the new contract. However, they also felt that the *difference* between the value of the new contract and the value of the old contract should be considered as it may give an appropriate indication of the "actual market value," which may give a better indication of the "actual loss" suffered by Shakhtar for their player unilaterally breaching their employment contract.

The Panel observed that the yearly remuneration of Matuzalem at Shakhtar at the moment of unilateral termination was approximately €1,200,000.

The Panel stated, after a series of calculations,[90] that the Player would be paid €1,000,000 plus bonuses for the 2007/2008 season and €2,445,600 plus bonuses in the 2008/2009 season.

The Panel took the view that because third parties (Zaragoza and Lazio) and the Player himself valued the services of the Player at this level that it would be appropriate to consider this as part of the calculation of the loss suffered by Shakhtar Donetsk.

The Value of the Services

The Panel was keen to acknowledge that the services provided by a player are traded and sought after and therefore worth legal protection when determining the economic value of a unilateral breach of contract.[91]

The Panel then examined how much both SS Lazio and Real Zaragoza valued the services of the Player per year by examining their loan agreement and the average yearly salaries they would pay the player.[92] SS Lazio had declared that they were willing to pay an average €14,000,000[93] to transfer the player, plus €7,112,267 in salaries to the player over three years time[94]; they valued the player at €7,336,800 per season. Real Zaragoza were willing to sell the player for an average of €14,000,000 plus pay the player €6,546,667 in salaries to the player over three years time[95]; they valued the player at €5,640,000 per season.

The Panel was not willing to consider the penalty clause of €22,500,000, should the player not return to Real Zaragoza following the loan, as an indication of the value of the services of the Player. They believed that from the evidence submitted

---

90 Found at paras 96–100 of the Decision.

91 Para 103 of the Decision.

92 Para 107.

93 The option clause in the loan agreement was between €13,000,000 and 15,000,000.

94 €2,445,600—Average yearly salary while on loan at SS Lazio.

95 2007/2008—€1,000,000; 2009/2010, 2010/2011—€2,320,000.

by Player and the Club that the amount of €22,500,000 was designed to act as a deterrent rather than a valuation.

Lost Earnings: Missed Transfer Fees

The Panel recognised that the loss of earnings or *lucrum cessans* could be included when calculating the damages for an unjustified termination of an employment contract.[96]

The major point of discussion regarding the loss of earnings is the club's lost opportunity to sell the player and receive compensation because they have terminated their contract early.

> [C]laim of his former club for the opportunity to receive a transfer fee that has gone lost because of the premature termination of the employment contract.[97]

The Panel stated that offers made by third parties for the player could help determine the value of the damage suffered by the club for two reasons.

i. Offers could help determine the value of the services of the player.
ii. The loss of the transfer fee may be a compensable damage head.[98]

The Panel said that the €7,000,000 offer for Matuzalem's services from Palermo should not be immediately disregarded because Shakhtar Donetsk turned said offer down. Although no direct damage was suffered by Shakhtar Donetsk, the offer could still be considered as a watermark in order to find the best valuation of the Player's services. The Panel did state that in the dispute, Shakhtar Donetsk was not entitled to claim the €7,000,000 offer from Palermo as a compensable loss of profits.[99]

The Fees and Expenses Paid or Incurred by the Former Club

According to Article 17 para 1 the fees and expenses that were required to obtain the player *should* be amortised[100] and taken into account when awarding compensation.

The Panel calculated the non-amortised value of the transfer fee to be 2/5 of €8,000,000 or €3,200,000 which was the fee Shakhtar Donetsk paid Brescia to

---

[96] CAS 2005/A/902 and 903, *Mexes and AS ROMA v/AJ Auxerre*, N 136; diss. CAS, *Webster Decision*, N 141 et seq.

[97] Para 117 of the CAS Decision; Cf. Haas 2009 at fn 156 et seq.

[98] A loss or hardship for which loses can be obtained—Depending on whether the club can prove that the timing of the termination infringed with their ability to accept an offer.

[99] Para 121.

[100] CAS 2006/A/1141, *Moises Moura Pinheiro v/FIFA and PFC Krilja Sovetov*, N 87; Ongaro 2009.

negotiate an employment contract with the Player. However, the Panel would not consider any solidarity contributions paid by Shakhtar as expenses[101] nor did they consider that the payment of agent's fees were linked to the transfer of the player, and they would not consider this in the amount to be determined for expenses incurred by the former club.[102]

Law of the Country Concerned

The Panel acknowledged that the amount of compensation awarded could vary depending on the laws of the country concerned, which is the law governing the employment contract between the player and the club; generally the laws of the country in which the club is domiciled.[103] However, the Panel concluded that in light of the submissions made by the parties to the dispute there were no particular arguments made in light of Ukrainian or Swiss law which could be taken into consideration by the panel in order to alter the amount of compensation due.

Additional Objective Criteria

It is important to note for future cases that the Panel stated that if the club could prove that as a result of the player's premature breach of contract that they were unable to fulfil their contractual obligations with a third party, such as a sponsorship agreement, then it would be possible to factor this into their determination of compensation.[104]

The Specificity of Sport

Finally the Panel considered the specificity of sport. The Panel recognised that sport plays an important role in society, as have sports organizations,[105] the courts,[106] the White Paper on Sport,[107] and even the European Commission.[108] They went on to justify the existence of the concept, and the concept serves the

---

[101] Para 128.

[102] The Panel also viewed agent's fees as potentially part of the costs incurred by the club to acquire the player, however in this case Shakhtar were not able to prove that such payments were linked to the transfer of the Player.

[103] FIFA Commentary on the FIFA Regulations, fn. 74.

[104] Para 151 of the Decision.

[105] http://www.fifa.com/aboutfifa/federation/releases/newsid=960669.html

[106] CAS, *Webster Decision*, N 131 et seq.

[107] COM [2007] 391 final.

[108] Treaty of Lisbon, 2007/C 306/01, para 124, revised Article 149.

Panel quoted the Panel from the *FC Pyunik*[109] decision to best explain what purpose the ideal serves.

> The criterion of specificity of sport shall be used by a panel to verify that the solution reached is just and fair not only under a strict civil (or common) law point of view, but also taking into due consideration the specific nature and needs of the football word (and of parties being stakeholders in such world) and reaching therefore a decision which can be recognised as being an appropriate evaluation of the interests at stake, and does so fit in the landscape of international football.[110]

In other words, the Panel will assess the amount of compensation that should be awarded according under Article 17, with adherence to the objective criteria listed in said article. Afterwards the Panel shall review the amount of compensation in light of the world of sport, and evaluate the decision's ability to protect the interest of sport. The Panel must make an award that is legally correctly and respects the specific nature of sport.[111]

4.5.3.3 Final Calculation

More criteria were considered by the Panel when discussing what should be the final amount of compensation awarded in light of the guidelines of Article 17,[112] the Specificity of Sport, and Articles 42.2 and 99.3 of the Swiss Code of Obligations[113]; however they did not sufficiently affect the outcome of the calculation to merit discussion in this article.

The Panel stated that the value of lost services of the Player would amount to €11,258,934, and the Player would have to pay an additional 6 months' salary because of the poor timing of his breach of contract.[114] Furthermore, in accordance with the request for relief from Shakhtar Donetsk and Swiss law,[115] the Panel awarded 5% annual interest on the sum of €11,858,934 payable from the 5th of July 2007.

---

[109] CAS 2007/A/1358, *FC Pyunik Yerevan v/Carl Lombe, AFC Rapid Bucaresti and FIFA.*

[110] CAS *FC Pyunik Yerevan* decision, N 104-10.

[111] Para 155 of the Decision.

[112] FIFA RSTP *et seq.*

[113] The Panel deemed that this was the applicable law to the present dispute: When a judge cannot establish the exact amount of ompensation then the judge may assess the amount of damages in a discretionary manner.

[114] The Player, who was the Club's most influential player and team captain, terminated his contract with the Club just a few weeks before the start of the qualification rounds of the UEFA Champions League.

[115] Article 104 para 1 of the Swiss Code of Obligations. NB. Swiss law was additionally applicable to the dispute because of FIFA's existence in Switzerland.

4.5.3.4 Joint and Several Liability

Article 17.2 of the Regulations says that the new club who contracts a player who has unilaterally terminated his contract shall be presumed jointly and severally liable.

The Panel confirmed the position of the DRC and the FIFA Regulations and held Real Zaragoza jointly and severally liable.

4.5.3.5 Costs

Both Parties had claimed costs against each other in the dispute, and the Panel took the view that because both parties had filed an appeal against the award of the DRC the costs should be shared by the parties. They stated that the costs would be paid 2/10 by Shakhtar Donetsk, 4/10 by Matuzalem and 4/10 by Real Zaragoza.

Finally, the arbitration costs of Shakhtar Donetsk would be equally split by Matuzalem and Real Zaragoza. They would have to pay CHF 7,000 each.

4.5.4 Commentary

This case was quite different from that of *Webster*, as the transfer amount was not amortised when the player terminated his contract, with two remaining years still existing and no renewal of contract was involved. So a sum was granted to the club for such pending amortization of the transfer fee.

Another amount was given on the basis of the "remuneration and other benefits due to the player under the previous and the new contract", which is a quite different position of the CAS award on Webster.

Finally, another amount was decided to compensate the "sports-related damage… in the light of the stability of sport" which is, also, a totally diverse application of Article 17 than that of the Panel in Webster's case.

All the parties appealed to the CAS and the novelty in the procedure at the CAS has been the presence of FIFA, which has requested to be a party, even though it was initially not admitted by Matuzalem and Zaragoza. This is a clear sign that FIFA wanted, at last, not to be taken out of the legal decisions of the CAS, contrary to its previous insistence not to be a party in the appeal.

4.5.4.1 The €25,000,000 "Buy Out" or Transfer Clause

The CAS clearly thinks that the way the clause was drafted indicates that it was a kind of a transfer clause or an offer to the player to ask a third club to pay the agreed amount as a transfer. This is acceptable, as the buy-out clause or indemnity clause should be drafted, in my opinion, clearly mentioning Article 17 and that the sum specified is "the one due as compensation in the event of a unilateral breach, respectively termination of the contract by either of the parties".[116]

4.5.4.2 The Decision

The factual circumstances of the case were completely different to those in *Webster;* therefore the CAS did not apply the "test" developed in *Webster.* Instead they used several criteria, mainly the loan agreement between Real Zaragoza and Lazio with which to determine the value of the player.[117] They reviewed the figure reached in light of the hotly debated "Specificity of Sport[118]" and gave an award in favour of Shakhtar Donetsk for the amount of €11,858,934.[119]

The amount is widely explained in the award itself but let us face that the new evidences requested by Shakhtar before the hearing and given at that time, had made a total change in respect of the claim by Shakhtar itself and that was the way the Panel decided to follow.

The importance of the loan agreement, the new contract (after the previous one signed) between Zaragoza and Matuzalem and the labour contract between Matuzalem and Lazio (the loan was for one year but the contract for three…) was an indispensable tool for the Panel to decide the final indemnification. What is important to mention is that such documents have to be requested by Shakhtar in order to know their contents and they were initially denied by Matuzalem and Zaragoza but finally disclosed in the very same hearing, which was a sort of luck to the Ukrainian club, as it served finally for its purposes as it was widely used by the Panel in order to settle the final indemnity amount. Of course, the whole request made in the statement of claim by Shakhtar has to be reviewed with those new documents but it was worth to do it.

The CAS reached the most equitable decision they could, and gave some of the proverbial power back to the clubs at a time when top Player's can behave as mercenaries and hold billion dollar businesses for ransom.[120]

However, they have not been given the tools with which to issue a confident decision which sets a precedent and gives clubs and players an indication of what

---

[116] Point 74 of the Decision.

[117] They took the value of the lost services as being approximately €14,224,534 and €13,093,334 minus the salaries which they would not have to pay to the Player.

[118] €600,000 or the equivalent of approximately 6 months' salary was awarded solely in light of the specificity of sport.

[119] Plus an interest rate of 5% from the 5th of July—shortly after the player had breached his contract. This was in accordance with Swiss Law, Article 339.1 of the Swiss Code of Obligations; and Jurisprudence, Decision of the Swiss Federal Tribunal of 4 May 2005, in *re X c/Y*, case no. 4C.67/2005, consid. 6; Decision of the Tribunal Cantonal du Canton du Vaud of 20 February 1980.

[120] http://news.bbc.co.uk/sport2/hi/sports_talk/1105037.stm, http://soccerlens.com/andy-webster-and-g14/5528/

value a unilateral breach of contract may carry in the future. But, as I said in the preamble, this is something difficult to venture as each case has so different issues that it would be quite impossible to pretend to know what kind of indemnity should be paid.

4.5.4.3 The "Right to Terminate a Contract" by Article 17

The CAS state in their decision that,

> The authors of Article 17 of the FIFA Regulations[121] achieved a balanced system according to which the judging body has on one side the duty to duly consider all the circumstances of the case and all the objective criteria available, and on the other side a considerable scope of discretion,

The statement made by the CAS is absolutely correct. The drafters of Article 17 did indeed create an article which gives the decision-making bodies ample room with which to make a discretionary decision based on equity and fairness. However, the purpose of Article 17 is the "Maintenance of Contractual Stability.[122]"

The CAS goes on to state that:

> [A]ny party should be well advised to respect an existing contract as the financial consequences of a breach or a termination without just cause would be, in their size and amount, rather unpredictable.[123]

Unfortunately, the previous statement is contrary to the very ethos of stability itself. We have seen how different the awards in a unilateral breach case can be in the *Matuzalem* and *Webster* decisions.[124]

In the situation of unilateral breach we will have players and clubs who take a chance to breach the employment contract unilaterally because they will believe that their result will be better than had they observed their contract.

And to clearly sustain that Article 17 is not a weapon to use in any case, CAS stated that:

> However, a termination of a contract without just cause, even if this occurs outside of the Protected Period and following the appropriate notice period remains a serious violation of the obligation to respect and existing contract… In other words, Article 17 FIFA Regulations does not give to a party, neither a club nor a player, a free pass to unilaterally breach an existing agreement…[125]

---

[121] FIFA Regulations on Status and Transfer of Players 2008 edition.

[122] Suggested by the title of Chap. IV of the FIFA Regulation on Status and Transfer of Players 2008 edition.

[123] CAS 2008/A/1519—FC Shakhtar Donetsk (Ukraine) v/Mr. Matuzalem Francelino da Silva (Brazil) and Real Zaragoza SAD (Spain) and FIFA; CAS 2008/A/1520—Mr. Matuzalem Francelino da Silva (Brazil) and Real Zaragoza SAD (Spain) v/FC Shakhtar Donetsk (Ukraine) and FIFA.

[124] Comparing and contrasting final awards of approximately €11,858,934 and £150,000.

[125] CAS award on Matuzalem, point 63.

4.5.4.4 Future of Article 17

The future is simple. Either the CAS sets out a test which has certain definable objective criteria which will govern each Article 17 dispute, or FIFA redraft Article 17 and make it more definitive, in order to increase contractual stability. Or clubs should agree with players on buy-out or indemnity clauses.

FIFA have stated that "Contractual stability is of paramount importance in football, from the perspective of clubs, players, and the public.[126]" The existence of Article 17 goes some of the way to address this issue; however, it is not drafted in a sufficiently comprehensive manner in order to ensure real solidity of contract between clubs and players.

The article mentions the calculation of compensation for breach of contract in light of the "specificity of sport," a concept which they fail to define in their regulations.[127] Furthermore they say that "any other objective criteria" should be defined without defining objective. This infringes the ethos of the word itself. It orders for something to be objective it must be defined, and not left for someone to give their *subjective* opinion of the constitution of objective. Perhaps an exhaustive list not entirely necessary but a list including more provisions than:

1. The remuneration and other benefits due to the player under the existing contract and/or the new contract, the time remaining on the existing contract up to a maximum of five years,
2. The fees and expenses paid or incurred by the former club (amortised over the term of the contract),
3. Whether the contractual breach falls within the protected period,[128]
4. The sporting loss and the specificity of sport.

The latest has been, for the very first time, included in a CAS award regarding a breach of contract and even though, the six months salaries that the Panel has thought would be enough for the sporting loss (within the specificity of sport) this should be discussed and surely would be in the future.

We have to face that players, when reaching a certain point of their career and due to personal or external matters as pressure of the club to renew, non-agreement on the new salaries, family issues, sporting needs of the player or whatever other reason, will utilise Article 17 and this should not be considered as an illegal treatment to the clubs but merely as an abrupt termination of the contract established in the Regulations that might permit clubs to obtain an indemnity for such termination.

The way resolve the issue of how much compensation shall be awarded in case of a unilateral termination of contract is simple: Contract.

---

[126] FIFA Circular Letter 769.

[127] It is arguable that nobody has managed to give an adequate definition of the specificity of sport—Not the EU courts, not the Lisbon Treaty, and not FIFA.

[128] Article 17.1 RSTP.

Where possible[129] the parties should seek to impose reasonable, variable, structured and tiered indemnification clauses where the contract specifically states how much the parties will have to pay each other in case of a unilateral breach. The value can vary based on the remaining years of the contract, the performance of the player,[130] the performance of the team or any other criteria the parties deem appropriate.

For example, a player signs a 5 year long employment contract. If in the first year of the contract either party breach, they will have to pay the other party 50 million. In the second year they will have to pay 40 million, and so on and so forth. Of course, this is only one of the criterion to be used with that kind of "changing clause" but we should think about it as the only way to avoid decision that could not be the one that we expect.

This is the future; a clause which encourages "*the maintenance of contractual stability*" and, if not, which permits to objectively know the detailed and contractually agreed criteria to apply when the contract is breached.

4.6 CAS 2005/A/876, 2006/A/1192, 2008/A/1644 Adrian Mutu v. Chelsea

Wil van Megen

In 2003 Mutu was transferred from AC Parma to FC Chelsea at a price of €22,500,000. But the extended 'Mutu saga' began in 2004 when Mutu had taken cocaine on several occasions. Mutu was thus terminated by FC Chelsea. Then several panels of judges (namely FAPLAC; FIFA DRC; CAS; Swiss Federal Court) were occupied with this dispute over several years. Ultimately the CAS ordered Mutu to pay compensation of €17,173,990 plus interest. The amount was based mainly on the non-amortised FC Chelsea transfer sum. The author believes this was not the right conclusion. Will van Megen draws a comparison with the Oliver Bernard ruling of the ECJ. In his view a transfer sum cannot be used as benchmark for calculating compensation. At its most extreme, Mutu became the victim of Chelsea's wealth, even if he did breach the rules.

4.6.1 Introduction

In the dispute between Adrian Mutu and Chelsea we now have landed at case nr. 7, the decision after an appeal against the last decision of the Court of Arbitration for Sport (CAS) of the Swiss Bundesgericht. The dispute is about the dismissal of Mutu by Chelsea for a positive doping test in 2006 and the consequences this termination has had for the player.

---

[129] In jurisdictions where indemnification clauses are permitted.

[130] It should be noted that performance-related unilateral breach clauses may not be the most desirable criterion as they encourage player's who seek to prematurely terminate their contract to perform poorly, thus encouraging either a sale or a lower level of contractual compensation.

In the latest decision CAS confirmed the FIFA DRC ruling that Mutu has to pay 17 million euros compensation to Chelsea.[131] The largest part of this amount consists of the non-amortised transfer sum that Chelsea paid to Mutu's former club Parma. Because of the approaching deadline for payment Mutu's current perspective is a career threatening ban as he almost certainly will not be able to pay this amount. The fact that the player had a recent new doping ban is not helpful either but irrelevant for this case.

4.6.2 Some of the Backgrounds

After a promising start with the club Chelsea became more and more dissatisfied with Mutu's performance. Chelsea admitted that they deliberately targeted the player because they suspected him of using drugs and subsequently dismissed him. According to Professional Footballers' Association boss Gordon Taylor, Chelsea target-tested the player with a view to getting rid of him. "The attitude may be zero tolerance but it's not a policy we would approve of." "Chelsea have a duty of care. We would expect an interest in the moral and social welfare of its employees." Additionally, the Premier League has always had a great tradition of rehabilitating addicted players.[132]

Taylor considers it astonishing that Chelsea is not prepared to discuss the situation with Mutu and set an example, encourage rehabilitation and get him back on track.

4.6.3 The Legal Aspects

It is time for an analysis to see how the case could end up like this. The result of a short overview is an astonishing range of mistakes and misconceptions by all deciding bodies.

4.6.4 Overview of the Separate Cases

We can see that in all cases a number of elementary things went wrong. Read and shiver.

---

131 CAS 2008/A/1644, 31 July 2009.

132 BBC Sport: Blues suspected Mutu of drug use, http://news.bbc.co.uk/sport2/hi/football/teams/c/chelsea/3964801.stm

4.6.5 The First Case

1. The first case was brought before the arbitration body of the English premier league, the Football Association Premier League Appeal Committee (FAPLAC). This panel concluded that the dismissal of Mutu was justified. However, the FAPLAC did not take a decision about the compensation to be paid by Mutu but referred this part of the matter to the FIFA Dispute Resolution Chamber (DRC). In fact this must be considered a strange decision. In order to judge whether a dismissal is justified it is absolutely necessary that the judging panel is aware of all relevant facts and circumstances of the case. The compensation to be paid is most certainly a relevant item in this process. By referring the case to another body for compensation this part of the circumstances could not be considered by the FAPLAC.
2. The second thing that comes to mind is the fact that the FAPLAC did not consider the specificities of sport in this case. There are hardly any examples of top players being dismissed by their club even after serious misconduct. There are several examples in the English Premier League. The Boyer—Dyer scuffle of 2 April 2005 is a notorious example. Before the eyes of millions of spectators two team mates fought with each other during a match. Craig Bellamy has been involved in several misconduct charges and Joey Barton was even imprisoned without being dismissed.
   The normal thing to do for a Premier League club in such a situation is to sanction the player with a fine and/or a period of non-payment of salary. The latter sanction is made possible by the collective bargaining agreement between the clubs and players' organization PFA. Eventually a transfer of the player to another club can take place. In this case the club chose for an immediate dismissal which was only possible because of the overwhelming wealth of the club. Chelsea simply could afford to take another direction and dismissed the player without being able to overlook the consequences. Most probably they did not care. In fact they took the risk of getting nothing but were prepared and able to accept that risk. In recent major transfers they did not see any problem with amortising large amounts for failed transactions like those of Shevchenko and Crespo. It is not a strange conclusion that Mutu is primarily a victim of the prosperity of Chelsea as no other club in the world would have acted in this way. Any other club that wanted to get rid of a player like Mutu would have transferred him to another club in order to control damages. In fact this is an obligation for a damaged party. This practice in English football is a very relevant specificity of sport which the FAPLAC did not take into account in their judgment.
3. The third point that pops up is the referral by the FAPLAC to the FIFA DRC for the establishing of the compensation. It has to be noted that the FIFA DRC is only competent in cases that have an international dimension. Such a dimension exists e.g. when a player has a different nationality as the country in which the club is based. In this case Chelsea is based in England whereas

Mutu has the Romanian nationality. This means that if Mutu would have been an Englishman the case could not possibly be referred to FIFA. In that case it would have been up to the FAPLAC to decide on the compensation themselves. Off course that would only have been possible according to the contract and relevant national regulations. This means that the case could only be referred to FIFA because of the nationality of Mutu. This distinction purely on the basis of nationality must be considered discrimination as described in national and international legislation.[133] As it concerns the nationality of the person concerned this is direct discrimination and as such it cannot be justified. At no stage this was recognised. The fact that Mutu agreed with the referral of the case cannot be considered decisive.

4. The fourth point is the problem that occurs when we look at Article 17 of the FIFA Regulations on the Status and Transfer of Players (RSTP). This article constitutes a liability for the player *and his new club* in the case where a player breached the contract with his former club without just cause.[134] Because of the fact that the case was brought before the English FAPLAC this made the involvement of Mutu's new Italian club in the procedure impossible as the FAPLAC has no jurisdiction over Italian clubs. It is the question if FIFA could have involved the Italian club after the referral to the FIFA DRC. As it did not happen this matter remains unsolved.
5. The FAPLAC decision was appealed by Mutu with CAS.[135] Also here it was not possible for the panel to judge the case in full because the financial consequences were not clear and still had to be decided. The specificities of sport as described above were not taken into account at all. The FAPLAC decision was confirmed by CAS after which the case went to the FIFA DRC.
6. The DRC declared the Chelsea claim inadmissible because of the fact that the parties initially chose to present their case at national level.[136] It is DRC case law that if the parties choose for another body to have their dispute decided the case will not be admissible before FIFA.
7. The FIFA DRC decision was appealed by Chelsea and CAS ruled that according to the applicable regulations FIFA should deal with the case.[137] CAS did not pay any attention to the fact that because of this way of litigation the new Italian club of Mutu, which according to FIFA regulations was jointly and severally liable for compensation, was excluded from the process. Maybe this was not argued by one of the parties and also not by FIFA.

   Confronted with this CAS decision the FIFA DRC was obliged to pass a new judgment only on the amount of compensation to be paid by Mutu. Thereto the

---

[133] The European Convention on Human Rights; Race Relations Act 1976.

[134] Article 17 para 2 If a professional is required to pay compensation, the professional and his new club shall be jointly and severally liable for its payment.

[135] CAS 2005/A/876,15 December 2005.

[136] FIFA DRC 106176, 26 October 2006.

[137] CAS 2006/A/1192,21 May 2007.

Chamber attempted to follow the guidelines of Article 17 of the Regulations on the Status and transfer of Players:

Article 17 Consequences of Terminating a Contract Without Just Cause

The following provisions apply if a contract is terminated without just cause:

1. In all cases, the party in breach shall pay compensation. Subject to the provisions of Article 20 and annex 4 in relation to Training Compensation, and unless otherwise provided for in the contract, compensation for breach shall be calculated with due consideration for the law of the country concerned, the specificity of sport, and any other objective criteria. These criteria shall include, in particular, the remuneration and other benefits due to the player under the existing contract and/or the new contract, the time remaining on the existing contract up to a maximum of five years, the fees and expenses paid or incurred by the former club (amortised over the term of the contract) and whether the contractual breach falls within a Protected Period.
2. Entitlement to compensation cannot be assigned to a third party. If a Professional is required to pay compensation, the professional and his new club shall be jointly and severally liable for its payment. The amount may be stipulated in the contract or agreed between the parties.

   The outcome of this case was that Mutu had to pay €17,000,000 to Chelsea.[138] The major part of this amount consists of the non-amortised transfer sum paid by Chelsea to Parma. When we look at the text of Article 17 then we can conclude that the transfer sum paid indeed is one of the components covered by this paragraph. However, this is only under the precondition as laid down under the strict precondition of para 2 of Article 17: "the professional and his new club shall be jointly and severally liable for its payment". The reason for this is that the payment of a transfer sum is a matter for clubs and not for players. The relevant amount is negotiated between clubs and lies totally outside of the scope of the player. In fact you can say that the better a player performs the higher the transfer sum will be.

   As we saw before, Mutu's new club was not involved in this dispute and therefore could not be held responsible for the payment of the amount of compensation. Because of this the whole amount of compensation was allocated to the player. In other words: because of the way the parties started their dispute Mutu had to bear consequences that normally would not be his problem. This aspect was wrongly ignored by the FIFA DRC. It is very peculiar that at no stage of the whole process one of the parties nor FIFA attempted to involve the new club.

8. The fact that the liability for compensation can be accounted to another party than the one that is directly involved is extremely relevant. We can see that in

[138] FIFA DRC 7 May 2008.

another football case in which liability for compensation also applies to the new club of the player: the Olivier Bernard case.[139] This case is about a young French player who transferred from the French club Olympique Lyonnais to Newcastle United FC in England after the termination of his training contract. According to the French regulations Bernard was obliged to sign a contract with the French club that trained him. The sanction for non-compliance with this rule is a three-year ban on national level. As this ban does not apply in England the club brought the case before a civil court in France in order to get a judgment on compensation. In appeal the French court presented the case to the European Court of Justice. Previously the Advocate General of the Court gave her opinion on the case.[140] In her considerations she made a very remarkable distinction between the situation that the successive employer can be held responsible for the compensation and the one in which the employee himself is the one to pay.

According to the Advocate General a system where the new employer is obliged to compensate the former employer that trained and educated the employee needs another standard for compensation than in the case the employee himself is liable. The standard for the first situation is that the new employer saved himself the costs for having a full training system that eventually delivered the outstanding employee. In fact here this is the talented professional player. In such a case it is considered reasonable that the new club pays a relevant part of the total of efforts from the former club in order to obtain the current result. The FIFA regulations on training and education follow this way of reasoning as laid down in Annex VI of the FIFA Regulations on the Status and Transfer of Players on training compensation and solidarity mechanism.[141] In case the individual employee has to pay the training costs another standard applies. In such a case only the actual individual costs for the training of the worker have to be taken into considerations as this employee cannot be held responsible for being a part of a broader system established by his employer according to the Advocate General; although less extensively the ECJ follows this way of reasoning in the ruling itself.

This Court decision implies that the fact that a new employer is liable for the payment of compensation is relevant for the outcome of a dispute regarding this compensation. A different standard applies if the individual worker is personally liable for the compensation. In that case only the actual costs for this individual must be taken into account.

As there in fact is a system regarding the compensation for breach of contract

---

139 ECJ,16 March 2010, Olympique Lyonnais v Olivier Bernard and Newcastle United FC, C-325/08.

140 Opinion of the AG Sharpston in the Bernard case.

141 http://www.fifa.com/aboutfifa/federation/administration/playersagents/regulationstatustransfertsplayers.html

by players similar to the system of compensation for training and education the distinction made by the Advocate General should also apply to transfer payments. In both situations it is the new club that pays for the compensation. When a transfer sum was paid by the former club it is reasonable that the new club pays compensation for that. As the player is not involved in the negotiations about the sum to be paid for him it is not reasonable that he has to bear all of the consequences. Looking at the Mutu case where the new club was not involved in the several disputes the implications of the Bernard case should have a drastic effect on the outcome of the case. The FIFA DRC should have disregarded the pro rata part of the transfer sum and not consider it a part of the compensation amount. According to Article 17 para 2 of the FIFA RSTP it would have been up to Chelsea to approach the new club in order to obtain compensation for the investments that were lost. Such outcome would have been much more appropriate than the current one in which we see that Mutu is threatened with a career ending ban as he—of course—will never be able to pay the compensation amount by himself. The outcome of the DRC decision is very dissatisfactory as the club that got him for free, Juventus, then transferred him for €8,000,000 to Fiorentina. As this is not a successive club it is not liable for the compensation claimed by Chelsea.

9. The appeal against the FIFA DRC decision was dismissed by CAS, disregarding all arguments brought forward inclusive of discrimination and the fact that Mutu is held liable for a claim that should at least partly be paid by Juventus.
10. Mutu's argument that in order to mitigate damages Chelsea had to take other measures than direct dismissal was explicitly rejected by the CAS panel. According to the CAS the obligation to control damages only exists after the occurrence and not before. What is disregarded here is the fact that Chelsea did not involve Mutu's new club. It is obvious that an Italian Series A club provides much more redress than an individual player. The fact that Chelsea chose not to involve the new club had certainly to be taken into account in the calculation of the damages.
11. This case offered an exquisite occasion for an application of the specificities of sport even in the case it might not be argued by the player. The fact that Chelsea did not do what any other club would have done just because of their financially dominant position should also have been reflected in the decision. Looking at the recent CAS case law in football matters it appears that CAS panels tend to be reluctant in applying specificities of sport.[142] If these specificities are applied they seem to work against the player.
12. In last instance the case is brought before the Swiss Bundesgericht in order to see whether the CAS ruling is against Swiss law or public order. This starting point only gives a very small margin to have a CAS award revised. The

[142] CAS 2008/A/1519, *FC Shaktar Donetsk v Matuzalem and Real Zaragossa*, www.tas-cas.org/dw2files/document/3229/5048/0/Award%201519-1520%20_internet_.pdf(September 2010) and CAS 1-6-2010, 2009/A/1856,1857, FC Sion/El Hadary/FIFA/Al- Ahly, www.tas-cas.org/d2wfiles/document/4267/5048/0/ Award%201880-1881.pdf.

decision of the Bundesgericht implied that the arguments brought in were not enough to reach the standard that is necessary in order to annul the CAS decision.[143] For Mutu this finalises a dramatic march through the institutions without getting anywhere.

4.6.6 Conclusions

The conclusion that can be drawn from the previous seven cases in this dispute is that despite the outcome of the Bosman ruling[144] a professional football player is still not regarded upon as a normal worker under an employment agreement with his club. The FIFA Regulations have anchored the specificities of sport concerning compensation matters, especially looking at Article 17 and Annex VI of the FIFA RSTP. It is obvious that Mutu did things he should not have done and that the relationship with Chelsea likely could not be continued. However, this is no reason to discard the relevant regulations and laws. On many occasions the panels should have chosen a different direction than they have done. Bottom line is that it cannot be the aim nor the result of the system that because of what he did a player's career is seriously endangered. Mutu is held liable for a claim that for the biggest part should not be accounted to him and under normal circumstances would not have to be paid by him. Chelsea abused their wealth by choosing direct dismissal instead of the usual way in which such cases are handled; a transfer in order to control damages. This fact was not recognised from the very start of the dispute and none of the panels that dealt with the case were able to put the case in the right perspective: that is that a professional football player is an employee like any other one. A mistake made should not confront a worker with the horrifying perspective of termination of his career, even if his name is Adrian Mutu.

4.7 CAS 2009/A/1880, 1881 FC Sion/Essam El-Hadary v. FIFA and Al-Ahly Sporting Club CAS 2009/A/1856, 1857 Fenerbahçe v. Appiah/Appiah v Fenerbahçe

Peter Limbert

In recent years the CAS has rendered several awards on calculating compensation for the unilateral breach of contract of a player's employment contract under Article 17 of FIFA Regulations for the Status and Transfer of Players. In analysing these awards it is apparent that the CAS exercises a great deal of transparency in calculating compensation. This is good news for those involved or who might become involved in future cases. The author

---

[143] Bundesgericht 10 June 2010 http://jumpcgi.bger.ch/cgi-bin/JumpCGI?id=10.06.2010_4A_458/2009

[144] ECJ, 15 December 1995, *Bosman*, C-415/93, ECR I-4921.

considers this development with particular reference to the FC Sion/Essam El-Hadary v FIFA and Al-Ahly Sporting Club (CAS 2009 A/1880/81) and Fenerbahçe v Appiah/Appiah v Fenerbahçe (CAS 2009/A/1856/1857) Awards.

4.7.1 Introduction

The last 3 years has seen a significant development in the CAS' approach to the calculation of compensation for the unilateral termination of a player's employment contract under the FIFA Regulations for the Status and Transfer of Players (the "FIFA Regulations"). The recent decisions in *FC Sion/Essam El-Hadary v FIFA and Al-Ahly Sporting Club* (CAS 2009 A/1880/81) and *Fenerbahçe v Appiah/Appiah v Fenerbahçe* (CAS 2009/A/1856/1857 mark the latest point in a line of authorities which have seen the CAS shift from the pro-player "residual value" approach exemplified by the decision in *Heart of Midlothian v Webster and Ors* (CAS 2008/A/1298/99/300), to the "positive interest" approach first set out in *Shakhtar Donetsk v Matuzalem and Ors* (CAS 2008/A/1519-20).

As set out below, the CAS decisions in *FC Sion* and *Appiah* develop and expand upon the positive interest approach and provide guidance on how future CAS Panels may assess damages under Article 17. While it remains to be seen whether such Panels will follow these authorities, it is arguable that to the extent they are consistent with each other and *Matuzalem* and demonstrate a reliable, transparent approach to the calculation of compensation, they represent a positive step for football.

4.7.2 The 3 Year Shift

FC Sion and *Appiah* should not be viewed in isolation. Rather, they should be considered against the background of relatively recent jurisprudence in which the CAS can be seen to have shifted its approach from the decision in *Webster,* to its current approach, the roots of which can be found in the decision in *Matuzalem.*

Following *Webster*, participants in football were particularly concerned to see whether future Panels would follow the formulaic, pro-player approach favoured by the CAS, or whether a new approach would be found. In *Webster* the fundamental issue centred on the measure of compensation due when a player unilaterally terminates his contract without just cause outside the Protected Period. Hearts (Webster's former club) argued that at its most basic, compensation under Article 17 should provide an effective remedy for the losses a party suffers as a result of the other's unilateral termination. It claimed (inter alia) that in Webster's case, compensation under Article 17 should comprise a sum equivalent to the value it had lost and that could be reflected in either the replacement cost of a player of similar age, ability and experience or the loss of the opportunity of securing a transfer fee for the player.

The CAS however, disagreed. It stated that for breaches of contract outside the Protected Period, compensation should be limited to a sum equivalent to the remaining value of a player's contract. This method—which became known as the "residual value" approach—created a misconception among some players, agents and clubs that a player could "buy himself out of his contract" after the expiry of the Protected Period by unilaterally terminating it and moving to another club.

The CAS decision in *Webster* left many questions unanswered. For example, it was not clear how the approach would be applied in cases where the termination occurred within the Protected Period. Similarly, it provided little (if any) clarification as to how the approach could be reconciled with the various criteria set out in Article 17 for the assessment of compensation. Lastly, and perhaps most importantly, it left unclear how a party (particularly a club) could be adequately compensated for a player's breach of contract if it could only recover what was left on his salary and bonuses and the point of termination. While it was one way of measuring the value a player represented to a club, it bore no proper relationship to a club's loss as a player's registration has a very significant value to a club which often far exceeds the value of his wages. Moreover, to common lawyers at least, the measure of compensation itself—i.e. the recovery of unpaid residual salary—seemed misconceived given that the remaining value of a player's contract would ordinarily represent a *saving* to a club, not a recoverable head of loss.

Some of these questions were addressed the following year in the CAS' decision in *Matuzalem*—another case involving a player's unilateral termination of contract outside the Protected Period. In *Matuzalem*, the CAS decided not to follow *Webster*, instead favouring an approach to the interpretation of Article 17 and the calculation of compensation which was reflected in both Swiss and common law legal systems. This principle—which became known as the "positive interest" approach—aims to put the injured party back into the position he would have been in had the contract been performed properly.

In *Matuzalem* therefore, the CAS found that contrary to the misconception created by *Webster*, Article 17 is not intended to provide a basis by which a party may terminate his contract with impunity. Rather, it is intended to protect and reinforce the principle of the maintenance of contractual stability in football. To that end, the Panel decided that the calculation of compensation under Article 17 should not be bound by a particular formula, but should be determined on a case-by-case basis, assessing the entire ambit of an injured party's loss—not just the remaining value on a player's contract.

4.7.2.1 FC Sion and Appiah: Applying and Developing Matuzalem

While the CAS decisions in *FC Sion* and *Appiah* turned on their own facts and had vastly differing results, they can each be viewed as applying *Matuzalem's* positive interest principle. Moreover, they should also be seen as developing the doctrine given that they deal with certain issues that remained outstanding following *Matuzalem*, including the relevance of the Protected Period to the calculation of compensation, the availability of replacement cost as a head of damage and the enforceability of unilateral options.

As set out below, in *FC Sion* and *Appiah* the CAS refused to follow the DRC's approach to the calculation of compensation and instead continued with a consistent line of jurisprudence since *Matuzalem*, applying a broad analysis to the calculation of an injured party's loss.

Appiah

The main significance of the CAS' decision in *Appiah* is that firstly it involved the application of the positive interest principle in a case involving unilateral termination inside the Protected Period. Secondly however, it also demonstrated that the application of that principle is flexible enough to lead to a result whereby the player is found to be not liable to pay over an amount of money in compensation.

The basic facts of the case are as follows: Appiah joined Fenerbahçe from Juventus for €8 million in July 2005. He entered into a four-year contract with the club until 2009 which included a unilateral option in favour of the club to extend the contract to five years. His salary and benefits under the contract ranged from approximately 2 million euros (in 2005/6) to approximately 2.4 million euros (in 2008/9).

In May 2007, Fenerbahçe organised for Appiah to have an operation on his left knee at a hospital in Istanbul. However, in December 2007 the player was diagnosed with deep vein thrombosis, which the Player alleged was as a consequence of him not receiving anticoagulants (blood thinning drugs) following the operation.

Appiah later alleged that Fenerbahçe had failed to provide him with adequate medical care by failing to treat him properly or diagnose him quickly enough. He claimed this amounted to a breach of contract without just cause which entitled him to treat the contract as terminated as from the end of the 2007/8 season. Appiah went to Italy for treatment by his own doctors and did not return to the club after January 2008. As a result of his medical condition he did not play professional football for another club until after the expiry of his contract in 2009.

The club denied any medical malpractice and demanded Appiah's return to the club. When he failed to do so, the club exercised a unilateral option to extend the contract until 2010, bought a replacement player and issued proceedings against Appiah before the DRC, claiming compensation of approximately 12 million euros and the imposition of sporting sanctions.

At first instance, the DRC decided Appiah should have returned to Fenerbahçe and that his failure to do so constituted his unilateral termination of the contract without just cause. It therefore ordered him to pay compensation to Fenerbahçe in accordance with Article 17 of the FIFA Regulations, which it calculated at approximately 2.2 million euros, based on the unamortised costs the club incurred in signing Appiah from Juventus.

Both Appiah and Fenerbahçe appealed to the CAS. The club maintained its claim for over €12m, arguing that compensation should comprise approximately

4.8 million euros in residual value (which it claimed should include the period of the unilateral option until 2010), 4.17 million euros in unamortised costs and 3 million euros for Appiah's breach in light of the "specificity of sport".

Contrastingly, Appiah firstly argued that if any compensation was due, it was due from the club to him as a consequence of his medical mistreatment. Secondly however, he argued that even if compensation was due from him to the club, such compensation should be reduced to €0 because the club's saving, by not paying him for the remainder of the contract, outweighed its loss through his termination.

The CAS agreed with Appiah. It found that whilst his failure to return amounted to a unilateral termination within the Protected Period, the application of the positive interest approach meant that he should not have to pay any compensation to the club. Appiah had been unable to play football between December 2007 and at least July 2009 (i.e. the entire period since before the termination until the expiry of the contract). There was no dispute between the parties that Appiah's injury was not his fault, therefore was no basis on which he should be liable for any loss caused to Fenerbahçe as a result of it. The injury effectively rendered Appiah of no value to Fenerbahçe (or any other club) during the remainder of his contract, and as such he could not be liable for either: (i) the club's failure to receive a transfer fee (which would have been impossible to achieve as Appiah was injured); or (ii) the club having to buy a replacement player (because the club would always have had to replace Appiah regardless of whether the contract was terminated).

Consequently, the amount Fenerbahçe saved by not having to pay Appiah the remainder of his contract—approximately 2.6 million euros—outweighed any loss it suffered through unamortised costs and disciplinary fines—approximately €2.5 million.

In calculating the unamortised costs under the contract until 2009, the CAS also agreed with Appiah's argument in relation to the unilateral option. It confirmed the commonly held view that as a matter of CAS, FIFA and Swiss law jurisprudence, unilateral options are unlawful and unenforceable.

FC Sion

The significance of the CAS' decision in *FC Sion*—which involved circumstances similar to *Webster* and *Matuzalem*—is firstly that it is another case involving a breach within the Protected Period. More importantly however, it can also be seen to develop the positive interest approach by explicitly accepting replacement cost as a valid head of damage in the calculation of compensation under Article 17.

The basic facts of the case are as follows: On 1 January 2007 the player, Essam El-Hadary, entered into an employment contract with an Egyptian club, Al-Ahly Sporting Club ("AA"). Under the contract, which was due to expire at the end of the 2009/10 season, he was paid approximately US $292,000 per year. On 25 February 2008, after meeting with AA a few weeks earlier regarding a possible transfer to FC Sion, El-Hadary wrote to AA terminating his contract. He argued that AA had previously agreed to let him join a European club and had agreed he could leave.

AA disputed this. It therefore issued proceedings against El-Hadary and FC Sion (the player's new club) claiming compensation and the imposition of sporting sanctions against the player and FC Sion.

At first instance the DRC agreed with AA, holding that El-Hadary had unilaterally terminated his contract without just cause within the Protected Period and that FC Sion had induced his breach. As a result, it ordered the player to pay compensation of €900,000 (jointly and severally with FC Sion), calculated in accordance with Article 17. The compensation took into consideration the residual value of the player's contract with AA and his contract with FC Sion over the same period (calculated at €300,000), plus the "sports-related damages" AA had suffered as a result of his breach (calculated at €600,000).

On appeal, whilst the CAS upheld the DRC's decision as to liability, it did not agree with its calculation of compensation under Article 17. Instead, the CAS followed the positive interest principle set out in *Matuzalem*, assessing (inter alia) the compensation due to AA by considering what it would cost AA to replace El-Hadary with one of similar value. The CAS took into account evidence adduced at the hearing that FC Sion would have been willing to pay US $600,000 for the player before he terminated the contract. It also considered that FC Sion was willing to pay the player US $488,500 until the end of the period in which he would have been registered with AA but for his termination. On this basis the CAS found that to be put in a position as if the contract had been performed properly—i.e. to return AA to the position equivalent to that as if El-Hadary had not terminated the contract—AA would have to spend US $1,088,500 (i.e. a transfer fee of US $600,000 and wages of US $488,500) to acquire a player of similar quality to El-Hadary.

Just as in *Appiah*, the CAS' decision in *FC Sion* represents an important step in the jurisprudence in this area. The CAS' approach in accepting that "replacement cost" is a valid head of damage brings the interpretation of Article 17 back to the argument Hearts made (but which was rejected) in *Webster*.

4.7.2.2 Life After FC Sion and Appiah

The decisions by the CAS in *FC Sion* and *Appiah* will be viewed as positive by most participants in football. Firstly, they make clear that the overriding intention of Article 17 is to protect the principle of contractual stability in football and to act as a mechanism by which an injured party may be adequately "compensated" for its loss.

Second, the decisions should allay any fears clubs had after *Webster* that their interests were not adequately protected by the CAS. Following *FC Sion* and *Appiah* it is clear that clubs' interests should be adequately protected by a line of authorities that aims to assess compensation in by taking into account the full spectrum of their loss.

Third, the decisions (and in particular, *Appiah*) also represent positive steps for players. *Appiah* confirms that CAS Panels are willing to take into account all of the circumstances in assessing compensation, even where there has been a breach within the protected period. In times of spiralling wages and fees, players should be encouraged that CAS Panels will not simply address compensation based on a formulaic approach considering the residual value of their contracts.

Fourth, it is hoped that these authorities lay to rest any lingering doubts as to whether compensation awards should be necessarily lower in cases of breach outside the Protected Period. This distinction—which was artificial in any event since in many cases the Protected Period bears little if any correlation to a party's loss in cases of unilateral termination—was responsible for the misconception that a player could "buy himself out of his contract".

Fifth, while the jurisprudence will continue to evolve, *FC Sion* and *Appiah* can finally be seen to provide clarity and consistency to an area which has been the subject of much debate over the last 3 years. By applying and developing *Matuzalem*, the CAS has created a line of authorities which participants in football can rely upon to deliver fair and reasoned decisions in cases of unilateral breach by a player or a club.

A note of caution however: whilst *FC Sion* and *Appiah* go some way to clarifying further points in relation to the calculation of compensation under Article 17, some fundamental issues remain. One of the most important of these relates to the extent to which the positive interest approach may be followed in circumstances where the parties have chosen a specific governing law. In *Webster*, *Matuzalem*, *FC Sion* and *Appiah*, the CAS decided to apply Swiss law in the absence of any explicit choice by the parties. The absence of a choice of law made it appropriate that the principle informing the calculation of compensation under Article 17 was governed by Swiss law. However, whether the positive interest principle is intended to be of general application—i.e. in circumstances where the parties have chosen a law other than Swiss law to govern the dispute—remains largely untested. It is possible that since the DRC and the CAS are organisations domiciled in Switzerland, this is the intention—i.e. because the interpretation of Article 17 will necessarily be governed Swiss law, however it is hoped that this issue will be clarified in due course.

References

Haas U (2009) Football disputes between players and clubs before the CAS. In: Bernasconi M, Rigozzi A (eds) Sport governance, football disputes, doping and CAS arbitration: CAS and FSA/SAV conference, Lausanne 2008. Editions Weblaw, Berne

Ongaro O (2009) The FIFA players' status committee and the FIFA DRC. In: Bernasconi M, Rigozzi A (eds) Sport governance, football disputes, doping and CAS Arbitration: CAS and FSA/SAV conference, Lausanne 2008. Editions Weblaw, Berne

Soek JW (2009) The prize for freedom of movement: the Webster case. In: Gardiner S et al (eds) EU, sport, law and policy. T.M.C. Asser Instituut, The Hague

Tercier Pierre (2003) Les contrats spéciaux. Zurich, Bale, Geneve

Wyler Rémy (2002) Droit du Travail. Berne

Chapter 5
Contractual Stability: Unilateral Options

Jean-Samuel Leuba, Robert Fox, Juan de Dios Crespo Pérez, Gerardo Luis Acosta Perez and Frans M. de Weger

Contents

Jean-Samuel Leuba—Attorney-at-Law.
Robert Fox—Attorney-at-Law.
Juan de Dios Crespo Pérez—Attorney-at-law, Ruiz Huerta & Crespo Sports Lawyers.
Gerardo Luis Acosta Perez—Attorney-at-law, P&A Grupo Consultor.
Frans M. de Weger—Legal Counsel, Dutch Federation for Professional Football Clubs.

J.-S. Leuba
Lausanne, Switzerland
e-mail: leuba-avocats@vtxnet.ch

R. Fox (✉)
Lausanne, Switzerland
e-mail: rofox@edeb.ch

J. de Dios Crespo Pérez
Valencia, Spain
e-mail: jddcrespo@ruizcrespo.com

G. L. A. Perez
Asunción, Paraguay
e-mail: gerardoacosta@pagrupoconsultor.com

F. M. de Weger
Maarn, The Netherlands
e-mail: frans.deweger@fbo.nl

A. Wild (ed.), *CAS and Football: Landmark Cases*,
ASSER International Sports Law Series, DOI: 10.1007/978-90-6704-808-8_5,

5.1 CAS 2005/A/973 Panathinaikos FC v. Sotirios Kyrgiakos

Jean-Samuel Leuba and Robert Fox

In the Kyrgiakos Award the CAS considered the validity of two unilateral options giving FC Panathinaikos the right to extend the player's contract unilaterally. The first option covered a period of two years; the second was for a one-year extension. Each extension would lead to the player receiving additional remuneration bonuses. In 2003 the club exercised the first option. However, things started go wrong when they tried to exercise the second one. Ultimately this dispute ended with the Panel's ruling for the validity of the unilateral extension options—much to the surprise of many lawyers, but mainly due to the contractual balance established between club and player. The authors comment on these matters as well as on the intriguing question of the applicable law and FIFA's competence in disputes between clubs and players.

5.1.1 Introduction

The arbitral award issued by the CAS on 10 October 2006 in the case *Panathinaikos FC versus Sotirios Kyrgiakos* (hereinafter: the "award") was noteworthy because it accepted the validity of a unilateral option enabling a club to renew a footballer's contract.

In this article, we will, of course, examine this particular question and the related reasoning of the CAS.

Nevertheless, this award also raises two other matters of interest: first, applicable law, and second, FIFA's competence to rule on the dispute between the club and the player. We will therefore examine these different issues in the order in which they are discussed in the award.

However, insofar as this publication contains the full text of the award, this article will not describe in full either the facts of the case or the reasoning adopted by the CAS.

Apart from a brief summary of the facts, only the elements relevant to the present article will be mentioned. Readers are therefore invited to read the full award first.

5.1.2 Summary of the Facts

In 2001, the Greek player, who was 22 years old at the time, signed a contract with an initial term of two years, which was due to expire at the end of June 2003. The contract contained two unilateral options granting the club the right to extend the contract, initially for a two-year period expiring at the end of June 2005, and then for a second period of one year, ending on 30 June 2006. The contract was duly registered with the relevant Greek authorities and placed under Greek law. With regard to remuneration, the parties had also jointly signed an agreement in 2001, entitling the player to additional bonuses. In June 2003, the club exercised its first two-year unilateral option, thereby extending the contract until June 2005. In January 2005, the player was loaned to Scottish club Rangers FC until the end of June 2005. The six-month loan agreement was signed in January 2005 by the Greek club, the Scottish club and the Greek player. Under this agreement, the Scottish club was granted an option to sign the player permanently at the end of the loan. The Scottish club did not exercise this option, although it had expressed interest in signing the player for a lower price. Instead, the Greek club exercised its unilateral option to renew the contract with the player for the 2005/06 season. The player, however, refused to return to the Greek club at the start of the 2005/06 season, claiming that the unilateral option was invalid. The file was therefore submitted to the FIFA Players' Status Committee, which ruled in the player's favour and considered the unilateral option to be invalid. The club appealed to the Court of Arbitration for Sport against FIFA's decision. In its award, the CAS found in the club's favour and recognised the full validity of the unilateral option.

5.1.3 Applicable Law

In the award, the panel clearly considered which law should apply (cf. award, p. 9, rec. 45–51).

The panel decided that the FIFA Regulations for the Status and transfer of players (in particular the 1997 edition) should apply in the first instance. This aspect was not discussed by the parties and did not prove to be relevant to the outcome of the dispute, since the FIFA regulations did not contain any provision authorising or prohibiting unilateral options to renew a contract. Therefore, the panel clearly had to consider whether national law should apply as an alternative to the FIFA regulations.

Referring to Article R58 of the Code of Sports-related Arbitration (hereinafter: "the Code"), the panel deemed it inappropriate to apply substantive Swiss law to the contract (actually comprising two documents) signed by the parties, i.e. Panathinaikos FC and the Greek player Sotirios Kyrgiakos, on 27 July 2001. The arbitrators held that the contract had no connection whatsoever with Switzerland. It was a contract signed in Greece between a Greek citizen and a Greek football club concerning activities mostly taking place in Greece. Furthermore, the contract contained numerous references to Greek law, particularly Greek Sports Law 2725/99.

The panel therefore decided that the contract was exclusively connected with Greek law.

Also with reference to Article 58 of the Code, the panel considered that any other aspect of the dispute which was not covered by the FIFA regulations should be governed by Swiss law, which is the law of the country in which FIFA is domiciled.

The panel therefore held that the dispute should be decided in accordance with FIFA regulations and, on a subsidiary basis, according to Swiss law, with the important exception of any issues related to the contract and agreement signed by and between the parties on 27 July 2001.

The award does not contain any further discussion of applicable law. The solution adopted by the CAS certainly appears complicated. Indeed, in a procedure concerning a possible breach of contract, it is never easy to determine what is related to the contract and what is not. In fact, every important point is inevitably related more or less directly to the contract. It therefore remains to be decided what constitutes a "relationship".

Furthermore, the award does not contain any indication of why the panel did not apply Greek law to all aspects of the case as an alternative to the FIFA regulations. In other words, the decision that Swiss law should apply to questions unrelated to the contract was based on the fact that FIFA is domiciled in Switzerland. Of course, Article R58 of the Code sets out this criterion for deciding which law should apply. However, this criterion is an alternative to that of "the rules of law, the application of which the Panel deems appropriate". On the basis of this provision alone, the panel might well have decided that a dispute with all the characteristics of a Greek dispute should only be subject to Greek law, as an alternative to the FIFA regulations.[1]

Some are bound to argue that, under the FIFA Statutes (Article 62 para 2), the FIFA regulations should apply primarily and Swiss law in the alternative.

[1] This solution also seems to have been chosen by the CAS on other occasions, cf. Haas 2008, p. 222, where he cites CAS 2004/A/678 *Apollon Kalamaris FC v Oliveira Morais*, award of 20 May 2005, para 5.3 et seq.

How should this provision of the FIFA Statutes be interpreted and applied in relation to Article R58 of the Code? Should it be assumed that Article R58 takes precedence over Article 62 para 2 of the FIFA Statutes and that the CAS is therefore free to apply whatever law it deems appropriate? On the other hand, should it be considered that Article 62 para 2 of the FIFA Statutes constitutes an element of the arbitration agreement and therefore limits the discretion of the Court of Arbitration for Sport?

The arbitral award does not examine these questions and therefore does not offer any kind of response to them. The solution chosen by the panel appears extremely problematic and uncertain. The phrase "with the important exception of any issues related to the Contract" is extremely vague and does not explain with any clarity or certainty which law applies to which issue.

It should also be noted that, in the present dispute, in addition to the two contracts signed by the parties on 27 July 2001, a loan agreement was signed by the two parties and by the Glasgow Rangers club in January 2005. According to the grounds of the award, this loan agreement, although it bound the club and the player in certain aspects, was not subject to Greek law, unlike the contract signed in July 2001. In other words, it should therefore be subject to Swiss law. It is hard to see what relationship this agreement might have had with Swiss law.

As we have just seen, the arbitral award raises a number of questions concerning applicable law. It does not provide all the answers that might be expected. But it is particularly clear that, by juxtaposing the application of the national laws of different countries, the award creates significant uncertainties. Indeed, if the same parties were to go back in time to when they signed the first contract in 2001, they would need to consider which law the Court of Arbitration for Sport might apply if a dispute should arise six years later. If it is feasible that the laws of several different countries might apply concurrently, it would be impossible to draft a contract with all the precautions that would be necessary.

Perhaps it would be useful to remember what another CAS panel indicated in award CAS 2005/A/983 & 984 rec. 68, reiterated in award CAS 2006/A/1180 *Galatasaray SK v Frank Ribéry & Olympique de Marseille*, rec. 12: "In this regard, the Panel considers that sport is, by its very nature, a phenomenon that transcends borders. It is not only desirable, but indispensable that the rules governing international sport are standardised and broadly consistent throughout the world. In order to guarantee respect at global level, such regulations must not be applied differently from one country to another, particularly on account of interference between state law and sports regulations. The principle that FIFA rules should apply universally.... satisfies the need for rationality, certainty and legal forseeability".[2]

The above excerpt gives logical reasons why the FIFA regulations should apply in a standardised way. However, this does not resolve the problem when the FIFA rules are silent and do not help to settle a disputed issue. Is it therefore necessary,

[2] Translator's own translation; not the official CAS wording.

for the sake of standardisation, to decree or create a lex sportiva, to be applied universally? Such a solution creates other problems that are at least as serious as the application of national law, particularly with regard to the foreseeability and certainty of the law. Another solution would be to impose Swiss law systematically as the alternative law. Such a solution would have the virtue of ensuring that the law was foreseeable and clear. However, it would force all stakeholders in the sports world to submit all agreements systematically to the requirements of Swiss law. It is worth remembering that Swiss employment law contains numerous subtle rules that are either fully or relatively mandatory.

This means that just as many stumbling blocks may be faced if the parties fail to examine their agreement down to the smallest detail. However, all these questions extend beyond the scope of this article.

5.1.4 FIFA Competence

In the award, the panel considered that FIFA was competent to rule on the dispute between the Greek club Panathinaikos and the Greek player Sotirios Kyrgiakos.

FIFA's competence was examined in the light of FIFA's 1997 regulations. In this article, we will not therefore look in too much detail at these 1997 regulations, which are quite clearly being applied less and less, almost not at all, bearing in mind the length of time that has passed since they were adopted. We will therefore limit ourselves to a few brief remarks. First, it should be pointed out that FIFA's 1997 regulations are much less precise than the 2005 version with regard to FIFA's competence. In the case at hand, the panel referred to Article 19 of the 1997 regulations, ignoring the fact that this provision was part of chapter 5 (transfer of players from one national association to another). No aspect of the dispute between the Greek club and the Greek player involved a transfer from one association to another. Only the employment contract between a club and a player of the same nationality was at issue.

This remark throws up a general and global question. Is it really logical, or even desirable, that a dispute between a club and a player of the same nationality, concerning a contract applicable in the same country, should have to be submitted to FIFA which, as we have seen, applies its own regulations and, in the alternative, Swiss law?

In other words, in order to avoid any future risk in case of a dispute, any contract signed between a club and a player from the same country should conform not only with the FIFA regulations and the relevant national law, but also with Swiss law, which might be applied to the dispute under Article 62 para 2 of the FIFA Statutes.

To put it in another way, a club from a small country on the other side of the world which wanted to recruit a player from the same country should be advised to ensure that the contract complies with Swiss law. If FIFA (or the CAS) decides that a dispute has an international dimension (cf. Article 22 of the 2005 FIFA regulations), Swiss law may be used to settle a dispute between a player and a club from the same country.

In other words, if FIFA is generally deemed competent as soon as a dispute has the slightest international dimension, the player and the club run the risk of seeing a future dispute resolved by FIFA, which will not apply the national law common to the club and the player.

In the award, the panel thought the dispute had an international dimension by virtue of the simple fact that it concerned whether the Greek player should resume his contractual obligations to the Greek club after a six-month loan in Scotland. However, the dispute did not concern any aspect of the loan agreement with the Scottish club.

Nobody disputed the validity of this loan agreement, nor that it had expired and had therefore ended.

Not even the question of the ITC could justify the international dimension, since this ITC had been the subject of a distinct, separate decision. The dispute therefore concerned only the contract signed between the Greek club and the Greek player in July 2001. This contract and all contractual relations between the two parties had only a national dimension, i.e. Greek.

Was it therefore necessary to decide that FIFA was competent to rule on a contract between Greek parties who were subject to Greek law, as the CAS decided? In other words, can FIFA's legal organs be expected to apply the national law of the player and club concerned?

FIFA's broad competence quite clearly has an objective and a consequence, i.e. a certain standardisation of applicable rules and judicial practices. However, it comes up against practical and legal obstacles when it is obvious that national law should apply to a dispute between a club and a player of the same nationality.

Therefore, in our opinion, while we can accept that the existence of an international dimension in the relations between the parties justifies, for the sake of legal certainty, a degree of standardisation, it is necessary, on the other hand, to show caution in a situation where the international element clearly has no direct, close link to the disputed issues.

5.1.5 Validity of the Unilateral Option Clause

Many sports law observers were surprised by the panel's decision concerning the clause granting the club a unilateral option. Unilateral options exist in practice, but they raise questions among lawyers. To the best of our knowledge, the CAS has been relatively hostile to such clauses,[3] although it has not ruled them out completely.

---

3 Cf. Haas 2008, pp. 225–226 and the awards quoted, particularly CAS 2005/A/983 & 984 *Penarol v Bueno, Rodriguez & PSG*, rec. 119; 2006/A/1157 *C.A. Boca Juniors v Genoa*, rec. 8.1.

This decision to recognise the validity of the unilateral option is certainly based on an extremely pragmatic analysis of the contractual relations between the two parties.

First, the panel considered that, in known case law, no unilateral option had ever been declared absolutely void under all circumstances.

However, known CAS awards had found such clauses to be invalid in the cases examined, although not as a matter of principle and based only on examination of the specific details of the case (cf. CAS 2004/A/678, for example).

But, in particular, the panel considered that the details of the case between Panathinaikos FC and Sotirios Kyrgiakos were such that the unilateral option was fully valid.

The panel based this decision on a number of elements, which are summarised below:

If the clause were exercised, the contract would be valid for five years in total. Such duration conforms with the FIFA regulations (Article 18 of the Regulations for the Status and Transfer of Players) and corresponds with what the player might have expected when he signed the contract.

The original contract expressly provided for substantial increases in the player's salary and bonuses. For example, at the end of the initial three-year period, the club had a first option (two years) which, if it were exercised, would result in a significant pay rise. But, in particular, if the second option (one year) were exercised, i.e. for the fifth year of the contract, the player's remuneration would be doubled (salary and bonus). In the panel's opinion, such an increase in remuneration showed that there was a fair balance between the concessions made by each of the parties in the contract. The club could not impose or amend certain clauses when exercising the option. It was obliged to pay the increased remuneration, which represented the price paid for the option.

Incidentally, the award points out that, when the initial contract was signed, the player was playing for a third division club for an extremely low salary. In other words, in order to acquire the option, the club had to make significant promises in terms of salary.

It is extremely interesting to note that the panel did not think it could take into consideration the fact that the player was offered, instead of a fifth year at the Greek club, a contract with a Scottish club with a much higher salary. This was deemed irrelevant. The panel's views on this matter are interesting, because they confirm the imbalance that exists in the market between certain rich clubs. Now, although this imbalance clearly exists, it does not mean that contracts can be broken. The panel noted that the player's motivation for not honouring the fifth year after the club exercised its option was almost certainly entirely financial, since he was able to earn much more by breaking his contract.

Furthermore, the panel noted that the player had never complained when the club had exercised its first option to extend the contract for the third and fourth years. The player met his obligations. It was only during the fourth year, when he was loaned to the Scottish club and realised that it was in his financial interest to dispute the contract that the player actually disputed the unilateral option.

To conclude, the award refers to the cardinal principle, "pacta sunt servanda". Although everyone, of course, knows what this phrase means, the panel's reference to it appears instructive. Indeed, having pointed out that this principle is fundamental in contract law, it is right to consider that, whenever a contract is allowed to be broken for whatever reason, the principle of respect for and the stability of contracts is breached, as well as, to some extent, legal certainty. It should be remembered that a contract often represents the law between parties.

Finally, the panel not only noted that the contract signed in July 2001 appeared perfectly valid and therefore allowed the club to exercise the option for the 2005/06 season; it also pointed out that, in January 2005, when the loan agreement was signed with Rangers FC, the player had himself signed the agreement, which included a clause under which the Scottish club could, at the end of the loan agreement, sign him permanently for a transfer fee of €1,500,000. This constituted an implicit acceptance, several months before the deadline, of the fact that the club was entitled to extend the contract for a further year, as this was the only reason a transfer fee would be due. Therefore, a refusal to accept the validity of this clause implies not only that part of the contract signed in 2001 by the player and club was considered invalid, but also that part of the loan agreement signed by the player in January 2005, five months before the option to extend the contract was exercised, was also deemed invalid.

5.1.6 Conclusions

This arbitral award raises a number of questions relating to FIFA's competence and applicable law.

In substance, it has the virtue of referring to the fundamental principle "*pacta sunt servanda*". As well as this principle, the panel emphasised that the player's attitude was not "*bona fide*".

Certainly, such an attitude in this case did not warrant increased protection, especially as the contract, when viewed as a whole, represented a contractual balance between the parties, containing reciprocal concessions.

There was therefore clearly no imbalance or obvious disproportion.

The unilateral option was therefore deemed perfectly valid and correctly exercised by the club. It is no surprise that the CAS ordered the player to pay damages to the club.

5.2 CAS 2005/A/983 & 984 Club Atlético Peñarol v. Carlos Héber Bueno Suárez & Cristian Gabriel Rodríguez Barrotti & Paris-Saint-Germain

Juan de Dios Crespo Pérez

This case is about the two players Carlos Bueno and Cristian Rodríguez who refused to renew their contracts expiring at the end of 2004. The dispute arose through the contractual use of unilateral options granting the Uruguayan club CA Peñarol the right to extend the contracts, which did not include any reciprocal benefits for the players. The players' refusal to comply with the Uruguayan Football Player Statute led to their right to play football being 'frozen', with contractual obligations suspended. In terms of these regulations the players were not free to leave their club until the end of their extended contracts. In its award the CAS stated the invalidity of these clauses. This fact and the fact that FIFA Regulations and international principles of law prevailed over the national rules at hand, turned this award into a milestone, the so called 'South American Bosman'.

5.2.1 Preamble

By the end of June 2005 I received a call from an agent, Mr. Francisco "Paco" Casal, who is well known as one of the leading intermediaries in football. He had apparently read an article I had written for the sports Spanish newspaper "MARCA" in which I was explaining briefly and with some wit (or at least that was my intention) the new FIFA Regulations for the Status and Transfer of Players. He seemed to like my approach and decided that the case he had in hand against the Uruguayan club CA Peñarol could be interesting for me.

We met, and when he described the situation of the players Carlos Bueno and Cristian Rodríguez, I was astonished. The players were under contract until the end of 2004 but with an option in favour of the CA Peñarol for an extension. The players refused to sign the new contract and immediately were involved into the Regulations in force in Uruguay for those kinds of situations: they were ousted from the club, they were deprived of any training or the possibility to use the club's premises as well as not paid but retained as licensed players of the club in what is called "Rebeldía" or "Rebellion".

It seemed to me that this kind of behaviour was a bit out of time but it was what was happening in Uruguay for a long time thanks to the "Estatuto del Jugador Uruguayo" (Uruguayan Football Player Statute). And then, things changed a lot after the CAS decision and it was a mini-revolution in the Oriental Republic, as Uruguay is also known.

5.2.2 Facts

The facts of the case were, in general terms, the following:

The Uruguayan Football Player's Statute[4] establishes that contracts signed between a club and a player may be extended by the club until the second 31 December following the date of termination of the initial contract. If the contract is signed during the second half of the season, the contract may then be extended until the third 31 December following the date of termination. Considering that the Uruguayan football season runs from January 1 to December 31, this essentially means that a club may unilaterally extend a contract signed with a player for an additional two seasons, and even two and a half seasons in some cases.

This possibility to unilaterally extend the contract does not implicate a reciprocal benefit to the player. The club had the sole obligation to adjust the salary of the player to the increase in the national Consumer Price Index, but had no obligation to provide better conditions whatsoever to the player. Furthermore, if the player refused to accept the contract extension, the club is entitled to list him as "rebellious" and to suspend its contractual obligations such as payment of the player's salary. The player would only be free to leave the club when the "rebellion" period ended, namely, when the contract (with the extensions allowed by the Statute) expired.

In this context, Carlos Bueno and Cristian Rodríguez, two Uruguayan professional football players, refused to agree to terms for a new contract with their club, Club Atlético Peñarol of Montevideo, Uruguay. The players were seeking a pay raise and other benefits to be included in their contracts.

The club, however, knowing that the Statute granted it the right to unilaterally extend the players' contract for a further two seasons by merely adjusting the players' salary in accordance with the Consumer Price Index, refused to negotiate and, when the players refused to sign a new contract, listed them as "rebellious" before the Uruguayan Football Federation and was thus exempted from fulfilling its contractual obligations (such as paying the players' salary). The players, in principle, were unable to sign with a different club.

Notwithstanding the above, and after being unable to play for approximately four months, the players proceeded to sign a contract with the French club Paris Saint-Germain for the season 2005/06, disregarding the Uruguayan Player's Statute which, in principle, established that they were still contractually bound to Peñarol even if listed "on rebellion".

As expected, Peñarol filed a claim against the players and Paris Saint-Germain before the FIFA Dispute Resolution Chamber, arguing that the players, induced by the French club, had breached their contract with Peñarol without just cause.

The DRC[5] rejected Peñarol's claim on the basis of the invalidity of an unilateral option clause in favour of a club, and the Uruguayan club proceeded to appeal before the Court of Arbitration for Sport.

---

[4] Now modified thanks to the *Bueno-Rodriguez* case.

[5] Decision of 24 October 2005.

5.2.3 Commentary

The decision taken by the Court of Arbitration for Sport (CAS) in the case of two Uruguayan footballers, Carlos Bueno and Cristian Rodríguez, who decided to disregard the extension clause that bound them to their employer, Uruguayan football club Club Atlético Peñarol, is of particular relevance in the world of football, due to the role that unilateral extension options in favour of clubs have maintained in the past few years.

It also established an important precedent as regards the law applicable to an international football case, as the CAS decided that the FIFA Regulations and international principles of law should prevail over national law considerations, when deciding over the validity of the unilateral extension option tying two Uruguayan players to a Uruguayan club.

Such has been the notoriety and impact of this case, that it has even been labeled the '*South American Bosman*'.

An extension option in professional football is the right of the player and/or the club to extend an employment contract for a certain period which is stipulated by the parties in the contract that binds them. The option can be reciprocal or unilateral. In the first case, both parties may agree on the extension, while in the second case, only one of the parties has the possibility to exercise the extension option without the need for the other party's consent.

In practice, unilateral extension options are normally established in favour of the clubs. The clubs establish this option in the contract to try to prevent the situation whereby their players leave freely at the end of their employment contract. Most clubs try to keep their players as long as possible, particularly when they expect their value in the transfer market to rise.

This practice has increased in certain regions of the world (particularly Latin America and China) as a consequence of the *Bosman* ruling and the end of the old transfer system which enabled the clubs to obtain a transfer fee when the player moved to a new club, even if the player was out of contract.

As a result of this practice, several players who have been affected by it have proceeded to legally challenge unilateral extension options included in their playing contracts, from which they obtain no benefits. The clubs have defended the inclusion of the said clauses on the basis that national laws, as a general rule, do not object or prohibit them.

However, in the purely sporting context, the decision taken by the Court of Arbitration for Sport (CAS) in the *Bueno-Rodriguez* case has produced sporting jurisprudence that should constitute the basis for future decisions regarding similar cases.

Despite the popularity and frequent use in international football of the unilateral extension clause, particularly after the Bosman ruling and the resulting changes to the FIFA Regulations, the latest editions of the Regulations on the Status and Transfer of Players (RSTP) have not included any provisions governing the validity of the aforementioned option. This has led the clubs into the belief that they are able to freely include this clause into players' contracts and therefore establish a mechanism to retain them when it suits the club's interest.

This type of clause has become particularly common in several countries in Latin America and other jurisdictions such as China. In Latin America, clubs have justified their inclusion by sustaining that this mechanism is their only defense against richer European clubs who take their players at a very young age, as they do not have the financial position to sign long-term contracts with players whose future development is yet uncertain.

However, several clubs in Europe have also included such a clause in the contracts signed with their players, constituting proof that the issue at stake is of global concern and not specific to a particular area of the world.

The appointed Panel of the CAS determined that the fundamental question of the dispute was precisely to determine whether the players Bueno and Rodriguez were still bound contractually to Peñarol when they signed employment contracts with Paris Saint-Germain. However, as an essential prerequisite to answer this question was to determine which law was applicable to the case at hand. Peñarol insisted on the fact that Uruguayan law should be applied as all parties involved in the employment contract were Uruguayan nationals.

However, the CAS determined that, since football is a global phenomenon, it is essential that the rules that govern the sport at the international level are uniform and coherent worldwide[6]:

> The Panel considers that sport is naturally a transnational phenomenon. It is not only desirable but indispensable that regulations referred to the sport at an international level have a uniform and coherent worldwide character. In order to ensure a respect at a worldwide level, such a regulation should not be applicable in a different way from one country to another, due to interferences established by a State Law or a Sporting regulation. The principle of the universality of the application of the FIFA regulations—or of any other international federation—is a need for the legal rationality, security and predictability. All the members of the football family are therefore under the same regulations, which are published. The uniformity that comes from it tends to assure the equality of treatment between all the addressees of such regulations, independently of the countries from which they are

The outcome of two cases with the same facts in two different jurisdictions should produce the same result. This is a kind of *lex sportiva,* a legal cousin of the *lex mercatoria* that is known in international commerce.

And it has to be said that as an international element came into the case, the Paris-Saint-Germain, rules of internal value, like the Uruguayan Football Players Statute, are not valid anymore in an international conflict.

Of course, there are a lot of detractors of *lex sportiva* but it is evident that if there is no common regulation that could be predictably understood by the entire football (or any other sport) family, the legal conflicts would be much more than at present.

[6] Point 68 of the award.

The Panel then asseverated the following:

> As it has been stated, the aim of the FIFA Regulations is to create uniform regulations that can be valid for all the cases of international transfers and in which all the actors of the football family are subject to. This aim would not be reached if all the applicable rules of one or other country had to be applied. It would be inconceivable that such national rules would affect parties that are not subject to the law of a country.[7]

Thus, it is crystal clear that the FIFA Regulations are applicable to the more than 200 of its members, with no obligation for any of them to be subject to the legal reality of another State.

Furthermore, the Panel reminded us the following:

> Then, unless you want to undermine the fundamental aim of the FIFA international Regulations, the agreements and other legal dispositions of national levels can only be applicable if they are in conformity, or at least complementary to the FIFA Regulations, but in no case if they are contrary to those. This necessity of uniform legality is, moreover, one of the most evident "specificities of sport" that article 25.6 of the FIFA Regulations refers to.[8]

It cannot be said more clearly and in lesser number of words. The "internationalist" scope of FIFA is therefore admitted, which is also strange when you talk about the body that controls the world of football, but I am not referring to the Marxist sense of the word…

Finally, we have to take into consideration that this is really the only way to deal with football when it comes to an international aspect as if the national legislation had to enter in conflict in order to know which one has to be applied, we can forget about a quick answer to any dispute.

Thus, let us keep the "internationality of football" that praises the Panel in the *Bueno-Rodríguez* case.

The CAS also determined, on the basis of Swiss International Private Law, that it had the possibility to apply a law that was not particular to a specific State, but of universal application such as sporting rules or federation rules, as long as the said rules were not in opposition to public policy.

The Panel then applied Article R58 of the Code of Sports Related Arbitration and Article 59.2 of the FIFA Statutes to conclude that the FIFA Regulations (and subsidiarily Swiss law) were applicable to the case. This conclusion was also supported by the fact that all parties involved are members of national federations that are, in turn, members of FIFA and thus subject to its rules and regulations.

Furthermore, considering that the dispute involves an international transfer and cannot be deemed a "local" dispute, Uruguayan law is not applicable, as there is a clear interest that the dispute be solved in accordance to unified rules and regulations of an international nature.

The Panel stated that sport is "a phenomenon that naturally expanded towards the borders" and that "it is not only preferable but also indispensable that the

---

[7] Point 101 of the award.

[8] Point 102 of the award.

regulations which control the sport at an international level have a regular and largely coherent character in the whole world."

In that sense, we must remember that the Switzerland Federal Code on Private International Law (LDIP)[9] had to be taken into consideration and the Panel said that:

> ... Consequently, the applicable regulations in first instance, FIFA Regulations in this case, cannot be superior to an imperative rule of Swiss Law if the result could be a contradiction in the essential values, duly recognized as per the Swiss legal concepts, that is to say, the Public Policy.[10]

Therefore, it clarifies the need of the FIFA Regulations to adapt itself to the Swiss public policy as the CAS and LDIP compel to do so, but also due to the fact that the FIFA Statutes are under Swiss Law too, as the world football regulator is an association of Swiss Law.

The Panel continues stating that:

> At first glance, the FIFA Regulations do not contain rules that might contradict the essential and well known values of the Swiss legal concepts. However, if a rule of article 25.6 of the FIFA Regulations is contrary to the public policy, it should not be taken into consideration. It would be also the case if an imperative rule of national law would be contrary to the Swiss concept of Law, if hypothetically such a national rule could be assumed as per article 19 of LDIP.

So, the Panel gives us a lot of weapons in order to make it clear that there are no ways to avoid Swiss Law, either by FIFA as it is a Swiss association of civil law, or by any national law of any other country.

It means that whoever wants to be a member of the football family, of FIFA family, cannot, in any way, withdraw from the *vis atractiva* of Swiss Law. The issue is not worthless, as the FIFA Rules and Statutes are the rules that must be accepted by anyone who is a member or wants to continue as a part of the family.

And as the Statutes are approved by the FIFA Congress, in which all the associations are members[11] and where the decisions are taken by majority,[12] it cannot be said afterwards that the legal duties of FIFA Regulations are unknown. The legal system of FIFA is accepted by all its direct (associations) members or indirect (leagues, clubs, players, agents, etc....).

As for the Uruguayan law, the Panel clarified as follows:

> As per article 19.2 of the LDIP, this solution would be even clearer if the application of the imperative Uruguayan law would come to a result that would be incompatible with the Swiss conception of the Law. Without anticipating the further considerations that shall be said in detail afterwards, the Panel observes that the litigious rules of the Uruguayan law, which is said to be mandatory, i.e. the unilateral option of renewal of the players' contracts and the so-called system of "rebellion", raise serious doubts as to their compatibility to

---

[9] Loi fédérale Suisse sur le droit international privé, dated 18 December 1987.

[10] Point 94 of the award.

[11] Article 25.2 m and 26 of FIFA Statutes.

[12] Article 27.4 of the FIFA Statutes.

the minimum standards of protection of employees in Swiss Law. It is to say that even though Uruguayan Law was to be directly applicable if its contents complied with the needs of legitimate interest stated in article 19.1 of LDIP, the Panel would have to refuse the applicability of rules that are potentially contrary to the Public Policy as defined hereinabove.

We have to point out, finally, that the simple fact that, as the appellant says, the whole system of Uruguayan rules that regulates the professional sport have been declared under Public Policy is not enough to raise them to the level of Public Policy in the sense of LDIP. Independently of what angle we might see the notion of Public Policy, its material content cannot be formed by anything else but rules and principles that have a particularly high material value. Therefore, it is not enough to proclaim that the rules are of Public Policy because they are related to certain relationships to give them such a quality.

In conclusion, even using article 19 of LDIP, the Panel considers that the Players' Status of Uruguay cannot be taken into consideration in the present case.[13]

Definitively, we must say that, even in the case that some national rules could be applied, thanks to Article 19 of LDIP, which permits that a Public Policy regulation of another State is applicable in Switzerland, if there is an evident connection with the facts, such rule should in any case be under the "Swiss conception of Law".

Then, this drives us to the point of saying that the entire Swiss legal system, depending on the case in question, had to encounter its home in any CAS award and in the present *litis*, Swiss Law has no possibility to admit the Uruguayan Players' Status which is contrary to the employees' rights in the *Confederatio Helvetica.*

Anyhow, a final remark must be made in this particular issue, as national law (Greek one) was used in the case between the Player Kyrgiakos and its former club Panathinaikos FC, both Greeks, as it was established that there was no *international element* in it.[14]

The CAS' stance regarding applicable law in this case constitutes a fundamental precedent, as the Panel determined that uniformity and legal certainty are essential for football to function globally as an organized sport, and only a universally applicable set of rules established by the sport's governing authority may achieve this objective. Thus, in a football-related case of international transcendence, FIFA's rules and regulations should be applicable over national law, as long as the aforementioned regulations are not contrary to public policy and fundamental principles of law.

When analyzing the dispute within the scope of the FIFA Statutes, the RSTP and Swiss law, the Panel determined that the players Carlos Bueno and Cristian Rodríguez were not contractually bound to Club Atlético Peñarol when they signed employment contracts with Paris Saint-Germain.

Thus, the players did not infringe Article 17 of the RSTP, which refers specifically to the consequences of a unilateral breach of an employment contract between players and clubs.

---

[13] Point 109, 110 and 111 of the award.

[14] CAS 2005/A/973 *Panathinaikos FC v Sotirios Kyrgiakos.*

The CAS sustained its decision on the argument that a contract, or Statute governing the same, that allows a club to unilaterally extend the duration of a player's contract with only a minimum adjustment to the player's salary, is clearly incompatible with the FIFA Regulations in regard to contracts, as these should always have a fixed duration and clearly stipulate the player's salary and other benefits.

The Uruguayan system allows a club, in practice, to establish a long-term contract with the player which, through the unilateral extension option, it may rescind at the end of only one year. The club can therefore refuse to extend the contract if a specific player does not progress as expected, but may retain players who have increased in quality and value, without having the obligation to increase the player's salary.

This leads to a system which is clearly disproportionate in favour of the clubs, and is contrary to the general principles of labour law, as the system gives the clubs undue control over the players without adequately rewarding the players in exchange. It is really a gambling on players but with all the cards in the hands of the club.

What a club should do, if it wants to control as much players as possible or at least the players it considers *previously* as potential transferable footballers, is to sign a long-term contract with them (three years for instance) and bet on them, but not just contract them for one year, in a sort of *period of proof* and only if they appeared to be good, to sign another year or if they are very good more than one only… This seems really unfair for the employees and this is what the CAS has understood.

Peñarol presented, on the very last day and before the hearing, the now well-known "Portmann report",[15] made by Prof. Portmann on the request of FIFA (and surely forced by the South American associations…) regarding the "unilateral option to renew a contract". That report makes clear that, according to Swiss Law, those kinds of options are valid, provided that they have certain points clearly stated in the contract.

Of course, it did not help the case itself, as those points were not, in any way, in the Uruguayan contracts, but would be a preparation for the future contractual labour agreements in Uruguay and some other South American countries that had a similar type of regulations.

But at the time of the case, the system imposed by the Uruguayan Statute of Players disregards the reforms contained by the FIFA Regulations of 2001 and 2005 that derogated the old transfer system, in which a club had the possibility to retain a player and block his move to a different club even if the player's employment contract with the club had expired.

By allowing a club to unilaterally extend a player's contract with no due consideration for the player, the Statute effectively allows Uruguayan clubs to maintain the old transfer system by retaining out-of-contract players, and declaring those that refuse to enter into a new contract as "rebellious".

---

[15] Dated 10 February 2006.

Furthermore, the Uruguayan *status quo* benefits the clubs when a player is signing a new contract, which is normally the point at which the player is in a weaker position and cannot truly negotiate fair terms. The player then has no possibility to escape the system and obtain more favourable employment conditions, or even the freedom to conclude a contract with a different employer.

The disproportion in the relation between club and player is contrary to contractual law, and a Statute that supports this system should be deemed illegal and unacceptable.

Despite the fact that the FIFA rules and regulations do not specifically touch the subject of unilateral extension of contracts, the aforementioned system is clearly contrary to the spirit of the said rules and regulations, and also to Swiss law as we have previously seen. The Panel took care to mention that such a system is not only contrary to a specific article or rule contained in a code, but is also contrary to the fundamental values of the Swiss legal order as a whole, as the employee is left completely at the mercy of his employer.

The provisions that enable a club to declare the player as "rebellious", contained by the Uruguayan Statute of Players, are also contrary to the Swiss Code of Obligations, as they enable an employer to suspend the payment of the salary to a player while simultaneously blocking his possibility to practice his profession. In general, a system that allows the employer to withhold an employee's revenue for several years is clearly contrary to the fundamental principles of law.

The Panel even considered that the "state of rebellion" in which a player supposedly incurs by refusing to sign a new contract with the club, voids the contractual relationship between the parties since the employer stops paying the salary at that time, and thus, if declared "rebellious", the player and the club are no longer linked by an employment contract.The said contract should be considered rescinded the moment the employer refuses to pay the player his salary while also preventing him from exercising his profession.

In conclusion, the CAS determined that a clause granting a club the unilateral right to extend a football player's contract without any due consideration for the player, such as a substantial increase in salary or other types of benefits, is contrary not only to the FIFA Regulations on the Status and Transfer of Players, but also to the Swiss Code of Obligations and the generally accepted principles of law.

The CAS thus proceeded to uphold the DRC's decision and determined that the players Carlos Bueno and Cristian Rodríguez did not have a valid contractual relationship with Club Atlético Peñarol when they proceeded to sign an employment agreement with Paris Saint-Germain.

This, of course, gave the start for a change in some countries, like Uruguay and also Argentina and Paraguay. In Argentina, for instance, the new official contract drafted by the association (AFA) had tried to introduce the Portmann's indications but failed to do it completely, so we will see what will happen in the future and we might have a potential Bueno-Rodriguez there also …

5.3 CAS 2006/A/1082-1104 Valladolid v Barreto, Cerro Porteño

Gerardo Luis Acosta Perez

This award revolves around the player Diego Barreto who signed a contract with Spanish club Real Valladolid CF SAD for the period after expiry of his contract with Cerro Porteño (Paraguay). However, Barreto had only considered his own position. The contract with Cerro Porteño covered a unilateral extension clause in the club's favour. For a number of reasons the player intended not to fulfil his contract with Real Valladolid CF SAD. He thus cited the unilateral extension clause of his prior club to breach the new contract. The CAS decided that such a unilateral extension of the player's contract would not be valid, and Barreto had to pay €1,500,000. In calculating compensation the Panel mitigated the amount of a buy-out clause of €6,000,000 established in the contract with Real Valladolid CF SAD. The author delves into the background to this ruling.

5.3.1 Introduction

The aim of this document is not to analyze the arbitration award with which the Court of Arbitration for Sport ended the dispute between the club Real Valladolid CF SAD and the player Diego Barreto and the club Cerro Porteño (Paraguay). Our discussion will focus on the background of the dispute, especially on the role played by another unknown stakeholder in this legal transaction.

In order to do so, we will begin with a description of Diego Barreto's legal situation in the club Cerro Porteño during the season of 2004 (I), and will then describe the circumstances surrounding the signing of the contract with the club Real Valladolid CF SAD (II) and we will conclude with a description of the breach of this contract (III). Finally in conclusion, we will briefly outline the outcome of the case in FIFA and the CAS.

5.3.2 Employment Relationship with the Club Cerro Porteño

Diego Barreto, born on July 16, 1981 registered with the Cerro Porteño at age 15, and completed all of his training as a footballer within this club. His outstanding performance in Cerro Porteño, led him to be chosen for the national team at a very early age, taking part in the under 17 and under 20 national teams. With both these teams, he received awards in competitions organised by the South American Football Confederation as well as in the World Championships.

When he was 19 years old, Diego Barreto and Cerro Porteño signed a Sporting Employment Contract under law 88/91 which "Establishes the Status of Professional Footballers" in Paraguay. The duration of the contract was four years from January 1, 2000 until December 31, 2004. In the contract, before the signatures, a special clause was included which enabled Cerro Porteño to extend the contract for two more years.

Under this contract, Diego Barreto played with the national team of Paraguay in the South American under 23 “Pre Olympics”, the “A” team of the Copa América and the Olympic Games in Athens, all in the year 2004, winning the silver medal in the two Olympic competitions.

5.3.3 The Contract with Real Valladolid CF SAD

In July 2004, more specifically on July 17, 2004, a day after his 24th birthday, while Diego Barreto was in Peru with the “A” national team of Paraguay due to his participation in the Copa América, the player’s father was contacted in Paraguay by a lawyer, Mr Pascual Barrios, who offered him an employment contract with Real Valladolid CF SAD, to begin on January 1, 2005, when the contract with Cerro Porteño would have expired, without taking into consideration the possibility that the extension agreed on by the parties in that contract would occur.

The player’s father was offered a sum of money (€300,000) for allegedly acting as his son’s representative, as stated in the FIFA Player’s Agent Regulations. The father obtained the consent of his son and a contract was created between Real Valladolid CF SAD and Diego Barreto.

In the contract, Pascual Barrios, is not named as the representative of Real Valladolid CF SAD, but as a lawyer acting on behalf of Diego Barreto. The contract was signed by the President of the Spanish club and by Pascual Barrios, on behalf of the player. Then, in order to avoid potential problems, Pascual Barrios faxed the document to Diego Barreto, who was in Peru, to seek his approval of it. The player signed the contract, confirming everything that Pascual Barrios had done on his behalf.

The contract stipulated that Diego Barreto was required to pay the fees of his agents and lawyers, which explicitly included Pascual Barrios. Until that point there were no problems.

However, when the date came around for the first payment of a sum of money to be made, which was to be paid in advance, Pascual Barrios, who acted as a representative of the Spanish club to the player and his father, but who, in the contract had a different role, provided his personal bank account details for the payment, and then only gave Diego Barreto and his father the sum of €50,000 (in the contract the amount was €100,000).

From the point when Pascual Barrios refused to hand over the full sum of the money to the player, Barreto also began to breach the contract, which culminated in the arbitration award of the CAS.

5.3.4 Breaches of Contract by Diego Barreto

Continuing to trust Pascual Barrios, Diego Barreto believed that he could claim that Real Valladolid had breached the contract which would have rendered that agreement null and void and he therefore considered himself free to sign a contract with any club of his choice. Real Valladolid, however, rejected this argument because it had paid the money owed according to the instructions of the player's "representative", Pascual Barrios.

At this point, in October 2004, Cerro Porteño requested that Diego Barreto sign a contract extension, in accordance with the clause in the contract that expired on December 31, 2004. Diego Barreto refused and a labour dispute was initiated in Paraguay.

Diego Barreto announced, through the media, that nothing had been signed with Real Valladolid, perhaps believing that the agreement between the two sides had been legally voided following Pascual Barrios' breach of contract, and initiated a series of training tests with UD Almería (Spain).

Diego Barreto's situation was therefore quite complex, involving three clubs. The first, Cerro Porteño, requested his compliance with the extension clause in the contract via the labour courts of Paraguay. The second, Real Valladolid CF SAD, having paid the player's "representative", required him to train at the club. The third, UD Almería, was where he was training and they wanted him to sign a contract with them.

Under these circumstances, Diego Barreto decided to end his disputes as follows:

(a) He accepted the extension of the employment contract requested by Cerro Porteño in the Paraguayan courts and signed a new two-year contract with them.
(b) He then informed Real Valladolid CF SAD and UD Almería SAD of this fact, so that they could contact Cerro Porteño, in accordance with the provisions of the FIFA Regulations on the Status and Transfer of Players.

Only UD Almería contacted Cerro Porteño and they eventually agreed to the transfer of Diego Barreto on the condition that they receive compensation of approximately €400,000.

The transfer occurred in July 2005, at which time Barreto was about to be declared eligible by the Royal Spanish Football Federation. At this time Real Valladolid CF SAD requested the fulfilment of the contract signed on July 17, 2004.

Through a legal procedure brought before the Royal Spanish Football Federation, Real Valladolid ensured that Diego Barreto would not be permitted to play for UD Almería until November 11, 2005. Before this, on June 7, 2005, Real Valladolid filed its dispute with the Dispute Resolution Chamber in order to obtain compensation for breach of contract. In other words, on the one hand Real Valladolid was opposing Diego Barreto being permitted to play at UD Almería, as the club had a valid contract with the player which preceded the UD Almería contract, and on the other hand, at the same time, they were pursuing legal means to obtain compensation from the player for breach of contract.

The legal process continued with FIFA deciding on January 12, 2006 that Diego Barreto would have to pay compensation of EUR 462,500, which was then increased to EUR 1.625 million by the CAS. In this regard we must remember that Real Valladolid CF SAD requested payment of €6,000,000 and Diego Barreto felt that he was only responsible for €150,000.

5.3.5 The Arbitration Award

Before presenting our findings on this particular case, it is worth analyzing the main arguments used by the Arbitration Panel, in ordering Diego Barreto to pay compensation of €1,625,000.

Diego Barreto's case was highly complex, given that the Panel had to resolve the following issues as mentioned in Section 59:

5.3.5.1 Validity of the Contract Signed on July 17, 2004

In this regard it ruled the following, using, at this point, Swiss law (Section 62): "Article 4 of the Regulations on the Status and Transfer of Players (2001 version) states that all professional players must have a written contract. In Swiss law, the validity of contracts is not dependent on a particular form of compliance but rather it comes under a special legal provision. The provision is based on the principle of autonomy and, consequently, on the principle of consent, which Swiss obligation law believes to constitute freedom of compliance with the rules. In this type of case, the individual employment contract signed between the parties is not subject to a particular form of compliance, in view of Article 319, Section 1 of the Swiss Company Law. Therefore, the criticism made by the player concerning the lack of a sufficient number of original copies of the contract of July 17, 2004 is deemed unfounded and cannot lead to any revocation or invalidity of the agreement."

5.3.5.2 Ruling on the Contract of July 17, 2004

In Section 66 the Panel ruled that: "The fact that entry into service has been agreed on for the future is not sufficient to conclude that there is a pre-contract. It is indeed clear from Article 320–322 of Swiss Company Law that the decisive factor in assuming the existence of an employment contract is an agreement on the performance of work in exchange for remuneration. So it is not therefore legally inconceivable that legal contracts are signed which are not to be fulfilled immediately. These agreements are contracts and not preliminary contracts or promises of a contract."

5.3.5.3 Supposed Unilateral Breach of Contract and Reasons for it

The panel mentioned (Section 69): "It has not been disputed that the player did not turn up at Real Valladolid to perform his duties. As a result of this fact, the player has violated his contractual obligations resulting from the agreement of July 17, 2004" and (Sections 71 and 72) "we must ask whether the player had reasons for not carrying out his duties which could justify the breach of contract. With regard to this, the player cited the existence of the renewal clause in his contract of December 27, 2000 with Cerro Porteño. It is not straightforward to distinguish, in this argument made by the player, if this fact is cited as a way to justify the unilateral breach of contract or as a circumstantial occurrence that should lead to a reduction in any possible compensation. Whatever the case may be, the panel considers that the contract renewal clause invoked by Cerro Porteño at the end of 2004 does not, on its own, constitute a valid reason in accordance with Article 21 and the following clauses of the aforesaid FIFA Regulations."

5.3.5.4 Principle and Amount of Compensation for Unilateral Breach of Contract

Regarding the validity of the clause, the panel said (Section 79): "So the indemnity clause in the contract of July 17, 2004 is considered as valid with regard to its beginning. We add, in the interest of clarity, that an employment contract providing compensation for a unilateral breach of contract by the worker cannot be considered as being in violation of the law. Swiss law, in accordance with the place of arbitration, does not object to this clause being invoked", adding that (Section 85) "under Swiss law, the judge should exercise caution when reducing the sentence, in order to protect the freedom of will of the parties. In doing so, the judge must take into account, in particular, the creditor's interest in the implementation of the obligation, the seriousness of the breach of the obligation and the debt owed and the economic capabilities of the parties" to conclude that (Section 89) "the panel also considers, in parallel, that the amount of the compensation clause for a unilateral breach of contract must be set in accordance with the interest of the club in the execution of this contract. That interest may correspond to the value of the player on the market, if that value can be demonstrated, as in the *Mexès* case. By default, the panel considers that this value should at least correspond to the remuneration the club was prepared to give the player under the repudiated contract, meaning the investment that the Club agreed to in order to secure the services of the player."

5.3.5.5 Obligation to Reimburse Payments made by Real Valladolid

On this issue the panel said that (paras 97 and 98): "Apart from compensation for unilateral breach of contract, the decision under review has awarded Real Valladolid the sum of €125,000 in reimbursement for the payments made by the Club in fulfilling the aforementioned contract of 17 July, 2004. On several occasions, especially before the Dispute Resolution Chamber and in the context of this procedure, the player has accepted this claim, both in terms of its principle as well as the specific amount. Therefore, in his statement of appeal, the player stated that he confirms the decision of the Dispute Resolution Chamber as "the repayment of €125,000 to Real Valladolid" and "we must emphasise that this issue is not being contested and that the decision reached can be confirmed at this point".

5.3.5.6 Sanctioning the Player

In Section 101, the panel says: "In this case, the panel finds no reason to stray from the clear language of the FIFA Regulations or to reverse the decision reached by the Dispute Resolution Chamber. In particular, the fact that the player has not been permitted to play in Spain for more than two months because of the administrative management of Real Valladolid opposing his registration in another Spanish club, means that the circumstances could not be considered as exceptional in the sense of Article 23 of the FIFA Regulations. There is not, therefore, any reason why the sanction imposed in the meeting with the player should be reduced, as he requested."

5.3.5.7 Sanction Against Cerro Porteño

The Panel finally rejects any sanction against Cerro Porteño saying (Section 105*):* "For the reasons given previously given, Real Valladolid does not have, in this case, any reason to challenge the ruling made by the Dispute Resolution Chamber in this regard. The decision made will be confirmed accordingly at this point."

5.3.6 Conclusion

Now that the arbitration award is known, certain pieces of information should be added to the analysis, which were not considered by the arbitration panel. These include the following.

(a) The ambiguous position, in this case, of Pascual Barrios and a company, who presented the offer from Real Valladolid to the player and his father, and later appeared in the contract as the player's representatives. In the legal procedure, numerous pieces of evidence were provided detailing the links between the president of the Spanish club and the lawyer Barrios and the company.
(b) The position of Real Valladolid CF SAD which, for four months, opposed the player's registration at UD Almería, so that he could not play, using the argument that he already had a valid contract and that he should be registering with Valladolid but, at the same time, initiating a legal procedure with FIFA's DRC to claim compensation for breach of contract. Either the player had a valid contract, or the player breached the contract. But not both at once.
(c) The decision made by CAS to disqualify the time during which the player was not permitted to play for UD Almería as a result of the opposition of Real Valladolid CF SAD, from counting towards the 6-month suspension.

However, it is clear that Diego Barreto signed two contracts with two different Spanish clubs and that also extended his contract with Cerro Porteño. And all this was done, not with the intent of defrauding Real Valladolid, but as a result of circumstances in which he was deceived by people who presented themselves as emissaries of Real Valladolid, but who, in the contracts, took on the role of the representatives of the player.

It has also not been mentioned at all that the *Diego Barreto* case effectively paved the way for the resolutions later reached by the CAS in the *Webster* and *Matuzalem* cases. Section 89 of the transcript shows the outcome of these two cases. The compensation for unilateral breach of contract by the player can be calculated either by the "value of the player on the market, if that value can be demonstrated, as in the *Mexès* case" (the solution in the *Matuzalem* case) or "the remuneration the club was prepared to give the player under the repudiated contract, meaning the investment that the Club agreed to in order to secure the services of the player" (the solution in the *Webster* case).

5.4 CAS 2006/A/1157 Club Atlético Boca Juniors v. Genoa Cricket and Football Club S.p.A.[/]

Frans M. de Weger

The Boca Juniors Award was about the move of a minor player, Fernando Martín Forestieri, from Club Atlético Boca Juniors to Genoa Cricket to Football Club S.p.A, ignoring a unilateral extension option exercised by Atlético Boca Juniors. Fernando Martín Forestieri moved to Italy as a consequence of his parents immigrating there. The CAS decided that in view of the minor player's prevailing interest in staying with his family, he did not have to go back to Argentina. Even though the Panel did not have to decide on the validity of the unilateral extension options, it took a critical view of the validity and enforceability of unilateral extension options, even from the perspective of the opinion of Prof Wolfgang Portmann, which encompasses the criteria for the validity of unilateral extension options (see: Unilateral option clauses in footballer's contracts of employment: an assessment from the perspective of international sports arbitration, International Sports Law Review (2007) no. 1, pp. 6–16). The author evaluates this award and the CAS' approach to the validity of unilateral extension options favouring clubs.

5.4.1 Facts

This case concerns a dispute between the Argentinian football club Club Atlético Boca Juniors (hereinafter referred to as: "Boca") and the Italian football club Genoa Cricket and Football Club S.p.A. (hereinafter referred to as: "Genua").

On 18 September 2005, the player Fernando Martín Forestieri (hereinafter referred to as: "Fernando"), born in Argentina and with dual Italian and Argentinean nationality, at the age of 15 entered into a contract with Boca. The contract was stated to end on 30 June 2006, when Fernando would have been 16 years old. In the contract his club Boca was given the right to unilaterally extend the contract twice for one year.

In December 2005 the player Fernando and his family moved to Italy, where he entered into a contract for a term of three years with Genua. Therefore, on 6 July 2006 the Italian Football association requested the Argentinean Football Association to issue the International Transfer Certificate (hereinafter referred to as: "ITC").

On 14 July 2006 the Argentinean Football Association responded to the request, stating that Fernando was still under contract to Boca. Boca asserted that on 31 May 2006 it had exercised the right to extend Fernando's contract for one year by sending the player a telegram to an address in Buenos Aires. Finally, the dispute was referred to FIFA and the FIFA Players' Status Committee (hereinafter referred to as: "Single Judge") had to decide whether or not a provisional registration should be issued.

The Single Judge referred to the jurisprudence of the FIFA Dispute Resolution Chamber (hereinafter referred to as: "DRC") and the Court of Arbitration for Sport (hereinafter referred to as: "CAS") which had concluded that unilateral options were, in general, void as being in unlawful restraint of trade. Boca relied upon a legal opinion from Dr. Wolfgang Portmann (hereinafter referred to as: "the Opinion").[16]

In the Opinion, Dr. Portman expressed the view that such provisions can be valid from the point of view of Swiss private international law. However, it was important that there had to be certain safeguards in relation to their exercise. The Single Judge noted that the extension option concerned did not meet these prerequisites. As result thereof, the Single Judge had doubts whether the option was enforceable and so whether a contractual relationship existed between the player Fernando and Boca.

[16] Dr. Wolfgang Portmann is a professor of private and employment law at Zurich University.

The Single Judge finally decided on 22 August 2006 that the Italian Football Federation could provisionally register the player Fernando as a Genua player.[17] Boca did not agree and appealed before CAS against the decision of the Single Judge. Boca's argument in appeal essentially was that the player Fernando should be required to play for their club. According to Boca the player should not be permitted to play for another club during the period of the disputed extension of his contract.

5.4.2 Decision

To go straight to the point: CAS agreed with the decision of the Single Judge. However, the CAS panel did not entirely concur with the Single Judge's reasoning.

According to CAS, the Single Judge appeared to place considerable weight on the Opinion, and implied that, if the Single Judge had not had such doubts about whether the unilateral extension option had been exercised in compliance with the conditions set forth in the Opinion, he would have refused the provisional registration. The CAS panel stated that it was not prepared to give the Opinion such weight. Even more, CAS emphasized in this case that it had great difficulty in following Dr. Portmann's reasoning, and in accepting the validity and enforceability of the extension option.

Fortunately, according to CAS, the CAS panel did not have to decide the issue of the option in the present case, because the panel would put its decision on a wider basis.

According to CAS, Boca's submission founders on a long and consistent line of CAS jurisprudence, as well as the jurisprudence of many systems of law, that will not require a person to perform a contract for personal services against his or her will.[18] CAS emphasized that the player Fernando was still a minor and it emphasized that it would be inconceivable that any tribunal anywhere in the world would require the player Fernando either to be separated from his family, and have to move back to Argentina against his will, or require Fernando's family once more to uproot itself from Italy to move back to Argentina. Finally, the appeal by the club Boca against the decision of the Single Judge on 22 August 2006 was dismissed by the CAS panel.

[17] The provisional registration can be seen as a first step in a case where there is an issue between clubs or associations as to whether an ITC should be issued. See Annex 3 Article 3 of the Regulations on the Status and Transfer of Players 2009.

[18] CAS refers to CAS 2006/A/1100 *Tareq Eltaib v Club Gaziantespor*.

5.4.3 Commentary

5.4.3.1 Intro

CAS explicitly emphasized in this award that nothing that it had stated had to be taken as an indication that CAS had formed any view as to whether the unilateral extension option in the player's contract was valid and enforceable. However, this case can still be seen as an interesting one with respect to the issue of unilateral extension options. More specifically, despite the fact that the aforementioned statements regarding the validity of the option concerned can be entitled as an Obiter Dictum, CAS did lift a corner of the veil regarding its point of view on the Opinion of Dr. Portmann. Therefore, I would like to lift out several relevant aspects with regard to this clause, more particularly related to the consequences for the future. In order to place this decision of CAS in the right perspective and to understand the commentary of this case well, first a short background, the relevant jurisprudence till so far and the criteria of Portmann regarding the unilateral extension option will be discussed.

5.4.3.2 Background

The extension option is the right of a player and/or club to extend their employment contract for a certain period which the parties have stipulated in their current employment contract. There are many kinds of extension options. There is the reciprocal extension option in favour of both the player and the club whereby both parties are entitled to prolong the contract for a certain predetermined period and there is the extension option in favour of only one of the parties. In the daily practice of international professional football, extension options mostly only favour the club.

After the Bosman case in 1995[19] in which the European Court of Justice decided that a club was not allowed to pay compensation for the transfer of a player who had ended his contractual relationship with his former club and that this was in violation of the free movement of persons within the European Union, there was a substantial increase in the use of the extension option in favour of clubs. By including options in their favour clubs attempt to prevent the situation whereby their professional football players serve out their employment contracts and are thereafter able to leave for free.

At the international level there is uncertainty regarding the validity of the unilateral extension option. The DRC as well as CAS, as the authoritative committees at the international level for professional football, have provided the

[19] Case C-415/93, *Union royale belge des sociétés de football association ASBL v. Jean-Marc Bosman, Royal Club liègois SA v. Jean-Marc Bosman. SA d'Economic Mixte Sportive de l'Union Sportive du Littoral de Dunkerque, Union Royale Belge des Sociétés de Football Association ASBL, Union des Associations Européennes de Football Union des Association Européennes de Football v. Jean-Marc Bosman*, judgement of 15 December 1995, [1991] ECR I-4837.

international football world with several decisions related to the subject of the extension option.[20] What conclusions can be drawn from analyzing DRC and CAS jurisprudence till date?

5.4.3.3 Jurisprudence Till Date

After analyzing DRC and CAS jurisprudence, it can be concluded that neither of the committees till date have found a uniform answer to the question related to the validity of unilateral extension options. The DRC seems to have a general way of analyzing the validity, maintaining that the clauses in general have a disputable validity. The DRC refers to its own jurisprudence constantly and has tried to formulate a starting point when assessing the clause's validity.[21] CAS does no such thing, dealing with each case individually and making the relevant circumstances decisive in each case. CAS is not bound to earlier jurisprudence due to the absence of the so-called 'Stare Decisis'-principle and as a result thereof, each case will be dealt with individually, making future jurisprudence quite uncertain.[22]

Nonetheless, one general conclusion can be drawn: unilateral extension options are—by their very principle—in general incompatible with FIFA regulations and the principle of global labor law. Indeed, both DRC and CAS have only once ruled in favour of a valid option.[23] In that respect it cannot be left unmentioned that both cases had the extraordinary circumstance of the player accepting an earlier extension that was based on the same option clause. Both players in these cases

---

[20] All published decisions of the DRC can be found on the FIFA web site: www.fifa.com. All published decisions of the CAS can be found on the CAS web site: www.tas-cas.org. Contrary to the dispute resolution committee DRC it must be noted that CAS is officially a court of arbitration. Without wishing to put too much emphasis on the possible differences it is important to remain aware that DRC decisions can only be enforced through regulatory measures. This means that only FIFA members, amongst other clubs and players, can be sanctioned. If a club or player fails to comply with a DRC decision, a disciplinary sanction can be imposed. CAS arbitration awards on the other hand can be much more difficult to enforce. The New York Convention on the Recognition and Enforcement of Foreign Arbitral Awards of 10 June 1958 applicable to the recognition and enforcement of arbitral awards made in the territory of a state other than the state where the recognition and enforcement of such awards are sought only applies to the Parties to this Convention. This means that non-Party countries lack the legal means to enforce arbitral awards. FIFA however is competent to respond directly to a party that infringes the rules by forcing the national association to impose a sanction. Parties therefore prefer the DRC as a sports deciding body given the possibilities that FIFA has to enforce decisions through its own FIFA channels. See also FIFA Commentary, explanation Art. 22, p. 65.

[21] DRC 22 July 2004, no. 74508, DRC 13 May 2005, no. 55161, DRC 24 October 2005, no. 105874, DRC 21 February 2006, no. 261245, DRC 23 March 2006, no. 36858, DRC 30 November 2007, no. 117707, DRC 7 May 2008, no. 58860, DRC 9 January 2009, no. 19174 and DRC 15 May 2009, no. 59081.

[22] It must also be noted that under CAS rules the parties have a formal say in the composition of the CAS committee.

[23] DRC 21 February 2006, no. 261245 and CAS 2005/A/973 *Panathinaikos Football Club v Sotirios Kyrgiakos*, 10 October 2006.

only started protesting when their clubs had already extended their players' contracts for the second time!

Despite the above-mentioned, both DRC and CAS have not gone so far as to declare unilateral extension options invalid *under any circumstance*. The DRC refers to its jurisprudence in similar cases, but rules every case on the basis of specific relevant circumstances. CAS does not sustain a clear line of reasoning by referring to its own jurisprudence, but bases its decisions solely on the circumstances of the case at hand.[24] For example, in a case before CAS of 10 October 2006 all relevant circumstances pointed towards the validity of the clause.[25] Apart from the fact that this is the first and only CAS-decision in which CAS declared a unilateral extension option valid, it is also an important decision since the CAS panel clearly emphasized that the relevant circumstances of each and every case can and will be decisive.[26] CAS emphasized in this case the value of FIFA's principle of contractual stability by using the *pacta sunt servanda* principle as a starting point and decisive factor.[27]

In another important CAS decision of 12 July 2006,[28] which can be considered as the landmark CAS-case of unilateral options, CAS refers to the Opinion of Dr. Portmann.[29] In his article, Portmann gives an explicit review of the case at hand. Portmann gives us five criteria on the basis of which a specific option right should be judged in order to answer the question whether the extension right is to be considered as an excessive commitment. In its decision of 12 January 2007, the DRC used Portmann's criteria as leading for valid options. Since then, the criteria are being used in football practice all over the world and are being highly valued.[30]

---

[24] An earlier decision that in a way covered the unilateral extension option is TAS 2003/O/530 *A.J. Auxerre Football c Valencia CF, SAD & M. Mohamed Lamine Sissoko*, 27 August 2004. In this case the club tried to convert a 'trainee' contract into a professional contract using an extension.

[25] CAS 2005/A/973 *Pananthinaikos Football Club v Sotirios Kyrgiakos*, 10 October 2006.

[26] An earlier CAS-case that dealt with a unilateral extension option was TAS 2006/A/1082–1104 *Real Valladolid CF SAD v Diego Barretto Cáceres & Club Cerre Porteno*, 19 January 2007. In this case the unilateral extension option was considered invalid, because of its incompatibility with FIFA regulations. In this case, CAS referred to its decision in the aforementioned CAS-decision of 12 July 2006, 2005/A/983 & 984, *Club Atlético Peñarol v Carlos Heber Bueno Suárez, Christian Gabriel Rodríguez Barrotti & Paris Saint-Germain*. One last CAS-case that handled some sort of unilateral option clause was the CAS-decision of 2006/O/1055 *Del Bosque, Grande, Miñano Espín & Jiménez v Besiktas*, 9 February 2007. In this case, however, the unilateral option clause referred to the right to terminate the relevant employment contract.

[27] See also dr. mr. S.F.H. Jellinghaus' annotation in 'Jurisprudentie in Nederland', Arbeidsrecht 194, May 2007, no. 5.

[28] TAS 2005/A/983&984 *Club Atlético Peñarol v. Carlos Heber Bueno Suárez, Christian Gabriel Rodríguez Barrotti & Paris Saint-Germain.*

[29] Prof. Wolfgang Portmann, *'Unilateral option clauses in footballers' contracts of employment: an assessment from the perspective of international sports arbitration'*, 7 Sweet & Maxwell International Sports Law Review (2007) no. 1, p. 6–16.

[30] Unfortunately this decision is not published on the web site of FIFA.

However, it is noteworthy in respect of the validity of unilateral extension options that after the mentioned cases before the DRC of 12 January 2007 and CAS of 12 July 2006, neither DRC nor CAS in later cases referred directly to the criteria of the Opinion. As mentioned previously, till date DRC and CAS have only once ruled in favour of a valid option. Moreover, in later cases the DRC is extremely reluctant in establishing options valid.[31] Also CAS, for example in a more recent case of 7 June 2010, is reluctant and states that the validity and enforceability of an option is not accepted.[32] So, a relevant question in that respect is, will the criteria of Portmann as laid down in the Opinion in fact be sufficient enough to establish a valid extension option?

5.4.3.4 The Criteria of Portmann

In the case between Boca and Genua the CAS panel explicitly, as pointed out earlier in the Introduction, lifted a corner of the veil regarding the Opinion of Dr. Portmann. CAS referred to the fact that it was not prepared to give the Opinion such weight as the Single Judge did. CAS even had great difficulty in following Dr. Portmann's reasoning, and in accepting the validity and enforceability of the extension option.

In the mentioned case before the DRC of 12 January 2007, for the first time the committee time gave us complete clarity and conditions under which the unilateral option can be valid. In this case the DRC first of all made note of the mentioned CAS case of 12 July 2006, the player referred to.[33] As mentioned, this CAS case could be seen as leading with regard to the option. The DRC finally decided that the system of the unilateral extension option in general is not compatible with the Regulations of FIFA. However, the DRC also referred to the Opinion of Dr. Portmann and his five criteria in order to establish whether an extension option can be valid.

Also CAS referred to Portmann's criteria in the mentioned CAS case of 12 July 2006 and applied them to the present case in one sentence under point 110 of its decision. However, it is important to note that Portmann's criteria are being mentioned and discussed in the part of the CAS-decision that assessed the question of applicable law. As from point 113 of its decision, CAS assessed the validity of a unilateral extension option. When CAS started assessing whether the option was valid, Portmann's criteria were never mentioned. Instead, the CAS came to the conclusion that the option was invalid for other reasons since it did not match with the FIFA rules.

---

31 See for example, DRC 30 November 2007, no. 117707, DRC 7 May 2008, no. 58860, DRC 9 January 2009, no. 19174 and DRC 15 May 2009, no. 59081.

32 CAS 2009/A/1856 *Fenerbahçe Spor Kulübü v Stephen Appiah*, CAS 2009/A/1857 *Stephen Appiah v Fenerbahçe Spor Kulübü*, 7 June 2010.

33 TAS 2005/A/983&984 *Club Atlético Peñarol v Carlos Heber Bueno Suárez, Christian Gabriel Rodríguez Barrotti & Paris Saint-Germain*, 12 July 2006.

It could be concluded after having studied both cases the DRC overestimated the value of Portmann's criteria in its case of 12 January 2007.

Nonetheless, and as said earlier, the criteria of Portmann are being considered as the general guideline by the professional football world in order to establish whether a unilateral extension option in favour of the club can be considered as valid.

According to the DRC in its decision of 12 January 2007, the following criteria are decisive in order to establish whether an option in favour of the club can be valid:

1. The potential maximal duration of the labour relationship shall not be excessive;
2. The option shall be exercised within an acceptable deadline before the expiry of the current contract;
3. The salary reward deriving from the option right has to be defined in the original contract;
4. One party shall not be at the mercy of the other party with regard to the contents of the employment contract; and
5. The option shall be clearly established and emphasized in the original contract so that the player is conscious of it at the moment of signing the contract.

With regard to the first condition, the DRC pointed out that the maximum duration can be five years as stated in the Regulations of FIFA.[34] The duration in this case was not excessive, because the total period (initial contract including the option years) did not exceed the five-year term. With regard to the second condition, the fact that the option must be invoked within an acceptable deadline before the end of the current contract, the DRC decided that five days before the opening of the transfer period was too short. The player was left in uncertainty till the last moment. This was a huge disadvantage for the player as a result of which the short term was not accepted by the DRC. In continuation, the DRC puts the third condition to the test and established that the salary reward deriving from the option right was defined in the original contract. The fourth condition contained that one party shall not be at the mercy of the other party with regard to the contents of the employment contract. The DRC in this respect made a match with the question whether a salary increase existed after the club invoked the option. The DRC referred in this respect to the CAS-case the club referred to.[35] In that matter in case the option was invoked the salary reward in the first year would be 25% and in the second year 100%. In the present case before the DRC the increase was 9% for the first year and 8.33% for the second year. The DRC concluded that the position with respect to the negotiations was not equal and that there was no apparent gain for the player as a result of the extension. For that reason the player

[34] See Article 18 para 2 of the FIFA Regulations on the Status and Transfer of Players, edition 2009.

[35] CAS 2005/A/973 *Pananthinaikos FC v Sotirius Kyrgiakos*.

was at the mercy of the club with regard to the content of the employment contract. With regard to the last condition the DRC was of the opinion that the clause concerned was established in the original contract. However, the DRC noted in that respect that the option was mentioned in the middle of both contracts without laying emphasis on it in a different manner. As a result thereof the unilateral extension option was not inserted in the contract in a correct manner. The player was not made fully aware of it. One of the safeguards as stated in the Opinion was to clearly highlight the option clause in favour of the employer.[36] At the end, the DRC decided in this case on the basis of the five elements that the unilateral option in this case could not be considered as valid.

It must be noted that the DRC in this matter also pointed out that the player in the relevant CAS-case the club referred to, explicitly accepted the first extension and solely disputed the second extension. According to the DRC, this was an important matter for the CAS to decide as it did. Finally, it is important to note that the DRC emphasized that the unilateral option, even if an option fitted in with all the five elements, can still be invalid. This can be derived from the words'If at all' as considered in point 9 of the DRC-decision. In other words, the DRC pointed out that even if the option can be seen as a valid clause, the five elements are at least of crucial importance.

5.4.3.5 Future of the Unilateral Extension Option

Although CAS explicitly emphasized in the case between Boca and Genua, as said above, that nothing that it had stated had to be taken as an indication as to whether the extension option in the contract was valid, one can now understand better—in relation to the jurisprudence of DRC and CAS—that this case is interesting with respect to the validity of unilateral extension options. The CAS seems to call in question the Opinion of Portmann and its criteria. What can be expected from future DRC and CAS decisions after this award? What will be the impact of this decision?

After having read the decision of CAS between Boca and Genua it can be concluded that the criteria of Dr. Portmann might not be interpreted as absolutely leading by CAS and DRC in future cases. In this case the CAS panel seems to give us a warning that in future cases CAS might be more than skeptical with regard to the validity of unilateral extension options. The message of this case: please be

[36] In the report '*Contractual Stability in Professional Football, Recommendations for clubs in a context of international mobility*', by Diego F.R. Compaire (Italy/Argentina), Gerardo Planás R.A. (Paraguay) and Stefan-Eric Wildemann (Germany), July 2009, reference is made to the case *Club Atletico Lanus/Javier Alejandro Almiron & Polideportivo Ejido SAD (FIFA 07/00789)*. However, this case is also not published. As far as I know and based on the report the unilateral extension option in the latter case was not valid because the decisive argument was that the player was absolutely aware of the unilateral extension option. According to the DRC the player therefore explicitly accepted this clause.

aware, meeting with the five criteria may not be sufficient. The particular circumstances of each case will now be even more decisive. One can say that after having analyzed the other relevant DRC and CAS jurisprudence, it still deems important to meet at least the five criteria mentioned in the DRC-decision of 12 January 2007 and the CAS-decision in the *Bueno & Rodriguez* case.[37] However, please be aware that the DRC does not refer to the criteria anymore in later cases and CAS—briefly put—seems to slightly distance itself from the value awarded to the criteria in the past.

Nonetheless, a general declaration of invalidity is not to be expected. The use of unilateral extensions is common in professional football all over the world, and openly declaring such clauses invalid under any circumstances would have serious consequences. In none of the decisions the DRC or CAS declare the unilateral extension option invalid *under any circumstance*. In that respect one should take into account that each case shall be decided on the relevant circumstances of that specific case. In my opinion, DRC and CAS will be more inclined to declare an extension option valid, if all five mentioned criteria are met. However, to be sure and to increase the chances, I would advise to add a sixth and seventh criterion to the list.

First, although this cannot be derived from the decisions of CAS and DRC, it would be advisable that the extension period is proportional to the main contract. For example, a main contract for the period of one year, with an extension option for four years does fall within the five-year maximum that is mentioned in FIFA Regulations. These clauses, however, can be considered as a disguised probation period solely in favour of the club and can therefore in my opinion not be considered as legally valid.

Second, it would be advisable to limit the number of extension options to one.[38] For example: a player's contract is signed for a period of one year. The contract contains a unilateral extension option that gives the club the right to extend the contract twice, one for year each, such as was the case in the matter between Boca and Genua. Again, the total period of five years (main contract of three years and two extensions of one year) falls within the FIFA Regulations and matches the five criteria mentioned by the DRC and CAS, but it still bears a substantial risk that this kind of option by the DRC or CAS will eventually be considered as an unreasonable commitment of the football player, being the weaker party in the employer–employee relationship.

It should be noted that from the analyzed jurisprudence one main criterion is deemed most important by DRC and CAS: the player should receive a significant increase in salary due to the extension. Furthermore, a club should explicitly mention the extension option in a contract by making the player sign the clause concerned, in addition to the player's contract. In order to avoid any

[37] CAS-decision of 12 July 2006, 2005/A/983 & 984, *Club Atlético Peñarol v Carlos Heber Bueno Suárez, Christian Gabriel Rodríguez Barrotti & Paris Saint-Germain.*

[38] See DRC 22 July 2004, no. 74508.

misunderstanding, I would say: put the unilateral extension option in bold characters above the player's signature.[39]

In conclusion, it can be said that even if all of Portmann's criteria (plus the additional ones) are met, this still does not automatically mean that the extension option will be valid. A declaration of validity appears dependent on another requirement, which cannot easily be put into words, but comes down to the fact that the relevant circumstances of a specific case shall always be decisive: has the player accepted an earlier extension? How did the player behave after the club's extension? Did the player play in any official matches and did the player keep training with his team after the extension? Did the club only extend the contract because it can then claim higher damages due to a player's breach? Did the player explicitly agree with the effects of the option (in writing, verbally or can it be drawn from his stance)? In short: apart from the aforementioned criteria, all relevant circumstances of a specific case should point towards validity of the unilateral extension, in order to establish a valid clause.

Following the decisions of CAS and DRC, one can come to the conclusion that the validity of a unilateral extension option increases in case the player accepted an earlier option in his contract or in case acceptance followed due to his stance, for example by continuing to take part in training sessions and official matches after the extension.[40] On the other hand, the DRC will be more inclined to come to an invalid option in case the contract is not provided with conditions that will bring the player a substantial advantage. Also, the fact that the extension option is extended by the club solely in order to claim higher compensation, will not speak in favour of the club.[41]

Finally, it is noteworthy to mention that recent developments in South America show us a decrease in the usage of unilateral extension options. For example, in South America where the unilateral extension option was extremely popular (and in some countries still is) the disputable validity of the clause has caused it to fall into disuse in certain countries. A recently published report even shows that in Chile the unilateral extension option is now completely banned and in Uruguay it only still exists because the players' union disagreed with its abolishment.[42] Furthermore, in Argentina the unilateral option can only be used

[39] The unilateral extension option could also be laid down in a document apart from the employment contract in which the player explicitly agrees to this clause. See DRC 23 March 2006, no. 36858.

[40] DRC 21 February 2006, no. 261245 and CAS 2005/A/973 *Pananthinaikos Football Club v Sotirios Kyrgiakos*, 10 October 2006.

[41] DRC 9 January 2009, no. 19174 and CAS 2009/A/1856 *Fenerbahçe Spor Kulübü v Stephen Appiah*, CAS 2009/A/1857 *Stephen Appiah v Fenerbahçe Spor Kulübü*, 7 June 2010.

[42] The unilateral extension option provides for employment. If the possibility of unilateral extension did not exist, fewer players would be provided with contracts. .

in contracts with players up to 21 years old and for a maximum of three years.[43] We will wait and see what happens here. In my opinion, there will still be enough options for players and clubs to come to a valid option.

Reference

Haas U (2008) Football disputes between players and clubs before the CAS, in sport governance, Football disputes, doping and CAS arbitration, 2nd CAS & SAV/FSA Conference, Lausanne 2008

[43] See the report '*Contractual Stability in Professional Football, Recommendations for clubs in a context of international mobility*', by Diego F.R. Compaire (Italy/Argentina), Gerardo Planás R.A. (Paraguay) and Stefan-Eric Wildemann (Germany), July 2009.

Chapter 6
Doping: Applicable Regulations

Claude Ramoni

Contents

Dr. Claude Ramoni—Attorney-at-law, Libra Law, Maison du Sport International.

C. Ramoni (✉)
Lausanne, Switzerland
e-mail: ramoni@libra-law.ch

A. Wild (ed.), *CAS and Football: Landmark Cases*,
ASSER International Sports Law Series, DOI: 10.1007/978-90-6704-808-8_6,

6.1 CAS 2008/A/1588 FIFA v. Malta Football Association & Claude Mattocks; CAS 2008/A/1629 WADA v. Malta Football Association & Claude Mattocks; CAS 2008/A/1576 FIFA v. Malta Football Association & Ryan Grech; CAS 2008/A/1628 WADA v. Malta Football Association & Ryan Grech; CAS 2008/A/1575/FIFA v. Malta Football Association & Gilbert Martin; CAS 2008/A/1627 WADA v. Malta Football Association & Gilbert Martin

In the Maltese cases the CAS stated that national rules can prevail over FIFA regulations under specific provisions. This led to the application of the Maltese Rules, given the Panel's opinion that the 2007 FIFA Disciplinary Code did not include its direct applicability at the national level. FIFA thus amended the direct applicability in the 2009 FIFA Anti-doping Regulations. But it should be noted that in the Dodô Award—under comparable circumstances—the CAS did not allow national rules to prevail over FIFA regulations. The author believes the Maltese cases confirm the need for all federations worldwide to adopt rules compliant with the International Federation Regulations and the WADC.

6.2 Background Facts

At the end of 2007 and the beginning of 2008, three Maltese football players, Mattocks, Martin and Grech tested positive for prohibited substances.

Following a test performed on 26 December 2007, the player Mattocks tested positive for 19-norandrosterone. He explained that the source of this prohibited substance was a contaminated food supplement. The Malta Football Association (MFA) accepted his explanation and suspended him for a period of four months.

Several days later, on 2 January 2008, two other Maltese football players tested positive for prohibited substances, as a consequence of excessiveness on the occasion of New Year's Eve:

- Grech tested positive for cocaine. He did not challenge the adverse analytical findings reported by the laboratory and explained to the MFA that cocaine was purportedly put in one of his drinks by one of his friends on New Year's Eve. The MFA Control and Disciplinary Board did not believe this explanation and imposed a one-year suspension period on Grech. Grech appealed this decision with the MFA Appeals Board, which reduced the sanction down to nine months.

- Martin tested positive for both cocaine and amphetamines. He admitted having taken both substances during a New Year's Eve Party and was suspended by MFA for a period of one year.

Both WADA and FIFA appealed all three decisions rendered by MFA. It seemed quite obvious to FIFA and WADA that the sanctions imposed by the MFA were not in line with the provisions of the then applicable FIFA Disciplinary Code (the 2007 FDC) or of the World Anti-Doping Code (WADC). According to the WADC or the 2007 FDC, a reduction of the ordinary two-year suspension period sanctioning the presence of a prohibited substance in a player's bodily sample may occur in exceptional circumstances only, where the player is able to demonstrate that his fault is not significant. The minimum period of suspension, except if the player is able to demonstrate that he bears no fault at all, is one year. FIFA and WADA therefore were of the opinion that all three sanctions imposed by MFA were too lenient. Furthermore, the sanctions of four months imposed on Mattocks, as well as the sanction of nine months imposed on Grech were not compliant with the set of sanctions provided for by the 2007 FDC and the WADC for the substances detected in the players' samples.

6.3 Admissibility of the Appeal

The 2002 edition of the MFA statutes (which were then applicable) contained a clause providing that:

> in so far as the affiliation to FIFA is concerned, the Association recognises the Court of Arbitration in Lausanne, Switzerland (CAS) as the supreme jurisdictional authority to which the Association, its Members and members thereof, its registered players and its licensed coaches, licensed referees and licensed players' agents may have recourse to in football matters as provided in the FIFA Statutes and regulations.

The CAS panel observed that the players were validly bound by the MFA Statutes. It therefore came to the conclusion that Article 61 of the 2007 FIFA Statutes providing, *inter alia*, for WADA and FIFA's right of appeal to the CAS in doping matters was validly incorporated by reference in the MFA Statutes. It therefore held that the CAS had jurisdiction.

This conclusion by the CAS panel is fully in line with a long-standing jurisprudence by the CAS, confirmed by the Swiss Federal Tribunal, admitting the validity of an arbitration clause by reference.[1]

---

[1] See e.g. CAS 2007/A/1370 & 1376 *FIFA, WADA v CBF, STJD & Dodô*; Swiss Federal Court, Judgement of 9 January 2009 4A_460/2008, published in ASA Bulletin Vol. 27, p. 540.

6.4 Applicable Rules on the Nerit: FIFA or MFA Regulations?

The key issue in all three cases was the one of the applicable regulations on the merits.

On the one hand, the MFA Statutes in force at that time provided that MFA was bound to "observe the rules, bye-laws, regulations, directives and decisions of the Federation International de Football Association (FIFA)". According to the 2007 FDC, which was adopted in compliance with the WADC, the duration of the period of ineligibility sanctioning the presence of a prohibited substance in a player's sample was *two years*.

On the other hand, MFA had adopted a "Doping Charter", which provided that the use of a prohibited substance by a player would result in the player being sanctioned with a *twelve-month* period of suspension (for a first doping offence). This suspension period could be scaled down or extended in particular circumstances.

In the present case, WADA and FIFA submitted that the Maltese players had to be sanctioned in accordance with the 2007 FDC and applied that the CAS impose a two-year suspension period on all three players. The MFA, as well as Martin, submitted that the only applicable rules were the Maltese rules, in particular the MFA Doping Charter.

6.5 Was the FIFA Disciplinary Code Directly Applicable?

In the proceedings, FIFA submitted that all FIFA anti-doping regulations in force at that time, namely the FIFA Doping Control Regulations and the 2007 FDC, which entered into force on 1 September 2007, were directly applicable to Maltese players, to the exclusion of MFA Doping Charter. FIFA in particular relied on Article 60 para 2 of the 2007 FIFA Statutes, which provided that "CAS shall primarily apply the various regulations of FIFA and, additionally, Swiss law".

The panel held that, as a matter of principle, national football federations were issuing their own national regulations and, then, retained their own regulatory competences, notably with regard to national competitions. FIFA regulations were applicable to international games only. However, the panel also held that FIFA was also entitled to issue regulations, which could be directly applicable at national level. When adopting regulations, FIFA can therefore decide whether such regulations shall be directly applicable to the whole football family, as a consequence of the affiliation of a national federation and its members to FIFA or, whether they need to be implemented by each FIFA member in order to then apply them at national level.

In order to answer this question, the panel made a thorough literal analysis of the then applicable FIFA anti-doping regulations. Article 2 of the 2007 FDC provided that the 2007 FDC applied to "every match and competition organised by FIFA", as well as, "beyond this scope [...] if the statutory objectives of FIFA are breached, especially with regard to [...] doping". This provision could mean that the 2007 FDC would directly apply in order to sanction any doping offence committed by a football player, even in the course of a control organised by a national federation.

However, the panel did not follow this interpretation based on Article 152 of the 2007 FDC, which provided for the obligation of the national federation to adapt their own provisions to comply with the code and to incorporate anti-doping regulations into their own regulations. Furthermore, FIFA circular number 1059 provided the national federations with a deadline to adapt their anti-doping regulations.

The panel therefore held that the 2007 FDC was clearly excluding its direct applicability at national level. It concluded that FIFA could therefore not claim that the 2007 FDC was applicable directly at national level, but that FIFA had to take disciplinary measures against national federations in order to ensure that they adopt national anti-doping regulations in line with the 2007 FDC and the WADC.

On the occasion of the entry into force of the revised WADC on 1 January 2009, FIFA amended its anti-doping regulations and replaced the provisions relating to doping in both the FDC and the FIFA Doping Control Regulations by the "FIFA Anti-Doping Regulations". According to Article 1 para 1 of these regulations,

> "These regulations shall apply to FIFA, its member associations and the confederations and to players, clubs, player support personnel, match officials, officials and other persons who participate in activities, matches or competitions organised by FIFA or its associations by virtue of their agreement, membership, affiliation, authorisation, accreditation or participation." Paragraph 2 of the same article further specifies that: "These regulations shall apply to all doping controls over which FIFA and, respectively, its associations have jurisdiction."

Therefore, the new FIFA Anti-Doping Regulations which entered into force on 1 May 2009 clearly state that they apply at both international and national levels. The ruling by the CAS panel in the *Maltese* cases with regard to the scope of application of FIFA anti-doping rules would therefore no longer be valid under the new regulations.

Nevertheless, according to the 2009 edition of the FDC, which is currently in force, the wording of Article 2 FDC has not been amended compared to the 2007 edition. Furthermore, the 2009 FDC also includes a provision similar to Article 152 of the 2007 FDC providing for the obligation of member federations to adopt regulations incorporating mandatory provisions of the FDC and sanctioning members' federations failing to comply with such obligation with a fine and, possibly, further sanctions (Article 145 of the 2009 FDC). Therefore, for all other offences, which are defined by the FDC and which have to be implemented by the national federations (such as, for example, infringements of the Laws of the Game, misconduct, offensive or discriminatory behaviour, threats, coercion, corruption, match fixing, etc.), the ruling by the CAS panel in the *Maltese* cases that the FDC is not directly applicable at national level, shall still be valid.

6.6 Did Article 60 Para 2 of the FIFA Statutes Compel the Panel to Apply FIFA Regulations?

Article 60 para 2 of the 2007 FIFA Statutes provided that "CAS shall primarily apply the various regulations of FIFA and, additionally, Swiss law". The appellants interpreted this provision as meaning that all parties, when agreeing to the arbitration clause contained in the MFA Statutes, by reference to the FIFA Statutes, also agreed that CAS had to primarily apply FIFA regulations. This reasoning was followed by the CAS in the *Dodô* case,[2] as well as in numerous other cases.[3]

However, the panel in the *Maltese* cases did not follow this approach. It held that the MFA regulations showed a lack of intention to extend the scope of application of the FIFA and the UEFA regulations per reference. Therefore, the CAS competence could not be interpreted as an admission of the applicability of the FIFA Regulations to national cases by virtue of Article 60 para 2 of the 2007 FIFA Statutes.

The conclusion of the panel in the *Maltese* awards with regard to the rules applicable to the merits of the case and the scope of Article 60 para 2 of the 2007 FIFA Statutes does not seem to be in line with a long-standing CAS jurisprudence. Does it mean that Article 60 para 2 of the 2007 FIFA Statutes is not *per se* sufficient in order to create a valid agreement between the parties as to the applicable rules in the meaning of article R58 of the Code of Sports-related Arbitration? We do not believe that the *Maltese* awards have to be interpreted this way. In our opinion, the ruling made by the panel as to the applicable rules should not be applied broadly, but only in very specific cases (for example in doping matters) where the CAS has jurisdiction to rule on matters involving national players, who are bound to comply with national rules, in purely internal matters. In such cases, one could understand that the panel does not feel comfortable in imposing the application of FIFA rules and Swiss law to national-level players in the absence of any decision rendered by FIFA and in the frame of a dispute, which does not have any international dimension. This is particularly true in doping matters where CAS arbitration is not agreed upon by the parties, but provided for by anti-doping rules.[4]

---

[2] CAS 2007/A/1370 & 1376 *FIFA, WADA v CBF, STJD & Dodô*, § 104.

[3] See CAS 2008/A/1519 & 1520, *Shakhtar Donetsk v Matuzalem, Real Zaragoza & FIFA*; CAS 2007/A/1298, 1299 & 1300 *Heart of Midlothian v Webster & Wigan Athletic FC*; CAS 2009/O/1808 *Kenya Football Federation v FIFA*.

[4] See in this respect Judgement of the Swiss Federal Tribunal of 22 March 2007, ATF 133 III 235.

6.7 Was the FIFA Disciplinary Code Applicable by Reference?

In the *Maltese* cases, WADA adopted a slightly different approach than FIFA in order to support that FIFA regulations were applicable to the players. WADA supported that the 2007 FDC was applicable as being part of the national anti-doping regulations by reference and that such rules prevailed in case of conflict. MFA Statutes stated that MFA had the obligation to comply with FIFA rules, by-laws, regulations, directives and decisions. The purpose of such provision was to implement, for the MFA, the obligation of FIFA members, provided under Article 13 of the 2007 FIFA Statutes, to fully comply with the Statutes, regulations, directives and decisions of FIFA bodies at any time. As a consequence of such, WADA submitted that FIFA regulations were applicable by reference and that, in case of conflict between FIFA rules and MFA rules, FIFA rules shall prevail, in order for MFA to comply with its own statutes.

In several awards, rendered prior to the *Maltese* awards, the CAS ruled that FIFA anti-doping regulations were applicable at national level in doping matters, ruling that the FIFA regulations had been validly implemented in national regulations.

- In an award rendered on 21 December 2007,[5] the panel noticed that there was a contradiction between the rules of the Football Association of Wales (FAW), which stated that the sanction for a first infringement of doping control regulations was, at least, a six-month suspension and a fine, and the FDC, which provided for the ordinary two-year suspension for a first doping offence. In this case, as the rules of the FAW expressly stated that, in case of a conflict between the FIFA rules and the FAW rules, FIFA rules prevail, the panel held that the FIFA rules, in particular the FDC, were applicable.
- In two awards rendered in August 2008 in connection with two Qatari players,[6] the panel observed that the Qatari regulations did not contain detailed provisions governing anti-doping. The regulations of the Qatar Football Association only provided that it was "prohibited to use illegal drugs for activation according to FIFA regulations…" and that players found guilty of doping offences were subject to several sanctions, among other a suspension period, whose duration was however not specified. The Qatari regulations also contained several references to FIFA rules and regulations. The panel held in both cases that FIFA anti-doping rules were applicable, inasmuch as the Qatar Football Association had not adopted national anti-doping rules. Nothing in the regulations of the Qatar Football Association prevented the direct application of FIFA statutes, regulations and directives in such cases.

[5] CAS 2007/A/1364 *WADA v FAW & James.*

[6] CAS 2007/A/1445 *WADA v QFA & Mohadanni*; CAS 2007/A/1446 *WADA v QFA & Alanezi.*

- In an award rendered on 11 September 2008 with regard to a Brazilian football player,[7] the panel held that the FIFA rules, in particular the FDC, were primarily applicable, the rules of the Confederação Brasileira de Futebol (CBF) being applicable subsidiarily. The panel relied on Brazilian law, which imposed on Brazilian sport federations and athletes the adherence to international sport rules. In this Brazilian case, the panel further referred to Article 65 of the CBF statutes, which provided that the prevention, fight, repression and control of doping in Brazilian football had to be done complying also with international rules.

In the *Maltese* cases, the CAS panel came to another conclusion. It held that the MFA statutes and the MFA anti-doping rules did not provide that FIFA rules and regulations were applicable by reference and/or should prevail in case of conflict between the 2007 FDC and the MFA Doping Charter. On the contrary, the panel held that the MFA Doping Charter should be applied "independently and without any reference to the FDC anti-doping regulations which [were] therefore not applicable in the present case[s]". The panel also took into consideration the fact that the players were national level football players.

6.8 Comment

The *Maltese* cases are among numerous cases, where a CAS panel had to deal with national regulations, which were contradicting international regulations. The panel came to the conclusion that the MFA national regulations were solely applicable on the merits by ruling (i) that the 2007 FDC was not directly applicable at national level without proper implementation by the national federations and (ii) that the MFA anti-doping rules did not leave room for the application of the 2007 FDC.

In case of conflicts between several sets of rules, the situation is clear if the national rules explicitly provide that, in such a case, international regulations prevail. In several cases, CAS panels relied on such provision to rule that the regulations of the international federation were applicable and prevailed over national rules.[8]

In the absence of such a provision, it is difficult to draw a final conclusion from the CAS jurisprudence. For example, in the *Maltese* cases, the CAS held that the MFA Doping Charter prevailed. In the Brazilian case of Dodô, the CAS panel came to the opposite conclusion, despite the fact that the rules applicable in this

---

[7] CAS 2007/A/1370 & 1376 *FIFA, WADA v CBF, STJD & Dodô.*

[8] See e.g. CAS 2007/A/1364 *WADA v FAW & James* where the rules of the Wales Football Federation stated that in case of conflict between FIFA and FAW rules, FIFA Rules shall prevail; CAS 2008/A/1558 & 1578 *WADA & FEI v SANEF & Gertenbach*, where the constitution of the South African Equestrian Federation stated that in case of conflict between national rules and rules issued by the International Equestrian Federation (FEI), the FEI rules will apply.

case (i.e. CBF rules, FIFA rules and Brazilian law) were similar or even identical to the rules applicable in the *Maltese* cases.[9] In another precedent about a Portuguese player, the panel held that the rules of the Portuguese Football Federation and Portuguese law were applicable (and not FIFA rules).[10] In the Qatari cases, the panel held that the absence of specific national provisions and the references to FIFA regulations provided for in national regulations resulted in the "direct" applicability of FIFA anti-doping rules to Qatari players.[11] On the contrary, in a Pakistani cricket case, the panel held that a general reference to the WADA Code in the Pakistani rules was not a valid arbitration clause by reference allowing WADA to appeal decisions rendered in doping matters with CAS.[12]

One should not forget that the ruling by CAS is influenced by the conduct of the parties during the proceeding and the argumentation they put forward. Most of the time, national football federations are reluctant to challenge the applicability of the FDC or to claim that national regulations shall prevail, as this would constitute a breach of their obligations towards FIFA.[13] In the *Maltese* cases, the MFA strongly submitted that FIFA anti-doping regulations were not applicable. On the contrary, in the Brazilian or the Qatari cases, the Brazilian Football Federation or the Qatari Football Federation did not fully exclude the application of FIFA rules in their submissions before CAS.

CAS panels face an uncomfortable situation when several contradicting sets of rules may be applied (national rules vs. international rules incorporated by reference; anti-doping rules adopted by an anti-doping organisation vs. international standard issued by WADA and incorporated by reference[14]). Most of the time, CAS panels start from a literal interpretation of the rules in order to come to a conclusion.

In our opinion, in order to solve such issues, CAS panels should refer to the general principles that govern the interpretation of disciplinary rules. It is undisputed that in order to impose a sanction on an athlete convicted of a doping offence, the offence and its consequences (sanction) have to be provided for in a rule which has to be accessible and predictable (principle of legality). In other words, the players must have access to anti-doping rules and be able—if need be with appropriate advice—to foresee the consequences, which a given action may entail.[15]

---

[9] CAS 2007/A/1370 & 1376 FIFA, *WADA v CBF, STJD & Dodô.*

[10] CAS 2006/A/1153 *WADA v Assis & FPF.*

[11] CAS 2007/A/1445 *WADA v QFA & Mohadanni*; CAS 2007/A/1446 *WADA v QFA & Alanezi.*

[12] CAS 2006/A/1190 *WADA v Pakistan Cricket Board & Assif & Akhtar.*

[13] See for example the statement by the Mexican federation in the Carmona case: CAS 2006/A/1149 & CAS 2007/A/1211 *WADA v FMF & Carmona*, § 66.

[14] See e.g. CAS 2008/A/1607 *Varis v IBU.*

[15] See Kaufmann-Kohler, Malinverni, Rigozzi, Legal Opinion on the Conformity of Certain Provisions of the Draft World Anti-Doping Code with Commonly Accepted Principles of International Law, 26 February 2003, available on the WADA website, §§ 76–77 & 86; CAS 2001/A/330 *R v FISA*, published in Digest of CAS Awards III, pp. 197 et seq., esp. p. 203.

Another principle, which is often applied in order to interpret sport regulations, is the principle that any provision with unclear wording has to be interpreted against the author of the wording (*contra proferentem*). As the CAS stated in an award rendered in 2008: "this means that in principle, if no other reasons require a different treatment, any ambiguous, or otherwise unclear, provision of the statutes has to be interpreted against the association that has drafted the statutes, and not against the members".[16] This would mean that any ambiguity due to contradictions between national and international rules should in no way be interpreted against the addressees of the rules, namely the players.

Nevertheless, in order to interpret anti-doping rules, one should not forget that the WADC has now been implemented worldwide in all sports and constitutes a standardised uniform set of rules providing clear definitions of doping offences, as well as the disciplinary consequences thereof. The WADC is furthermore an appendix to the International Convention against Doping in Sport, adopted under the patronage of UNESCO and now in force in 137 countries throughout the world. In good faith, nowadays, no player or athlete may support that he/she is unaware of anti-doping rules adopted in compliance with the WADC, or at least of the main principles of the WADC. We remind however that neither the UNESCO Convention nor the WADC are of direct application and that, therefore, contradictory regulations should not be automatically overruled by the WADC or the UNESCO Convention.

Based on the foregoing, it is interesting to note that the panel in the *Maltese* cases has adopted a relatively strict "legalist" approach, by deciding that Maltese national rules prevailed over the 2007 FDC adopted in conformity with the WADC. As a result, the awards rendered in the *Maltese* cases did not hesitate to adopt the interpretation of the rules, which was more favourable to the players, even though the panel did not refer to the principle "*contra proferentem*".

6.9 Sanctions

The panel, applying the MFA Doping Charter, examined whether the periods of suspension imposed on each of the players by the MFA were admissible in view of Section 6 MFA Doping Charter, which provided for a one-year sanction for a first doping offence, which may be scaled down or extended in certain circumstances. The panel did not agree with WADA's submissions that the MFA Doping Charter should be interpreted in compliance with the 2007 FDC, which would mean that the suspension period should be extended up to two years unless the nature of the substance, or particular circumstances, justify a less severe sanction. The panel

---

16 See CAS 2008/A/1622, 1623, 1624 *FC Schalke, SV Werder Bremen & FC Barcelona v FIFA*, §§ 50–51, published in Court of Arbitration for Sport, CAS Awards Olympic Games 2008, 2009, pp. 219 et seq.

held that the objective of the MFA Doping Charter was clearly to impose a one-year sanction for doping offences, to be scaled up or down in specific circumstances and that the provisions of the 2007 FDC providing for a two-year sanction were not a circumstance justifying a departure from the clear wording of the MFA Doping Charter.

The panel then ruled as follows with regard to the sanctions imposed on the three Maltese players:

- Mattocks, sanctioned by the MFA to a suspension period of four months for use of a contaminated supplement.
  The panel held that the risk related to contaminated supplements was well-known and that Mattocks did not demonstrate that he had made any inquiry as to the content of the nutritional supplements he was taking nor that he exercised any caution when using such products. On the contrary, the panel relied on the well established CAS jurisprudence on contaminated supplement, which constantly refused to consider as an exceptional circumstance justifying a reduced sanction the contamination of supplements, unless the athlete demonstrate that he exercised a specific caution to enquire whether the supplement was "reliable".[17]
  Therefore, the panel ruled that no specific circumstance justified a reduction of the ordinary one-year suspension period provided for under Section 6 of the MFA Doping Charter and increased up to one year the sanction imposed on Mattocks;
- Grech, sanctioned by the MFA Appeals Board to a suspension period of nine months, further to an appeal by the player against the twelve-month ban imposed by the MFA Control and Disciplinary Board.
  The panel held that it did not believe the player's explanation that the origin of the cocaine found in his bodily specimen was due to a spiked drink. On the contrary, the panel ruled that taking cocaine on the occasion of a New Year's Eve party could not be considered as an exceptional circumstance justifying to depart from the ordinary sanction of one-year suspension provided for under the MFA Doping Charter. The panel therefore increased the sanction imposed to Grech up to twelve months.
- Finally, regarding Martin, who was sanctioned by the MFA to a one-year period of ineligibility for use of cocaine and amphetamine on the occasion of a New Year's Eve party, the CAS panel confirmed this sanction, which was the ordinary sanction provided for under the MFA Doping Charter.

[17] See e.g. CAS 2005/A/847 *Knauss v FIS*; CAS 2008/A/1510 *WADA v Despres & CCES*; CAS 2008/A/1597 *Akritidis & al. v IWF*.

6.10 Conclusion

The ruling by the CAS panel in the *Maltese* cases that national rules shall prevail over FIFA regulations seems justified in view of the wording of both the MFA rules and regulations, as well as of the 2007 FDC. This award confirms the necessity that all federations worldwide adopt rules compliant with the International Federation regulations and the WADC, in particular in order to ensure that all athletes worldwide are submitted to the same treatment in case of an anti-doping rule violation, albeit their nationality, domicile or origin.

The systematic of the FIFA rules in force at that time, which provided for FIFA and WADA's right of appeal to the CAS in the FIFA Statutes, when the provisions applicable on the merit of the case were contained in the FDC and the FIFA Doping Control Regulations results however in a somehow contradictory result, with regard to the *Maltese* case.

The appeals by WADA and FIFA were held admissible. The purpose of such appeals is mainly to ensure that decisions rendered by anti-doping organisations, such as a national football federation, comply with FIFA regulations governing doping and/or the WADC. However, in the case at stake, the panel ruled that the FDC was not applicable, and chose to apply rules, which were not compliant with the WADC.

In application of the MFA Doping Charter, the panel increased the sanctions pronounced in two out of the three cases.

Therefore, the effect of the appeals lodged by FIFA and WADA in the cases of the Maltese players was to allow the CAS to review decisions rendered in application of national Maltese rules, which do not provide for a right of appeal by FIFA or WADA. The panel partially upheld two out of the three appeals, imposing however, sanctions which are not in line with the FDC or the WADC. This (practical) result does not seem in line with the purpose of the appeal by FIFA and WADA in doping matters as provided for under the FIFA Statutes.

Chapter 7
Doping: CAS Jurisdiction

Claude Ramoni

Contents

Dr. Claude Ramoni—Attorney-at-law, Libra Law, Maison du Sport International.

C. Ramoni (✉)
Lausanne, Switzerland
e-mail: ramoni@libra-law.ch

A. Wild (ed.), *CAS and Football: Landmark Cases*,
ASSER International Sports Law Series, DOI: 10.1007/978-90-6704-808-8_7,

7.1 CAS 2007/A/1370 FIFA v. Superior Tribunal de Justiça Desportiva do Futebol & Confederação Brasileira de Futebol & Mr Ricardo Lucas Dodô; CAS 2007/A/1376 WADA v. Superior Tribunal de Justiça Desportiva do Futebol & Confederação Brasileira de Futebol & Mr Ricardo Lucas Dodô

In the Dodô Award the CAS had to resolve two main issues: the CAS jurisdiction in doping matters and the sanctioning of a doping verdict. In the author's words: 'The CAS panel ruled that the general reference to the FIFA Statutes provided for under the rules of the CBF constituted a valid arbitration clause, allowing WADA and FIFA to appeal decisions rendered by CBF in doping matters.' But care is needed; the author notes that this could not be extended to all decisions rendered by a sports federation, outside the scope of doping-related decisions. As to the merits, the author concludes that the CAS confirmed its jurisprudence on the burden of proof and the duty of care of the athlete.

7.2 Background Facts

On 14 June 2007, the Brazilian football player Ricardo Lucas Dodô (Dodô) underwent an anti-doping test on the occasion of a football match between his club Botafogo and Vasco de Gama. The sample provided by Dodô revealed the presence of Fenproporex, a prohibited stimulant.

After receiving the notification that the B sample analysis confirmed the adverse analytical finding, the Botafogo football club sent several nutritional supplements used by the team to the laboratory of the São Paulo University. Such laboratory issued a report stating that some capsules sent by Botafogo contained Fenproporex. These capsules, packed in two sealed containers and one unsealed and partially used container, were supposed to be caffeine capsules manufactured by a pharmacy called *Farmácia de Manipulação*.

Dodô submitted in the disciplinary proceedings before the Disciplinary Commission in Brazil that he had been administered, without his knowledge, contaminated caffeine capsules prepared by *Farmácia de Manipulação* and that he had absolutely no reason to doubt the products given to him by the medical team of Botafogo.

The Disciplinary Commission did not believe Dodô's explanations and imposed a 120-day suspension on him. Dodô then appealed the decision with the *Superior Tribunal de Justiça Deportiva de Futebol* (STJD). Contrary to the Disciplinary Commission, the STJD was convinced by Dodô's submissions and acquitted the player, setting aside the Disciplinary Commission's decision.

Both WADA and FIFA appealed to the CAS, the decision rendered by the STJD, requesting that the CAS impose a two-year suspension on the player Dodô in accordance with the then applicable FIFA Disciplinary Code and WADA Code.

7.3 Admissibility of the Appeal

7.3.1 The "Independence" of STJD

Dodô challenged that the CAS had jurisdiction over his case. He first submitted that the STJD was an independent appeal body and that the decision of such body could not be appealed to the CAS as:

- The STJD statutes did not provide for an appeal to the CAS; and
- The decision rendered by the STJD should not be considered as a decision "taken by FIFA, Confederations, Members or Leagues", which may be appealed to the CAS by FIFA or WADA pursuant to Article 61 para 5 and 6 of the 2007 FIFA Statutes.

It is true that in some countries, the authority to issue decisions in doping matters is not exercised by the national federations themselves, but by independent bodies organised by the National Anti-Doping Organisation (NADO). This is, for example, the case in the United States where, if an athlete does not agree with the suspension period imposed on him or her by the anti-doping authorities, he or she may raise a claim with the American Arbitration Association (AAA). In Switzerland too, all decisions in doping matters are rendered by a disciplinary commission established by the Swiss National Olympic Committee (Swiss Olympic), in cooperation with the Swiss national anti-doping organisation. As long as the statutes or regulations governing the sanctioning authorities provide for a right of appeal of WADA or of the international federation to the CAS—in compliance with the World Anti-Doping Code (WADC)—WADA or FIFA's right of appeal derives directly from the (national) rules governing such bodies. For example, in the cases of the Italian football players Cherubin or Mannini and Possanzini,[1] the CAS had jurisdiction to decide on the appeals lodged by WADA under the Italian anti-doping regulations. In those cases, the FIFA rules were not referred with regard to CAS jurisdiction.

In the case of Dodô, the legal status of STJD did not appear clear. Therefore, WADA and FIFA chose to name STJD as a Respondent in their appeals, as if it was an autonomous party. However, after careful analysis of all Brazilian rules and regulations—which were provided after the filing by WADA and FIFA of their appeal—the CAS panel came to the conclusion that STJD had to be considered part of the organisational structure of the *Confederação Brasileira de Futebol* (CBF). The CAS panel relied on the criteria of the "stand-alone test" to conclude that STJD was part of CBF. The panel ruled that, if the CBF did not exist, the STJD would not exist and would therefore, not perform any function.

---

[1] See CAS 2008/A/1551 *WADA v CONI, FIGC & Cherubin*, §§ 49 *et seq.*; CAS 2008/A/1557 *WADA v CONI, FIGC, Mannini & Possanzini*, §§ 28 *et seq.*, this award was later rescinded by the CAS panel, but the CAS jurisdiction was never challenged by the parties.

As the STJD had no autonomous legal personality but was just one of the bodies of the CBF, even though it benefited from independence when taking its decisions, the decision rendered by STJD was to be considered as CBF's decision, i.e. a decision of a FIFA member in the meaning of Article 61 of the 2007 FIFA Statutes. Dodô tried to challenge this ruling by the CAS before the Swiss Federal Tribunal. However, in recourses against international arbitral awards, the Swiss Federal Tribunal does not review the facts established by the panel. In the case at hand, the Swiss Federal Tribunal considered that the factual ruling by the CAS panel that the STJD was part of CBF, which was supported by evidence in the file, was binding upon the Swiss Federal Tribunal; Dodô's submissions in this respect were dismissed.[2]

As a consequence, the CAS panel held that, as the STJD did not have an autonomous legal personality, the decisions rendered by such body could be appealed to the CAS as decisions rendered by CBF, but that the STJD may not be considered as a Respondent in the procedure.

The award rendered by the CAS in the Dodô case confirms that, even though national or international federations set up independent bodies in order to decide on doping offences,[3] such bodies are nevertheless an integral part of the sports federations. Decisions rendered by such bodies are therefore—legally speaking—decisions of the concerned federation, which may be appealed to the CAS.

The situation would have been different if STJD would have had an autonomous legal personality and would stand alone if CBF did not exist. In such a case, it would have been quite doubtful that decisions of such an organism could be considered as decisions of a FIFA member in the meaning of Article 61 of the 2007 FIFA Statutes. The wording of Article 61 of the 2007 FIFA Statutes was "too narrow"; a literal interpretation of such provision seemed to indicate that if a decision was not rendered by FIFA, a confederation, a FIFA member or a league, but by another body, such decision could not be appealed to the CAS as per the FIFA Statutes. This issue has been cured under the FIFA Anti-Doping Regulations that entered into force further to the adoption of the new WADC. Under Article 62 of the 2010 FIFA Anti-Doping Regulations, decisions rendered by the body passing the decision (including a "national-level reviewing body" as provided in the National Anti-Doping Organisation's rules or even a state body), may be appealed to the CAS.

7.3.2 Arbitration Clause by Reference

Dodô also challenged the CAS jurisdiction on the basis that the CBF bylaws and regulations did not expressly provide that the CAS has jurisdiction in doping matters.

---

[2] See Judgement of the Swiss Federal Tribunal of 9 January 2009, 4A_460/2008, § 6.3, published in ASA Bulletin Vol. 27, p. 540.

[3] *According to WADA Model Rules for International Federations, the hearing panel deciding on anti-doping rules violation shall be "fair and impartial" (Article 8.3 WADA Model Rules for International Federations, Version 5.0, June 2010).*

It is true that the CBF Statutes or regulations do not contain an express arbitration clause providing for an appeal to the CAS. However, such regulations state that all players affiliated to CBF must comply with the rules of FIFA. The key issue in the case at hand was therefore whether the global reference contained in the CBF statutes to the FIFA rules, including Article 61 of the 2007 FIFA Statutes, did constitute a valid arbitration clause by reference.

In several cases, CAS panels held that, in order for the CAS to have jurisdiction as per Article R47 of the Code of Sports-related Arbitration (the "CAS Code"), the statutes or regulations of the body that rendered the decision should expressly provide for the ability of a party to appeal to the CAS.[4] In a case rendered about the sport of Cricket in Pakistan, a CAS panel held that the very broad reference to "IOC/WADA law" in the Pakistani rules under the heading "Matters not provided for" was not a valid arbitration clause by reference.[5] However, in this latter case, the Pakistani rules did not contain, contrary to the CBF Statutes, any express reference to the rules of the international federation (the International Cricket Council).

In the case of the player Dodô, the CAS panel held that the general reference in the CBF statutes to the FIFA rules was a valid arbitration clause by reference. Dodô was bound to comply with FIFA rules, including FIFA and WADA's right of appeal provided for under Article 61 para 5 and 6 of the 2007 FIFA Statutes. The CAS therefore had jurisdiction. Dodô tried to challenge the admissibility of such arbitration clause by reference before the Swiss Federal Tribunal, but the Court dismissed this argumentation, confirming that a general reference to statutes providing for an arbitration clause was a valid arbitration agreement.[6]

In view of the CAS jurisprudence, a distinction should be made, in the FIFA Statutes, between para 5 and 6 of Article 63 of the 2009 FIFA Statutes (Article 61 of the 2007 FIFA Statutes), which provide that FIFA and WADA are *entitled* to appeal any internally final and binding decision and Article 63 para 1 and Article 64 of the 2009 FIFA Statutes (Article 61 para 1 and 62 of the 2007 FIFA Statutes), which provide for an obligation of FIFA members to recognise CAS, with a reference that decisions of FIFA members shall be appealed with CAS within 21 days. Para 5 and 6 of Article 63 of the 2009 FIFA Statutes are sufficiently explicit to constitute a valid arbitration clause by reference if the rules of the national federation contain a global reference to the FIFA Statutes.[7] On the contrary, the mere reference to the obligation of FIFA members to recognise CAS or the indication of the deadline to appeal *do not constitute* valid arbitration clauses

---

4 See e.g. CAS 2005/A/952 *Cole v Premier League*, § 8.

5 See CAS 2006/A/1190 *WADA v Pakistan Cricket Board & Akhtar & Asif.*

6 See Judgement of the Swiss Federal Tribunal of 9 January 2009, 4A_460/2008, § 6.2, published in ASA Bulletin Vol. 27, p. 540. See also ATF 133 III 235 c. 4.3.2.3.

7 This was accepted by the CAS not only in the *Dodô* case, but in other cases, see e.g. CAS 2007/A/1445 *WADA v QFA & Mohadanni*; CAS 2007/A/1446 *WADA v QFA & Alanezi.*

by reference, should the rules of the national federation not contain explicit provisions with regard to the CAS jurisdiction.[8]

On one hand, this reasoning is convincing, in particular in view of the specificity of doping and the obligation made to all anti-doping organisations to recognise the right of appeal by WADA and the applicable international federation provided for under the WADC. On another hand, the distinction made by the CAS between para 5 and 6 of Article 63 of the 2009 FIFA Statutes (Article 61 of the 2007 FIFA Statutes) and para 1 of the same provision could consequently make an undue distinction between WADA's or FIFA's right of appeal and the player's right of appeal. The CAS reasoning could have an adverse effect in that WADA or FIFA may be entitled to appeal a national decision in doping matter (as ruled by the panel in the *Dodô* case), but that the player would not be granted the same right to appeal the decision with CAS, due to the lack of proper implementation of a CAS arbitration clause in the rules of the national federation (as ruled by the panel for example in the *Cole* case), and as para 5 and 6 of Article 63 of the 2009 FIFA Statutes (Article 61 of the 2007 FIFA Statutes) only provide for FIFA or WADA right of appeal and not for the player's right of appeal.

As of 2009, this issue is solved as the FIFA Doping Control Regulations contain explicit provisions governing the appeal against doping-related decisions (in accordance with the WADC). Such provisions (i) reinforce Article 63 para 5 and 6 of the 2009 FIFA Statutes for appeals against doping-related decisions and (ii) confirm that doping matters are governed by specific rules with regard to the CAS jurisdiction.

In fact, it is fully justified to adopt different rules and to distinguish doping-related disputes, as the right of appeal to the CAS is provided for under the WADC and has been (or should have been) implemented by all anti-doping organisations worldwide, from other sports-related disputes, where sports organisations or parties are free to adopt the dispute resolution mechanism they find the more appropriate (jurisdiction of the ordinary court, CAS jurisdiction, other arbitration clause, constitution of a specific arbitral tribunal, etc.).

7.4 Applicable Rules on the Merit

In the *Dodô* case, the panel noted that both the CBF Statutes and Brazilian law impose players to comply with international rules, in particular with reference to doping or anti-doping controls. The panel further relied on Article 60 para 2 of the 2007 FIFA Statutes, which provided that "CAS shall primarily apply the various regulations of FIFA and, additionally, Swiss law" to rule that the "applicable

[8] This reasoning was expressly followed by a CAS panel in the case CAS 2008/O/1694, *CSKA Sofia v BFU*.

regulations" governing the dispute according to Article R58 of the CAS Code were primarily the rules of FIFA and, subsidiarily, the rules of CBF.

The *Dodô* award is, in this respect, in line with well-established CAS jurisprudence about the interpretation of the choice of law provided for under Article 60 para 2 of the 2007 FIFA Statutes[9] and the integration by reference of FIFA rules in rules of a national federation.[10] We note however that, in three cases about Maltese football players, the CAS panel came to the opposite conclusion and ruled that national rules overruled FIFA regulations in national matters.[11]

This conclusion as to the applicable law nevertheless raises two issues.

1. In the *Dodô* case, the panel justified its ruling that FIFA rules shall prevail over CBF rules by the fact that the player was "of international status", without further defining this concept. We observe that, under the WADC, an international-level athlete is defined as an athlete included in the registered testing pool of an international federation. Cases arising from the participation in an international event[12] are also considered as cases involving international-level athletes for the purpose of the appeal rights provided under Article 13 of the WADC.
   Certainly, the player Dodô played with the national Brazilian team in 1997 and was employed by clubs outside Brazil, in South Korea, Japan or the United Arab Emirates. Nevertheless, it has not been submitted that, in 2007, Dodô was registered in the FIFA registered testing pool. Furthermore, he tested positive during a doping control organised on the occasion of the national Brazilian championship. Therefore, even though Dodô is without any possible doubt a football player of international calibre, he does not qualify as an international-level athlete in the meaning of anti-doping rules. The finding by the CAS panel with regard to the "international status" of Dodô is therefore quite surprising.
2. According to Article 60 para 2 of the 2007 FIFA Statutes, the CAS panel is to apply the various regulations of FIFA and Swiss law. Several international federations have adopted similar rules, such as for example the UCI.[13] However, national federations, such as for example, the CBF in the case of

[9] See CAS 2008/A/1519 & 1520 *Shakhtar Donetsk v Matuzalem, Real Zaragoza & FIFA*; CAS 2007/A/1298, 1299 & 1300 *Heart of Midlothian v Webster & Wigan Athletic FC*; CAS 2009/O/1808 *Kenya Football Federation v FIFA*.

[10] See CAS 2007/A/1364 *WADA v FAW & James*; CAS 2007/A/1445 *WADA v QFA & Mohadanni*; CAS 2007/A/1446 *WADA v QFA & Alanezi*; CAS 2008/A/1558 & 1578 *WADA & FEI v SANEF & Gertenbach*.

[11] See CAS 2008/A/1627 *WADA v MFA & Martin*; CAS 2008/A/1628 *WADA v MFA & Grech*; CAS 2008/A/1629 *WADA v MFA & Mattocks*, commented by C. Ramoni in Chap. 6 of this book.

[12] International event is defined by the WADC as an event where the International Olympic Committee, the International Paralympic Comittee, an International Federation, a major event organisation (defined as a continental association of National Olympic Committees or other international multi-sport organisation that function as the ruling body for any continental, regional or other international event), or another international sport organisation, is the ruling body of the event or appoints the technical officials for the event.

[13] See CAS 2007/A/1396 & 1402 *WADA & UCI v Valverde & RFEC*, § 5.

Dodô, will probably primarily apply their national rules and national law when sanctioning an athlete in the course of a national proceeding. In the case of an appeal against the national decision by WADA or FIFA before the CAS, it is quite likely that the CAS panel will not apply the same set of rules or the same governing law than the body which issued the challenged decision.

This confirms that the appeal to the CAS by WADA or an international federation against a decision rendered by a national sports federation is not a proper "appeal". Such appeal departs from the right to submit a decision of an association to the control of a judge or arbitrator recognised by Article 75 of the Swiss Civil Code.[14] The appeal by WADA or an international federation before CAS in doping matters is a totally new proceeding, aiming at ensuring that the WADC/the FIFA rules are properly applied worldwide. The CAS panel does not automatically apply the same sports regulations or governing law as the first instance decision-making body. It has full power to review the facts and the law (Article R57 of the CAS Code) and is not bound by specific issues that may have affected the procedure at national level.[15]

Nevertheless, when an appeal is lodged by WADA or an international federation with the CAS, the panel shall first determine whether the initial decision was erroneous or not. It is only if the panel comes to the conclusion that the first decision has to be set aside that it has the full power to review the facts and the law and to issue a new decision.[16]

7.5 Sanction

The anti-doping rule violation by Dodô, namely the presence of the prohibited stimulant Fenproporex in his bodily sample, was undisputed.

With regard to the sanction, Dodô applied that the prohibited stimulant came to be present in his system because the caffeine capsules that were administered to him by the medical team of his club before the match, were contaminated with Fenproporex. He therefore submitted that no fault at all was attributable to him and that he should not be sanctioned for the presence of a prohibited substance in his body.

---

[14] Article 75 of the Swiss Civil Code: "Each member shall be entitled by force of law to challenge in court, within one month of his having gained knowledge thereof, resolutions that he has not consented to and that violate the law or the articles of association" (translation by the Swiss American Chamber of Commerce).

[15] See CAS 2007/A/1396 & 1402 *WADA & UCI v Valverde & RFEC*, § 7.10, whereby the CAS panel held that it was not bound by the orders issued by the Spanish Justice, banning the use by the RFEC of the copy of the record of the Spanish criminal proceedings; CAS 2006/A/1153 *WADA v Assis & FPF*, whereby the CAS panel held that any possible irregularities in the proceeding before the Portuguese authorities had been cured before CAS.

[16] This reasoning in two steps has been well described by a CAS panel in the case CAS 2008/A/1471 & 1486 *FINA & WADA v CONI, FIN & Tagliaferri*. On the contrary, the reasoning of the panel on this issue in the case CAS 2007/A/1396 & 1402 *WADA & UCI v Valverde & RFEC* is difficult to follow (see in particular section 7 of the award).

According to Article 106 para 2 and 65 para 2 and 3 of the 2007 FIFA Disciplinary Code, in order to obtain a reduction or cancellation of the ordinary two-year suspension period provided for under Article 65 para 1 (a) of the 2007 FIFA Disciplinary Code, the player had to demonstrate:

- How the prohibited substance entered his body; and
- That he bore no fault or negligence or no significant fault or negligence.

Even though, in 2007, the FIFA Disciplinary Code did not expressly mention that a reduction or elimination of the ordinary two-year suspension period may occur in exceptional circumstances only, the CAS panel relied on the wording of the WADC and the CAS case jurisprudence to rule that those principles instituted by the WADC were also applicable with regard to FIFA rules.

7.5.1 How did Fenproporex Enter Dodô's System?

Dodô relied on analyses performed by the laboratory of the University of São Paulo (USP) to submit that the cause of the Fenproporex found in his urine was contaminated caffeine pills manufactured by *Farmácia de Manipulação*. Despite the report issued by the USP, which confirmed that pills contained in boxes provided by Botafogo football club were containing Fenproporex, the panel did not find this evidence conclusive to demonstrate that Fenproporex entered Dodô's system by the ingestion of contaminated caffeine pills.

The panel noted the following:

- The report issued by the USP did not contain details as to the number of pills analysed and whether all of them were contaminated or not;
- The USP issued a warning that it did not assume liability for the origin of the material delivered for the analysis;
- Nobody from the USP was called to give evidence on the analysis performed;
- Dodô delivered urine samples at three other doping controls, which show no presence of Fenproporex, even though Dodô ingested the allegedly contaminated caffeine pills before the matches preceding such controls;
- Dodô did not declare on the doping control form that he took caffeine pills before the match;
- The other players of the Botafogo team, who were controlled after the same match as Dodô, stated in the doping control form that they ingested caffeine pills. They did not test positive for Fenproporex, even though they ingested pills from the same source;
- None of the Botafogo football players ever tested positive for Fenproporex, despite their massive ingestion before matches of caffeine capsules manufactured by Farmácia de Manipulação Pharmacy;
- The head of the *Farmácia de Manipulação* testified that Fenproporex capsules and caffeine capsules were produced at different times and in different places;

- Caffeine capsules could easily be opened and closed again, while containers could also be unsealed and re-sealed.

The reasoning by the panel shows that, in order to bring scientific evidence—such as the analysis of products by a laboratory, one should clearly define the protocol of any testing in order for such analysis to be conclusive. The football club should at least have taken the appropriate measures to demonstrate which pills were analysed. It would also have been useful to ask the laboratory to identify all substances in the capsules, in order to see whether the concentration of Fenproporex was compatible with an accidental contamination or whether such concentration was very low, which could have explained why Dodô or other football players of the Botafogo football club had never tested positive for Fenproporex after having ingested such capsules.

This case also shows that doping control forms have to be filled-in carefully by indicating all substances taken before the control. Any failure in providing all the requested information is often interpreted as evidence, which excludes any reduction of the ordinary two-year period of ineligibility for no significant fault or negligence.[17]

7.5.2 Dodô's Duty of Care and Degree of Fault or Negligence

The panel also examined whether, in the event that Dodô had provided a plausible explanation of how Fenproporex entered his system (*quod non*), the player duly exercised his duty of care.

At the hearing, Dodô confessed that he simply trusted his club and the team doctors and that he did not know exactly how and where the products given to him were manufactured. He was unable to mention the names of the products regularly administered to him.

The WADC clearly states that "it is each athlete's personal duty to ensure that no prohibited substance enters his or her body" (Article 2.1.1). The definition of "No fault or negligence" provided for under the WADC states that the athlete has to establish not only that he did not know or suspect that he had used or been administered a prohibited substance, but that he *could not reasonably have known or suspected* such use or administration.

The award rendered by the CAS in the *Dodô* case confirms a long standing jurisprudence ruling that athletes, who do not comply with their personal duty of care and do not exercise caution before ingesting products, do not deserve any reduction of the ordinary two-year period of ineligibility.[18] We hope however that, more than five years after the entry into force of the first WADC, players and clubs

[17] See e.g. CAS 2008/A/1597 *Akritidis* et al. *v IWF*, § 7.2.21. On the contrary, in the case CAS OG 06/001 *WADA v USADA, USBSF & Lund*, the fact that Lund indicated on the doping control forms that he was taking a medication, containing a prohibited substance, played a key role in the decision of the panel to accept that Lund bore no significant fault or negligence.

[18] See e.g. CAS 2008/A/1597 *Akritidis* et al. *v IWF* ; CAS 2003/A/484 *Vencill v USADA*.

are now aware of their duties and obligations as per the anti-doping rules and that negligence, such as the one observed by the CAS panel in the case of Dodô, would be avoided in the future.

7.6 Conclusion

The *Dodô* award is key with regard to the CAS jurisdiction in doping matter. The CAS panel ruled that the general reference to the FIFA Statutes provided for under the rules of the CBF constituted a valid arbitration clause allowing WADA and FIFA to appeal decisions rendered by CBF in doping matters. This ruling was confirmed by the Swiss Federal Tribunal.

The reasoning by the CAS as to the jurisdiction cannot, in our opinion, be extended without limitation to all decisions rendered by a sports federation, outside the scope of doping-related decisions.In doping matters, the CAS arbitration is specific:

- The CAS jurisdiction is not agreed upon "freely" by the parties, but it is a mandatory rule, which is applied worldwide.
- Article 13 of the WADC allows WADA, the international federation and in some cases the IOC to appeal doping-related decisions. Therefore, the parties to the appeal to the CAS are not necessarily the same as the parties in the procedure that led to the decision, which is appealed against.
- With regard to the applicable law on the merit, it may well happen that the CAS panel applies a different law or different rules than the national federation, by virtue of Article 60 para 2 of the 2007 FIFA Statutes.

On the contrary, the CAS jurisprudence, which requests that the CAS arbitration clause be specifically included in the rules of the body rendering the appealed decision in order for CAS to have jurisdiction, remains valid for other disputes than doping cases.

As to the merit, the *Dodô* case confirms that, in order to obtain a reduction or elimination of the ordinary two-year suspension period, the player needs to bring satisfactory evidence showing how the substance entered his or her body and that he exercised specific caution in avoiding the ingestion of any prohibited substance.[19]

---

[19] For a recent example of an award admitting that the athlete bore no fault or negligence, see CAS 2009/A/1926 & 1930 Gasquet, WADA, ITF (where Gasquet got contaminated with cocaine by kissing a girl named Pamela, whom he met in an "unsuspicious environment like an Italian restaurant"). For a recent example of an award accepting that the fault of the athlete was not significant, see CAS 2009/A/1870 *WADA v Hardy & USADA* (where Hardy was contaminated with clenbuterol by using a supplement, but who was told by the manufacturer of the supplement that its products were tested by an independent company for purity, who purchased the supplement from a reliable source unrelated to prohibited substance, who consulted with the team nutritionist and the USOC sport psychologist about the supplement, and who used the same supplement (and no other) for a long period of time).

Chapter 8
Doping: Request of Review/Revision

Philippe Schweizer

Contents

8.1 CAS 2008/A/1557, Federazione Italiana Giuoco Calcio (FIGC), Daniele Mannini, Davide Possanzini and Comitato Olimpico Nazionale Italiano (CONI) v. World Anti-Doping Agency (WADA)

The Mannini/Possanzini Award concerns two players whose conduct in undergoing the applicable anti-doping urine tests was open to question: they passed the test, but there was a half-hour delay. The CAS had originally ordered that the players be banned from

Dr. Philippe Schweizer—Attorney at Law, KGG Associés.

P. Schweizer (✉)
Neuchâtel, Switzerland
e-mail: philschweizer@bluewin.ch

A. Wild (ed.), *CAS and Football: Landmark Cases*,
ASSER International Sports Law Series, DOI: 10.1007/978-90-6704-808-8_8,

participating in official matches for 350 days. The FIGC filed a 'Request for Arbitration' with the CAS submitting three 'new' witnesses. The CAS eventually set aside its original decision. The author describes the revision of arbitration in Switzerland and the CAS arbitration rules. He analyses whether the admissibility of the revision was justified, and concludes that the Swiss Supreme Court would never have admitted a request for revision based on new evidence such as that which was submitted to the Panel.

8.2 The Facts

The dispute arose from certain irregularities in connection with an anti-doping test carried out after the game between Brescia and A.C. Chievo Verona on 1 December 2007. Two of Brescia's players, Messrs Daniele Mannini and Davide Possanzini (the players), did not fully comply with their "urinary duties" pursuant to the applicable anti-doping regulations (implementing the WADA Code in Italian football), including the *Istruzioni Operative della Commissione Antidoping* and the *Procedimento disciplinare e Istruzioni operative relative all'attività dell'Ufficio di Procura Anti-doping* (*Instructions*). More precisely, they did comply, but with a delay of half an hour, which was considered excessive and led to a request for a sanction for non-cooperation. The FIGC's Court of First Instance acquitted the players, considering that there was no sanction provided for under the *Instructions* for their behaviour. But upon appeal by the *Ufficio di Procura Antidoping*, Italian judge of final jurisdiction in doping matters (*Giudice di Ultima Istanza*) suspended the players for a period of 15 days.

The World Anti-Doping Agency (WADA) brought an appeal against this decision before the CAS. Based on Article 2.3 of the WADA Code, WADA claimed that the players' behaviour constituted an undue refusal to submit to a sample collection and requested the CAS to impose a suspension of 2 years.

On 29 January 2009, the CAS Panel rendered an award, ruling as follows: a) the decision issued on 20 March 2008 by the Italian judge of final jurisdiction on doping issues was set aside; b) the players were suspended for a period of 350 days. In accordance with Article 57 of the CAS Code, the Panel had reviewed both the facts of the case and the applicable law and determined that the players had committed an anti-doping rule violation as they had failed to immediately report to the anti-doping station without an authorisation or a compelling justification, and they had not remained under the direct control of the anti-doping officer during the period between the end of the match and the anti-doping test.

On 12 February 2009, FIGC filed with the CAS a "Request for Arbitration", submitting that new evidence (three witnesses, among others) was made available, which would prove that the players were not guilty of any rule violation. The CAS was asked to set aside the award rendered on 29 January 2009, to confirm the decision issued on 20 March 2008, and to rule that no anti-doping violation was committed by the players. This is where the going got rough.

The Secretary General of the CAS transmitted that request to the other parties on 16 February 2009, with the following statement: "It is understood that such 'request for arbitration' is to be considered as a request for review of the arbitral award rendered by the CAS on January 29, 2009 based on new facts and/or new evidence (*recours en révision*). Although the Code of Sports-related Arbitration does not provide for a possibility to reopen an arbitration procedure when an award has been rendered, the CAS can accept to reopen an arbitration procedure which is terminated if all parties involved in the arbitration agree to do so. Basically, such general agreement would then be considered as a new arbitration agreement which would enable the CAS to reopen the procedure. In case of disagreement between the parties, any request for review could be addressed to the Swiss Federal Tribunal which would then initiate a specific procedure in accordance with Swiss law".

On 18 February 2009, WADA's counsel wrote to the CAS as follows: "WADA has no objection that the same Panel who rendered the Award (…) examines, on the basis of the conduct of the proceeding (including the tapes of the hearings), whether there is any ground to reopen the case. If the Panel determines that such a ground exists, WADA will abide to such decision".

On 25 February 2009, the Secretary General of the CAS acknowledged receipt of the various letters sent to him by counsel to the parties involved in the case and stated: "Considering that all parties have agreed that the arbitration procedure be reopened, this matter will now be submitted to the Panel for consideration".

WADA's counsel then submitted that WADA did not agree at all that the case be reopened and that "it (would) be up to the Panel to decide whether the request filed by FIGC based on allegedly new evidence permits or not to reopen the case". Furthermore, the reopening of an arbitral procedure closed by a CAS award should occur only in exceptional circumstances, and a party should not be allowed to request the reopening of a case in order to file evidence which such party renounced to file in the previous procedure. In WADA's opinion that condition was clearly not met in the present case.

8.3 The Award

The following findings of the Panel are relevant for our purposes:

1. Neither the Swiss Private International Law Act (PILA) nor the CAS Code provide for the revision of international arbitral awards, but if the parties agree to submit a request for revision to an arbitral tribunal directly, the latter is competent to undertake such revision under the rules which govern a "révision" of court decisions applied *mutatis mutandis* to a revision of international awards.
2. In the present case, there was no agreement by WADA to a new arbitration, as requested by the FIGC, but the parties agreed nevertheless that the Panel should have jurisdiction to determine whether there was any ground for a revision of the first award, applying by analogy and for guidance those rules which govern

a "révision" of court decisions, including Article 123 § 2a of the Swiss "*Loi sur le Tribunal fédéral*". According to that provision, the applicant must establish that, through no fault of his own, he was prevented from or otherwise unable to adduce the relevant facts or evidence in the course of the proceedings. This means that the applicant must prove that he acted diligently and did everything to elucidate the facts deemed relevant to his case.

3. In this respect, the three "new" witnesses mentioned by the FIGC were not admissible, in the Panel's opinion. The applicant and the players did not show why they should have been unable to call these witnesses to testify in the previous proceedings before the Panel.
4. As regards the award rendered by the CAS in another case (the so called *Cherubin* Award, where the CAS was quite soft with a player who did not strictly comply with the anti-doping-control proceedings), the Panel stated that this award was published approximately two months after the first award in the present case was rendered, and that new jurisprudence cannot, in principle, be a ground for the revision of an award.
5. Examining the admissibility of that part of the evidence adduced by the FIGC and the players to show that there was a lack of understanding and some confusion about the regulatory requirement of immediately proceeding to the doping-control after the game while being continuously chaperoned, the Panel found that the three conditions of admissibility were met: (a) the practise invoked, which allegedly prevailed in Italian football between 2005 and 2008 pre-existed the rendering of the first award; (b) the additional evidence was relevant enough to possibly have an impact on the outcome of the case; (c) considering the evidence relating to the due diligence criterium, the Panel found that the players themselves were unaware of various discussions surrounding the nature of the doping-control procedures and were unable to realise how important it was for them to explain in detail what their perception was of the nature of the doping-control they were subject to after the games.
6. For the reasons mentioned above, the Panel found that the conditions for admitting a revision of the case were met with respect to the additional evidence adduced about the practise and beliefs which allegedly prevailed in Italian football between 2005 and 2008 as to the nature and conditions of the post-match doping controls that regularly took place.
7. Considering the new evidence, including the testimony of a witness who had already been considered inadmissible[1] (!), the Panel found that in this case the players could not be deemed responsible for their lack of knowledge and understanding of the nature of the anti-doping test and corresponding duties to which they were subject on the relevant date.
8. On these grounds, the Panel retracted its first award and confirmed the decision issued on 20 March 2008, by the *Giudice di Ultima Istanza*.

---

[1] Cf. supra, 8.2.3).

8.4 Short Analysis

8.4.1 The Revision of Arbitral Awards in Switzerland

In view of the foreign seat, respectively, domiciles of the parties concerned, this was an international arbitration and, since the CAS is seated in Lausanne, Switzerland, the proceedings were governed by Chap. 12 of the PILA.[2] The PILA contains no express provision on the revision of arbitral awards. However, the Swiss Supreme Court has held that the Swiss legislator could not reasonably be assumed to have wanted to exclude such a remedy altogether; thus, the Court has found the revision of arbitral awards to be admissible *praeter legem.*[3]

To do so, the Supreme Court had to be creative, notably with respect to issues such as the designation of the court of competent jurisdiction to hear such requests, as well as the admissible grounds for revision and the applicable time limits. As far as jurisdiction is concerned, the Supreme Court has found that it is competent to hear requests for revision in all cases (including with respect to partial awards[4]). As for time limits and the admissible grounds for revision, the Court has chosen to apply, by analogy, the *Loi fédérale d'organisation judiciaire*, i.e. the statute governing proceedings before the Swiss Supreme Court at the time when the question was first raised, in 1982. That said, this procedural framework will only apply where the parties have not agreed, whether directly or by reference, upon a specific procedure for revision, for instance by providing that the arbitral tribunal itself may revise its own awards. The new statute governing proceedings before the Swiss Supreme Court, the *Loi sur le Tribunal fédéral* (LTF), in force since 1st January 2007, has not modified the previous system in any significant way. As seen above,[5] the remedy of revision is available when the applicant has discovered relevant facts or found conclusive evidence which he/she could not have invoked in the previous proceedings, excluding, however, any facts or evidence which have come into existence after the rendering of the award. The time limit for filing a request with the Supreme Court is 90 days from discovery of the ground(s) for revision.[6]

8.4.2 The CAS Arbitration Rules

As was rightly observed by the Panel in the present case, the CAS Code does not provide for the possibility of revision proceedings *stricto sensu*, i.e. where a request is filed unilaterally by a party that considers it has reasons to request the

---

[2] Article 176 PILA.

[3] DTF 118 II 199, 204; see also 129 III pp. 727, 728.

[4] Federal Tribunal, 1st November 1996, *P. v A.*, in RSDIE 1997, p. 279, with note PhS.

[5] Cf. supra, 8.2(2).

[6] Article 124 al. 1 lit. D LTF.

reopening of the proceedings which had been closed by a final award, without the agreement of the other party. That said, the CAS Code does not exclude an agreement between the parties providing for the reopening of the proceedings after the award has been rendered.

8.4.3 The Theoretical Admissibility of the CAS System

At first blush, the permissive approach of CAS in interpreting the CAS Code in favour of allowing revision by agreement is in accordance with the principle of party autonomy, although such a procedure (resulting in a party-agreed reopening of the proceedings) may elicit some reservations with respect to the *res judicata* character of arbitral awards (which is the same as that of court judgments). Indeed, in Switzerland, *res judicata* has to be raised *ex officio* by courts, since it deprives the parties of a legal interest in bringing anew before the judge a matter which has already been adjudicated. On the other hand, since it is undisputed that a party may validly forgo the execution of an enforceable decision it has obtained in its favour, one cannot see why the parties could not resubmit a matter to an arbitral tribunal if they agree that the tribunal was not apprised of all the relevant elements at the time when it rendered its award.

8.4.4 In Case, was There a Unanimous Agreement on the Reopening of the Proceedings?

In the case under discussion, the Panel found, as we have seen, that WADA had not unconditionally consented to the reopening of the proceedings, but rather that it had agreed that the Panel was competent to determine whether the conditions for such a reopening were met. In this respect, the Secretary General's letter of 25 February 2009[7] is instructive. It makes it clear from the start that the parties' agreement may extend to the recognition of the CAS's competence to deal with a request for a reopening of the proceedings *where a ground for revision has been validly invoked*, without, however, entering into any detail. The Secretary General's letter notes that absent an agreement between the parties, such a request should be dealt with within the normal procedural framework, meaning that it should be brought before the Swiss Supreme Court (which in turn implies that the conditions set forth in the Swiss law, i.e. the LTF, are to apply in such cases). Indeed, upon receipt of the Secretary General's letter of 16 February 2009, WADA had seized the opportunity to plead that no valid ground for revision had been established.

---

7 Supra 8.1.

8.4.5 The Panel's Reasoning on the Parties' Agreement to the Reopening of the Proceedings

Starting from the premise that WADA had only accepted the competence of CAS to decide on its own competence, the Panel chose to limit the scope of its examination to the question whether the case submitted to it was one that would call for revision in accordance with Article 123 (2)(a) of the LTF, which it found to be applicable by analogy. One can only say that, in so doing, the CAS has certainly not opted for the easiest solution—*ad augusta per angusta*—all the more so in view of the final outcome, i.e. the retracting of its first award. To arrive at *that* result,[8] the Panel could have said that by giving it the full power and authority to decide whether to reopen the proceedings, the parties, including WADA, had in reality authorized it to render a decision based on considerations of fairness or equity, on the basis of a "new" request for arbitration providing it with a full power of review (as submitted by the FIGC—whose counsel were clearly aware that a proper application of the requirement of Article 123 LTF would have very little chance to succeed…). The Panel preferred, instead, to give a restrictive interpretation of WADA's first letter (i.e. before WADA changed its arguments), by finding that WADA had only agreed for it to determine whether it was competent to decide that a valid ground for revision had been put forward, what's more, by analogy. This was obviously done to avoid creating a precedent in the system which could result in many more cases where the parties would attempt to reopen the proceedings. However, one should not lose sight of the fact that such a reopening would require the unanimous agreement of the parties, a condition which will make it a relatively rare occurrence, although it can happen that all the parties are unhappy with an award, whether because they find it too lenient or too strict, meaning that one cannot altogether exclude the potential for such a procedural "vicious circle", running counter the principles of *res judicata* and legal certainty. Thus, since the Panel had chosen not to redirect the applicant to the Swiss Supreme Court, it was left with the option of treating the new request for arbitration as a request for revision, which it admitted and which led it to retract its previous award. Although little detail has transpired as to the new evidence offered by the applicant, the summary made in the award leaves one slightly perplexed. The Panel, finding that the three newly offered witnesses could just as well have testified in the prior proceedings, held that their testimonies should be disregarded. Then, referring to the confusing manner in which the anti-doping legislation had been enacted in Italy between 2005 and 2008 and to the players' assumed understanding of that legislation at the relevant time, it retracted its previous award, rendered relying on the circumstantiated evidence submitted to it, which

---

[8] Rejecting the applicant's request would have been easy, on various grounds which will not be developed here, including the principle of *res judicata*, the silence of the CAS Code, the applicability of the *Loi sur le Tribunal fédéral*, or the absence of any ground for revision, as the case may be.

evidence was again comprehensively administered and completed before the second award. As a result, the Panel ended up dividing by more than 23(!) the length of the suspension it had originally imposed on the players. One may wonder whether, in so doing, the Panel has not set an even *more* dangerous precedent than the one it was trying to avoid. Furthermore, for those who are familiar with the Swiss Supreme Court's case law relating to the revision of arbitral awards—even if, in this case, the CAS emphasized that it would only rely on it "by analogy and for guidance"—it is absolutely clear that the Supreme Court would never have admitted a request for revision based on such new evidence as that submitted to the Panel, at least as it was summarized in the award discussed here.

Chapter 9
Doping: Sanctioning of a Football Team

Tim Kerr

Contents

9.1 CAS 2004/A/593 Football Association of Wales v. UEFA

In the Football Association of Wales v. UEFA Award the CAS had considered the question as to whether it is appropriate to impose a sanction on an entire football team, where the evidence shows doping by only one of the team's players. In the first leg between Wales and Russia Titov, a Russian player, tested positive and was ordered to sit on the bench for this match. In the return match Titov played until the 59th minute, not knowing the result of the first test; Russia won that match. Ultimately Wales was relegated by Russia's victory. This launched the dispute. The CAS did not impose a sanction on the entire team. The author discusses this dispute and the CAS ruling.

1. This case demonstrated the difficulty in persuading UEFA's disciplinary bodies, and the CAS, to impose a sanction on an entire football team where the evidence shows doping by only one player in the team. The Football Association of Wales (FAW) succeeded in establishing that CAS had jurisdiction to hear its appeal against the decision of UEFA's Appeals Body, but failed in its attempt to get the decision overturned and in its ambitious

Tim Kerr—QC, Barrister.

T. Kerr (✉)
11 KBW, London, United Kingdom
e-mail: kerr@11kbw.com

A. Wild (ed.), *CAS and Football: Landmark Cases*,
ASSER International Sports Law Series, DOI: 10.1007/978-90-6704-808-8_9,

quest to obtain a ruling effectively substituting Wales for Russia among the qualifying teams for Euro 2004.

2. Russia had eliminated Wales by winning 1–0 on aggregate over two matches in a play-off. The FAW argued that this achievement may have been secured through illegal and corrupt sporting advantage, i.e. doping of a player, and not fairly according to the rules of the game. The FAW's central proposition was that UEFA's rules should be interpreted as requiring that the benefit of the doubt should not go to the team whose player has cheated, but to the team whose players have not cheated.
3. The facts were these. On 11 November 2003 a Spartak Moscow player, Titov, tested negative for banned substances. The Football Union of Russia (FUR) found him eligible for selection for the national team. On 15 November Titov was a non-playing substitute at the 0–0 draw in Moscow, in the first leg of the play-off between Russia and Wales. After the match, he was selected for drug testing.
4. Before the result of that test was known, the return match was played in Cardiff on 19 November. Titov played until the 59th minute when he was substituted, with the score standing at 0–1 to Russia. This was also the final score, so Russia was declared the winner and Wales eliminated. Titov was not tested on that occasion. But on 3 December the IOC accredited laboratory reported to UEFA that Titov's sample taken in Moscow had tested positive for bromantan; a performance enhancing banned substance known to have been used by Soviet military pilots as well as by sportsmen and women, to increase their endurance.
5. On 22 January 2004, UEFA's Control and Disciplinary Body suspended Titov for 12 months and fined him CHF 10,000. It also fined his club, Spartak Moscow, CHF 20,000, but expressly absolved the FUR from all responsibility. The FAW protested but after correspondence and written submissions, on 3 February 2004 UEFA's Control and Disciplinary Body rejected the FAW's complaint, reasoning that it had not been shown that Titov was doped in the second match, in which he actually played; and that even if that had been shown, neither UEFA's rules nor the (then newly promulgated) World Anti-Doping Code provided for sanctions to be imposed on entire teams unless more than one player from the team had committed an anti-doping rule violation.
6. The FAW appealed against that ruling. The FUR was joined to the appeal as an interested party. At a hearing on 1 April 2004 in Lausanne, UEFA's Appeals Body rejected the appeal and upheld the decision appealed against. The Appeals Body pointed out that Titov had not been disqualified when he played in the second match, before the result of the test in Moscow was known; that on the true construction of UEFA's rules (Articles 6 and 12.4 of UEFA's Disciplinary Regulations 2002), a national federation could be held responsible for a doping offence only if it was *implicated* in the offence, and that this could not be proved in the present case.
7. The Appeals Body heard disputed evidence from scientists called by both parties, but did not find it necessary to resolve a scientific dispute over whether the effect of bromantan on Titov's performance would have lasted from 11

November 2003 (the date of the first match) until 19 November 2003 (the date of the second match). This was because the Appeals Body reasoned that even if Titov was still doped when he played during the second match, he was eligible to play and his subsequent ban for 12 months had not then yet been imposed and was not retroactive.

8. On 10 April 2004 the FAW appealed to the CAS. The language of the appeal was English and the applicable law was Swiss law, in the absence of any other choice of law by the parties. The hearing of the appeal took place on 12 May 2004 in Lausanne. At the hearing, the author spoke for the FAW (instructed by Michael Culley, of Loosemores, solicitors in Cardiff) except in relation to matters specifically concerned with Swiss law, which were addressed by Dr Marco Niedermann, a distinguished commercial lawyer practising in Zürich. UEFA was ably represented by M. Ivan Cherpillod, also an eminent Swiss lawyer practising in Lausanne.
9. UEFA contested the jurisdiction of the CAS. The question of jurisdiction turned on whether (per Article 62.1 of UEFA's Statutes) the decision of the Appeals Body was a "decision under civil law (of a pecuniary nature)". UEFA submitted that it was not, but rather that it was a decision "of a sporting nature" (per *ibid.* Article 62.2) and thus excluded from challenge on appeal to the CAS. The FAW submitted that the exception in the case of decisions "of a sporting nature" should be narrowly construed and relied on witness evidence of the substantial financial consequences attendant on qualification for, or elimination from, Euro 2004.
10. In their decision, the CAS arbitrators (Professor Michael Geistlinger, Mr Peter Leaver QC and Professor Massimo Coccia) looked at the Swiss law genesis of Article 62 of UEFA's Statutes and noted that the expression "of a pecuniary nature" corresponded to the phrase "*de nature patrimoniale*" in Article 177 of the Swiss Federal Code on Private International Law. After considering Swiss Federal Tribunal case law dealing with that provision, the CAS panel decided that it did have jurisdiction to determine the appeal, on the following basis (para 33 of its decision):

> in cases in which it is not clear whether the sporting or the pecuniary nature of the decision is predominant, it should normally be the case that the matter will be considered to be of a pecuniary nature. .... a dispute is of a pecuniary nature if an interest of a pecuniary nature can be found in at least one of the parties.....

11. The panel therefore went on to consider the merits. The FAW submitted that the doping offence occurred while Titov was on international duty, not club duty, and that the FUR must be regarded as implicated because it was involved in the offence in that Titov was under the direction and control of the FUR, not Spartak Moscow, when the offence was committed.
12. The FAW relied on the award in the *Eindhoven* case, TAS 2002/A/423 as establishing the principle of a host association or club's strict liability under UEFA disciplinary rules for the conduct of supporters; and that *a fortiori* that reasoning applied to strict liability for the conduct of players. Alternatively,

the FAW contended that if negligence was required, the evidence of negligence on the part of the FUR was very strong and the burden of proof should rest with the federation of the cheat, not the federation which is the victim of the cheat.

13. Finally, the FAW submitted that the CAS should not apply UEFA's unwritten rule whereby a team would not be sanctioned unless more than one player was found to be doped; there was no express provision in UEFA's disciplinary regulations to that effect, and it would be unfair and would encourage cheating to apply that principle given the small number of tests carried out after football matches.
14. UEFA submitted that, on the contrary, implication in a doping offence by a national federation required intent or, at least negligence on the part of the federation and that there was no evidence of such intent or negligence on the part of the FUR. UEFA also submitted that provisions in other sports which allowed for disqualification of an entire team where only one member of the team is doped, were not appropriate in the case of football and would violate the principle of proportionality, given the interest of the undoped players in the team concerned.
15. The panel's decision was squarely against the FAW and in favour of UEFA. The panel started by assuming, without deciding, that Titov remained under the effects of bromantan during the second match. Even on that basis, the FUR was not liable for Titov's offence. While a host association and host club are responsible for order and security before, during and after matches (Article 6.2, as interpreted in the *Eindhoven* case), culpability is required before a sanction can be imposed.
16. In the case of a doping offence, Article 12.4 imposes liability on host associations and clubs only where they are "accomplices or abettors", and this must be interpreted in accordance with Swiss civil and criminal law as requiring that:

> before a person can be fixed with liability he must at least have participated in the violation of a law and been aware of the violation and, therefore, [this] is more than just being 'involved' (para 50).

17. In the context of the case before the panel, that would mean that in order for the FUR to be liable for Titov's doping offence, the FAW would have had to show "participation of an association [the FUR] in the voluntary or negligent use of a banned substance or method by a player being aware of his doing so" (para 51).
18. Turning to the evidence, the panel rejected the FAW's alternative case that if it were necessary to show fault on the part of the FUR, circumstantial evidence pointed overwhelmingly to Titov's doping offence having been committed after and not before Titov had joined the national squad, i.e. while Titov was on international duty and under the direction and control of the FUR, not Spartak Moscow.

19. The panel assumed in the FAW's favour, without deciding, that Titov's body was free from bromantan on 11 November 2003 and that his doping offence was committed while under the direction and control of the FUR. But even on that basis, the panel rejected the *res ipsa loquitur* argument advanced by the FAW and held that "there is no evidence at all that the FUR cooperated intentionally or negligently in the use of this banned substance by Titov" (para 53).
20. In other words, it is not enough to show that a doping offence is committed while a player is on international duty under the direction and control of his national association rather than his club. The challenger must perform the almost impossible task of adducing evidence that the national association was aware of and participated in the doping offence. The panel commented that:

> ... it is impossible for a federation or club to control a player every day for 24 h; the player will always have a chance sooner or later to hide and take by himself a forbidden substance. (para 53).

The FAW's appeal therefore failed and the FAW was ordered to pay CHF5,000 as a contribution to UEFA's costs. The panel did, however, state that it "understands and sympathises with the FAW's concerns at having played a team with a cheat, at least in the first match ..." (para 55). Perhaps of greater consolation to Welsh football fans was Russia's early exit from Euro 2004 after losing to Portugal and Spain, despite being the only team to beat the eventual winners, Greece.

Chapter 10
Hooliganism

Ivan Cherpillod, Peter T. M. Coenen and Juan de Dios Crespo Pérez

Contents

Ivan Cherpillod—Attorney-at-law, BMP Associés. The commentary reflects the author's personal view.
Peter T.M. Coenen—University of Lucerne School of Law.
Juan de Dios Crespo Pérez—LL.M., Attorney-at-law, Ruiz Huerta & Crespo Sports Lawyers.

I. Cherpillod (✉)
Lausanne, Switzerland
e-mail: ivan.cherpillod@bmp.ch

P. T. M. Coenen
Lucerne, Switzerland
e-mail: peter.coenen@unilu.ch

J. de Dios Crespo Pérez
Valencia, Spain
e-mail: jddcrespo@ruizcrespo.com

A. Wild (ed.), *CAS and Football: Landmark Cases*,
ASSER International Sports Law Series, DOI: 10.1007/978-90-6704-808-8_10,

10.1 CAS 2002/A/423 PSV Eindhoven v. UEFA

Ivan Cherpillod

This CAS Award concerns a very important matter for clubs: strict liability. On 25 September 2002 PSV Eindhoven and Arsenal FC played in the UEFA Champions League. Racist incidents occurred during the match, with Thierry Henry becoming a particular victim subjected to spectator 'monkey noises' accompanied by plastic lighters being thrown. The UEFA Control and Disciplinary Body imposed a CHF 30,000 fine on PSV Eindhoven, later increased to CHF 50,000 by the UEFA Appeals Body. The club was also warned of severe sanctions should there be a repeat offence. The CAS did not state any failure on the part of the club, but it did consider the strict liability regime of Article 6 para 1 of the Disciplinary Regulations to be valid. The fine was ultimately reduced to CHF 30,000. The author analyses this award, especially from the perspective of the validity of the principle of strict liability and its application under Swiss law.

10.1.1 The Appealed Decision

The CAS case *PSV Eindhoven v. UEFA* deals with a very important issue in sports law: strict liability. In that case, the UEFA Control and Disciplinary Body had inflicted a fine (amounting to CHF 30,000) to PSV Eindhoven because of racist incidents which had occurred during the match Eindhoven–Arsenal on September 25, 2002 (in particular, a group of supporters were screaming like monkeys in Thierry Henry's direction). On appeal by the UEFA Disciplinary Inspector, the UEFA Appeals Body increased the fine to CHF 50'000 and issued a clear warning that a severe sanction would be applied to the club in case of repeated offence.

This decision was based on Article 6 of the UEFA Disciplinary Regulations (ed. 2002), which reads as follows:

> Member Associations and clubs are responsible for the conduct of their players, officials, members, supporters and any other persons exercising a function at a match on behalf of the association or club.
>
> The host association or club is responsible for order and security both inside and around the stadium, before, during and after the match. It is liable for incidents of any kind, and can be rendered subject to disciplinary measures and bound to observe directives.

The UEFA Appeals Body considered that this provision could be applied even if the club had committed no fault (strict liability). However, it held that the club was at fault as it had not done its best to prevent this kind of incidents. Therefore, it inflicted a fine of CHF 50,000 to the club because of the racist incidents which had occurred. In addition, it took into account the fact that the club had already been fined for similar incidents in a recent past. PSV appealed to CAS against this decision and challenged the validity of a strict liability regime.

10.1.2 CAS Decision

In short, CAS considered that the club was not at fault, but agreed that Article 6 para 1 of the Disciplinary Regulations provided for a regime of strict liability, and affirmed its validity.

The CAS Panel however decided that Article 6 para 2 had not been infringed by the club: it held that the club had done its best to secure order and prevent incidents in the stadium. In contrast with para 1, Article 6 para 2 does not institute a regime of strict liability. The Panel therefore considered that the fine had to be reduced to CHF 30,000 (taking into account the fact that this was a repeat offence). It also held that a warning was superfluous.

10.1.3 Validity of a Regime of Strict Liability Under Swiss Law on Associations

10.1.3.1 The Autonomy of Association and its Limits Set Forth by Article 28 CC

UEFA, like FIFA, is an association formed under the laws of Switzerland.

Swiss law on associations is highly flexible (and this is certainly one of the reasons which explain why so many sports federations are associations organised under Swiss law). In particular, it is admitted that associations are free to define their organisation within the limits of the few mandatory rules set forth by law. This freedom is recognised as a basic principle which is called the "autonomy of association". In furtherance of this autonomy, the statutes will define the rights and obligations of the members. They will also define the sanctions which may apply.

In a normal situation, nobody may be forced to adhere to an association, and if someone becomes a member, this is by choice. Those who freely choose to adhere to an association will therefore accept the statutory rules—and those who do not want to accept these rules are normally free to refuse membership. At least, this is how the situation was perceived by the lawmaker when it enacted the law on associations at the beginning of the 20th century.

Against this background, sanctions may be inflicted even without fault if this is clear from the statutes (or if this is provided by a regulation which has been validly enacted on the basis of the statutes). Under Swiss law on associations, this is largely admitted.[1]

Further, any association is free in principle to accept or refuse new members. In addition, it may exclude any member even without grounds (Article 72 of the

1 See Riemer 1990, Art. 70 N 210; Bütler 1986, p. 96 s) ; Corbat 1974, p. 89 f; Keller 1979, p. 36 f.

Civil Code). Some authors in the Swiss legal literature therefore contend that if the association has such a power to exclude any member, it may inflict other sanctions which are less stringent (a *majore minus*).[2] In the present case, CAS expressly referred to this opinion: "Article 72 para 1 of the CC allows associations to expel their members without giving their reasons for doing so. It would therefore seem paradoxical if an association were able, through its statutes, to expel its members without having to show that they had committed some kind of violation, whilst only being allowed to sanction its members if it could prove that they had breached their obligations".[3]

However, the right to exclude any member has been restricted by the Federal Supreme Court for professional or economic associations which "appear in the public and vis-à-vis authorities and clients of their members as being the relevant organisation for the profession or for that economic sector": these associations "cannot claim the full benefit of the autonomy to exclude members". In particular, the right to develop an economic activity is protected by Article 28 of the Civil Code (which provides for general rules on the protection of personality); therefore, the Federal Supreme Court decided that members of such associations may be excluded only in the presence of justified grounds.[4]

Therefore, it is quite certain that sports federation cannot enjoy the same degree of autonomy as any "standard" association. To a certain extent at least, their situation is similar to that of a professional or economic association. Thus, it is not possible to apply the same rules as for "standard" associations, in particular as to the right to expel members or to inflict sanctions. As shown by case-law concerning professional or economic associations, limits are set forth by Article 28 of the Civil Code (CC).

Article 28 CC protects "personality" in very broad terms. This protection extends to "all essential values which are inherent to personality". In the field of high-level sports, it has been decided that this protection includes a right to sports activity and, for professional sports, a right to develop an economic activity.[5] Further, Article 28 CC also protects reputation, professional and social esteem. Thus, pecuniary sanctions imposed to professional players or clubs may infringe the right to develop an economic activity. More generally, disciplinary sanctions—at least if they are imposed for violation of ethical standards—may damage reputation.[6]

---

[2] See Scherrer 1985, p. 15.

[3] CAS decision, at para 17.

[4] Federal Supreme Court decisions ATF 123 III 193 and 131 III 97 (translation by the author). The right to exclude any member may also be restricted by the possible application of competition law.

[5] Federal Supreme Court decision ATF 134 III 193.

[6] Same decision.

Article 28 para 2 CC provides that any breach of the rules protecting personality "is unlawful unless it is justified by law, by the consent of the victim, or by an overriding public or private interest".[7]

In the case of an association as envisioned by the lawmaker (e.g. a philatelists' club), sanctions might be justified by the consent of the member who has accepted these sanctions when adhering to the association.[8] Even in this case however, if a sanction was to damage reputation or to cause any other breach of the rules protecting personality, Article 28 CC may apply and—in the absence of any justification provided by law—the association which inflicts such a sanction would have to demonstrate the existence of an overriding interest.[9] This will *a fortiori* apply in the field of disciplinary sanctions pronounced by sports federations.

As regards anti-doping regulations, it has been held by the Federal Supreme Court that a regime of strict liability—at least as regards disqualification if a prohibited substance has been found—is justified by an overriding interest: otherwise, rules against doping would lose their efficiency; the need for efficient rules against doping has thus been viewed as an overriding interest in the meaning of Article 28 para 2 CC.[10]

The validity of regulations enacted by sports federations against racism has not been dealt with by Swiss courts. However, it must be assumed that the fight against racism justifies a regime of strict liability. This has been stressed by CAS in the present case:

> If clubs were able to extricate themselves from any responsibility by claiming that they had taken all measures they could reasonably be expected to take to prevent any breach of the UEFA rules, and if supporters still managed to commit such an act, there would be no way of penalising that behaviour, even though it constituted a fault in itself. UEFA's rules of conduct would therefore be nothing more than vague obligations, since they would be devoid of any sanction. By penalising a club for the behaviour of its supporters, it is in fact the latter who are targeted and who, as supporters, will be liable to pay the penalty imposed on their club. This is the only way in which UEFA has any chance of achieving its objectives. Without such an indirect sanction, UEFA would be literally powerless to deal with supporters' misconduct if a club refused to take responsibility for such behaviour.

Therefore, a regime of strict liability is valid under Swiss law on associations insofar as it is necessary to protect overriding interests—because less stringent sanctions would be regarded as inefficient. However, such a regime should not be admitted in any case: if the imposition of disciplinary sanctions without fault infringes the rights which protect personality (Article 28 CC), it will be necessary

---

[7] Translation by the author.

[8] Riemer 1990, Art. 70 N 217.

[9] See Riemer 1990, ibid.: if excessive, damage to reputation will be unlawful, notwithstanding consent of the aggrieved party.

[10] Federal Supreme Court decision ATF 134 III 193.

to demonstrate the existence of an overriding (public or private[11]) interest which justifies such a regime.

Further, pecuniary sanctions will be subject to judicial review: if excessive, a penalty may be reduced by the judge. This is expressly provided by Article 163 para 3 of the Code of obligations (CO). Although this provision relates to penalties stipulated in a contract (while sanctions imposed by an association are not of a contractual nature: they rely on the competence which is attributed by the statutes to the organs of the association[12]), it is admitted that it applies by analogy to those imposed by an association. Therefore, even if a pecuniary sanction is in itself justified, it is still possible to claim application of this provision, which cannot be waived in advance by the debtor. On the basis of this provision, the judge will reduce penalties which are obviously disproportionate and thus incompatible with the rules of law and equity[13]; this assessment has to be made in the case at hand.

10.1.3.2 The Grounds Invoked by the Appellant

The appellant raised three objections against the regime of strict liability instituted by Article 6 para 1 of the UEFA Disciplinary Regulations:

- Immorality in the sense of Article 20 CO
- Breach of Article 163 para 2 CO
- Abuse of a dominant position (competition law).

Immorality?

The appellant first argued that a regime of strict liability would be immoral in the sense of Article 20 CO. This provision stipulates that a contract is void if its subject-matter is impossible, illicit or contrary to morality.

However, sanctions imposed by an association are not of a contractual nature: they rely on the competence which is attributed by the statutes to the organs of the association.[14] It was therefore dubious whether this provision could be invoked in this case.

Further, a contract will be "immoral" if it runs against ethical principles and values which are inherent to the Swiss legal system.[15] As seen above, it is widely admitted under Swiss law on associations that statutes may provide for sanctions even in the absence of any fault. The limits which are set forth to this power laid

---

[11] See Article 28 para 2 CC quoted above (footnote 7).

[12] Heini/Scherrer 2006, Art. 70 N 20; Riemer, Art. 70 N 236. However, non-members may accept the rules of a competition by contract; in this case, law on contracts would apply.

[13] Federal Supreme Court decision ATF 133 III 201 with further references.

[14] Cf. footnote 12.

[15] Federal Supreme Court decision ATF 132 III 458.

down by Article 28 CC. Against this background, the argument based on "immorality" could not succeed and thus has been rejected by CAS.

The appellant also argued that Article 6 para 1 of the UEFA Disciplinary Regulations should be declared immoral and void because it would violate foreign law; in this respect, the appellant invoked a provision of Dutch law concerning the principle of equal treatment. The CAS Panel rightly dismissed this argument: the UEFA regulations are governed by Swiss law, and the relevance of this provision of Dutch law—to the extent that it could have had any influence in this case—was unsubstantiated.[16]

Breach of article 163 para 2 CO?

The appellant also invoked Article 163 para 2 CO, which provides that—except if otherwise agreed—a contractual penalty may not be claimed if performance of the violated obligation was rendered impossible by circumstances for which the debtor was not responsible.

Again, sanctions imposed by an association are not of a contractual nature. For this reason, Article 163 CO should not apply here. However, it has been considered that it could apply by analogy to pecuniary sanctions pronounced by an association.[17] In the present case, the CAS Panel followed this view.[18] Nevertheless, Article 163 para 2 CO allows for the possibility to agree that the penalty may be due even if non-performance has become impossible by circumstances for which the debtor was not responsible. Therefore, this provision does not prohibit a regime of strict liability and CAS rejected the appellant's arguments based on Article 163 para 2 CO.

Abuse of a dominant position?

The appellant also argued that UEFA would abuse its position by inflicting sanctions without fault. However, in the absence of any indications as to the relevant market as well as to the existence of any abuse of a dominant position, in particular, this argument has been rejected by CAS as being unsubstantiated.[19]

Competition law requires evidence as to the relevant market, the effects of the restriction on that market, the possible justifications etc. so that application of competition law appears as being quite complicated. Against this background, the limits set forth by Article 28 CC as regards disciplinary sanctions[20] provide for a

---

16 CAS decision, at para 38.

17 Federal Supreme Court decision ATF 119 II 165, 80 II 133.

18 CAS decision, at para 25.

19 CAS decision, at para 42.

20 See 10.1.3 above.

sufficient basis to tackle the issue. Further, it is hard to imagine that disciplinary regulations which satisfy the requirements of Art. 28 CC could be seen as being abusive under competition law. Therefore, it does not seem that competition law would bring any further remedy against a regime of strict liability.

10.1.4 Conclusion

Under Swiss law, validity of a regime of strict liability has been admitted by the Federal Supreme Court in the field of anti-doping regulations (at least as regards disqualification if a prohibited substance has been found). Although the imposition of disciplinary sanctions may infringe the rights which protect personality (Article 28 CC), a regime of strict liability may be justified by an overriding interest in the meaning of Article 28 para 2 CC; the existence of such an overriding interest has been recognised as regards the rules against doping (otherwise, these rules would lose their efficiency).

Even if Swiss courts have not dealt yet with the validity of regulations enacted by sports federations against racism, it must be assumed that a regime of strict liability is also justified by an overriding interest (the fight against racism), as this has been admitted by CAS in the present case.

As regards other disciplinary regulations, it should be kept in mind that sanctions may infringe the rights which protect personality. In case of such an infringement, a regime of strict liability will be valid only insofar as it is necessary to protect overriding interests; if less stringent sanctions would be efficient to protect these interests, a regime of strict liability should not be admitted.

Further, Article 163 para 3 of the CO may be applied by analogy to pecuniary sanctions, which will be reduced by the judge if they are obviously disproportionate.

In conclusion, it is certain that the limits set forth by Article 28 CC and the possibility for the judge to reduce pecuniary sanctions still leave some room for further legal battles. Under Swiss law however, a regime of strict liability may be applied, and this has been recognised both by CAS and by the Federal Supreme Court.

10.2 CAS 2007/A/1217 Feyenoord Rotterdam v. UEFA

Peter T.M. Coenen

The Feyenoord Rotterdam Award demonstrates the consequences of strict liability for a club. On 30 November 2006, Feyenoord played the French team AS Nancy–Lorraine in the UEFA Cup. A number of factors led to rioting inside and outside the stadium, with the match having to be interrupted for half an hour. The CAS asserted that in terms of Article 6 of the UEFA Disciplinary Rules, Feyenoord bore strict liability for the incidents caused by its supporters, even if these 'supporters' were not recognised as such by the club. The CAS ultimately confirmed UEFA's sanction, the disqualification of Feyenoord from the current UEFA Cup competition 2006/07 and the fine of around CHF 100,000. The author believes this was the correct signal to send, both legally and as a deterrent.

10.2.1 Introduction

Feyenoord is perhaps the most popular football clubs in the Netherlands. The club has strong support throughout the whole of the Netherlands, thanks to its working-class image. Contrary to its rival Ajax Amsterdam, Feyenoord supporters do not expect great technical prowess from their team. Rather they expect the players of the club to live up to the club's motto: 'geen woorden maar daden', which roughly translates as 'no words, but deeds'.

The last couple of years have not gone very well for Feyenoord. The results have been meager, but more importantly the club has struggled to keep pace financially with other clubs in the Netherlands. Traditional powers PSV Eindhoven and Ajax have a lot more money to spend yearly than Feyenoord and the club has been surpassed in many levels even by AZ Alkmaar and FC Twente. One of the catalysts for this lack of success has been the failure of Feyenoord to perform well in European matches.

The events on November 30, 2006 serve as an illustration of the current state of the club. A match in the French city of Nancy on November 30, 2006 ended in complete pandemonium, with scenes of fan violence broadcast all over the news throughout the whole of Europe.[21] This ultimately led to the club being suspended from European football for rest of the season, adding to an already woeful season for the club.

This case review deals with football hooliganism. Football hooliganism is still a huge problem; it is not a phenomenon of the 1980's. Clubs get a bad reputation based on the behaviour of their fans. They are fined or suspended from play by their national associations and international associations. As a result of fan behaviour, sponsors might decide not to attach their brand name to a certain team and its fans.[22] This costs clubs lots of income. Furthermore, hooliganism gives the whole of professional football a bad reputation. In the last years, it seems that the problem of football (and sports) related violence has intensified again in places all over the world and Europe, which is the focus of this article.

This case review deals with an award from the Court of Arbitration for Sports (CAS) that confirmed the exclusion of Dutch team Feyenoord from the UEFA

---

[21] NOS, *Rellen met Feyenoord fans in Nancy*, http://www.nos.nl/nosjournaal/artikelen/2006/11/30/301106_feyenoord_rellen.html (Nov. 30, 2006).

[22] T-Online.de, *Hansa Sponsor droht mit rückzug*, http://sport.t-online.de/fc-hansa-rostock-sponsor-droht-wegen-hooligans-mit-rueckzug/id_41688126/index (May, 14, 2010).

Cup, following riots instigated by Feyenoord supporters at the UEFA Cup match between the club and French team AS Nancy. The legal issue in this award is whether a club has strict liability for the acts of people associated with that club, even if that club does not want to recognize these individuals as supporters of their team. Feyenoord tried to argue against UEFA's strict liability rule with regard to supporter misconduct. The strict liability rule states that a club is responsible for the conduct of their supporters, regardless of whether the club itself is at fault. Feyenoord tried to argue that their exclusion from the UEFA Cup tournament was unjustified since the supporters that were responsible for the misconduct in Nancy were not supporters of their team. Feyenoord argued that these individuals had just come to Nancy to misbehave and were not connected legally to the team itself. In the end, CAS denied Feyenoord's appeal, but the award and the reaction by UEFA shows there may be an upcoming shift in UEFA's stance on supporter violence.

10.2.2 What Happened that Day in Nancy?

Feyenoord Rotterdam is a professional football club based in the Dutch harbor city of Rotterdam. The club has a rich history, having won numerous national and international prizes.[23] Feyenoord was the first Dutch club to win the European Cup competition in 1970, the predecessor of the UEFA Champions League. Being one of the traditional 'big three' teams in the Netherlands, the club has a large fan base at home and abroad. The club's motto is '*geen woorden maar daden*', which translates as 'no words, but deeds'.[24] This reflects the origin of the club, being founded by hard-working laborers in the city's harbor.[25] It also reflects the no-nonsense style of football favoured by the supporters.[26]

Feyenoord is also known for its devoted and die-hard fan base.[27] Most of these fans are great supporters who never cause any problems for the club, but a small portion of these supporters have exhibited a tendency towards violent behaviour.

---

[23] Feyenoord, *Hoogtepunten*, http://www.feyenoord.nl/pages/feyenoordcontent/s2/10010000000002-10010000000068/de+club+-+historie+-+hoogtepunten.aspx (accessed June 13, 2007).

[24] Feyenoord, *Het Legioen, Van het volk,door het volk, in het volk*, http://www.feyenoord.nl/pages/story/s2/de+club+-+historie+-+van-door-in+het+volk.aspx (accessed June 13, 2007).

[25] Feyenoord, *De accomodatie, Put en Afrikaanderplein*, http://www.feyenoord.nl/ pages/story/s2/de+club+-+historie+-+put+en+afrikaanderplein.aspx (accessed June 13, 2007).

[26] Feyenoord, *Het Legioen, het Feyenoord gevoel*, http://www.feyenoord.nl/ pages/story/s2/de+club+-+historie+-+het+feyenoord-gevoel.aspx (accessed June 13, 2007).

[27] Feyenoord, *Het Legioen, Intro*, http://www.feyenoord.nl/pages/story/s2/10010000000002-10010000000073/de+club+-+historie+-+het+legion.aspx (accessed June 13, 2007).

This development can be traced back to 1974 when Feyenoord won the UEFA Cup against London team Tottenham Hotspur.[28] More importantly for this review, that match signified the introduction of hooliganism into Dutch football. Before and during the match, Tottenham supporters fought with Feyenoord fans and police.[29] Since this incident, a number of Feyenoord fans have built up quite a reputation for violence throughout the Netherlands and Europe, being involved in numerous incidents during games of the club.

On November 30, 2006, Feyenoord was scheduled to play an away game against French team AS Nancy–Lorraine (hereafter AS Nancy), as part of the group phase of the 2006/2007 UEFA Cup tournament. UEFA is the framework European Football Association, which organizes among others, the Champions League and the UEFA Cup Tournament.[30] On November 2, 2006, officials of Feyenoord and the Dutch police met with officials from AS Nancy and the city of Nancy in preparation for the game.[31] As a result of this meeting, Feyenoord received about 1400 tickets for the game.[32]

On November 27, 2006, Feyenoord warned AS Nancy that the number of supporters traveling to Nancy for the game would far exceed the number of tickets allocated to them.[33] A lot of fans who did not have tickets for the game would still make the trip to the French city.[34] Feyenoord also informed AS Nancy that about 400 tickets, allocated to AS Nancy and bought at the stadium, had been purchased by supporters who could be linked to the Rotterdam side, outside the realm of the normal away ticketing system.[35] In most cases, Feyenoord tries to regulate the allocation of tickets for away games so they can ensure that tickets for these games do not end up in the hands of people they do not know, or even in the hands of known troublemakers.[36] Because these tickets had been allocated to AS Nancy, Feyenoord had no information on who exactly bought these 400 tickets, but they feared these tickets had indeed come into the hands of known hooligans. The 'supporters', who bought these tickets outside the normal away ticketing system, would end up in sections with supporters of AS Nancy.[37] Under these circumstances, it was likely that a large

---

28 Www.sportgeschiedenis.web-log.nl, *Feyenoord en de voetbalrellen van 1974*, http://sportgeschiedenis.weblog. nl/sportgeschiedenis/2007/01/feyenoord_en_de.html (January 12, 2007).

29 Id.

30 UEFA, www.uefa.com (accessed June 13, 2007).

31 *Feyenoord Rotterdam N.V. v. Union of European Football Associations*, CAS 2007/A/1217, 2.

32 Id.

33 Id.

34 Id.

35 Id.

36 Ernst Bouwes, *ESPN.com, The final irony*, http://soccernet.espn.go.com/columns/story?id=404445&root=europe&&cc= 5901 (accessed May 2007).

37 *Feyenoord v. UEFA*, at 2.

number of known troublemakers would end up in the stadium, mixing amongst the supporters of the other team.

On November 28, 2006, AS Nancy acknowledged that tickets had been sold to Dutch supporters outside Feyenoord's away-ticketing system.[38] AS Nancy stated this information had been known since November 20th, and that it had taken a number of measures to avoid problems during the game. Police would check the tickets of fans coming to watch the game at the stadium entrance and would direct any Feyenoord supporters to the away sections; an extra 100 stewards were designated to the match, thus bringing the number of stewards to 400; a police force of about 300 officers was designated to patrol the match; the away sections of the stadium were to be isolated from the sections in which the supporters of the home side would watch the game; and a special entrance to the stadium would be created for supporters of the Dutch club.[39]

Unfortunately these measures proved to be insufficient. Feyenoord supporters were present long before the match started in the city centre of Nancy.[40] Amongst them were a number of people had stadium bans in the Netherlands.[41] Fearing destruction or riots, several bars and restaurants closed at the sight of the large numbers of football fans.[42] Fans roamed the city centre, looking for something to do. Riots broke out in the city centre of Nancy hours before the match was even supposed to start.[43] Police moved the troublemakers from the city centre towards the stadium and opened the doors to the sections reserved for the away supporters to all Feyenoord supporters, with or without tickets.[44] The police attempted to isolate the troublemakers within the confines of the stadium, rather then let them roam free in the city centre. This decision had to be made on short notice by the chief of police of Nancy, motivated by the immediate need to halt the riots, without consulting Feyenoord representatives or UEFA delegates in Nancy.[45] The consequence of this decision was that the rioters and other supporters who did not have a ticket were driven into a section of the stadium immediately adjacent to the regular away section.[46] The hooligans quickly tore down the fence between their section and the regular away section and mixed with the Feyenoord supporters who had received their tickets through Feyenoord's normal ticketing system for

---

38 Id.

39 Id. at 3.

40 www.voetbalprimeur.nl, *Waar het mis ging in Nancy,* http://www.voetbalprimeur.nl/index.php?t=article&id=2772 (accessed May 15, 2007) (this is an eyewitness report of the riots in Nancy, send in by a Feyenoord supporter and placed on the website, since it gives an interesting inside perspective in what transpired in Nancy).

41 Id.

42 Id.

43 Id.

44 *Feyenoord v. UEFA*, at 3.

45 Id.

46 www.voetbalprimeur.nl, *Waar het mis ging in Nancy,* http://www.voetbalprimeur.nl/index.php?t=article&id=2772 (accessed May 15, 2007).

away games.[47] As the match progressed, the riots continued within the stadium. The police finally used tear gas to stop the rioting in the stands.[48] The game had to be interrupted for about half an hour because of the effects of the tear gas on the players, referees and fans.[49]

After the match had ended and the dust had cleared, the fans, media, players and staff of Feyenoord braced themselves for UEFA's response to the riots in Nancy.[50] The UEFA Control and Disciplinary Body came with a ruling on 7 December 2006. Feyenoord was to pay a 200.000 CHF fine and the two next games of Feyenoord in any of the European cup competitions needed to be played without any supporters present.[51] However, this order was deferred for a probationary period of three years.[52] UEFA appealed this decision on 13 December 2006, asking for a more severe punishment for Feyenoord.[53] Even though this penalty was not as severe as some around the Rotterdam club might have feared, Feyenoord decided to also appeal the decision of the Control and Disciplinary body on 11 January 2007, asking for annulment of the decision and an acquittal for the Rotterdam club.[54]

After a hearing was held on 19 January 2007, the UEFA Appeals body returned on January 25th' 2007, with an even harsher verdict this time, excluding Feyenoord from the 2006/2007 UEFA Cup tournament and setting the fine at 100.000 CHF.[55] The team's worst fears had materialized. The decision of the UEFA Appeals Body was felt to be too harsh by the Rotterdam team, and Feyenoord decided to file an appeal against this decision with the Court of Arbitration for Sports (hereafter CAS) on 26 January 2007.[56]

CAS is the highest appeals institution with whom an appeal was possible against the ruling of the UEFA Appeals Body.[57] CAS is an independent arbitration body set up to arbitrate and/or mediate sports related disputes[58] and its arbitrators are generally considered to be high level jurists.[59] CAS also has a good reputation

---

47 Id.

48 *Feyenoord v. UEFA*,at 4.

49 Id.

50 NOS,*Uefa toont zich mild voor Feyenoord*, http://www.nos.nl/nosstudiosport/artikelen/2006/12/7/07121734uefatoontzich mildvoorfeyenoord.html (Dec. 7, 2006).

51 *Feyenoord v. UEFA*, at 4.

52 Id.

53 Id.

54 Id.

55 Id.

56 NOS, *Feyenoord in beroep*, http://www.nos.nl/ nosstudiosport/artikelen/2007/1/26/26011524 feyenoordinberoepcas.html (Jan. 26, 2007).

57 NOS,*'zaak Feyenoord' snel aan bod bij CAS*, http://www.nos.nl/ nosstudiosport/artikelen/2007/1/29/29011300zaakfeyen oordsnelbehandeld.html (Jan. 29, 2007).

58 Matthieu Reeb, *The Role and Functions of the Court of Arbitration for Sports (CAS)*, ISLJ 2002/2, 21.

59 Id. at 23.

in the sports community,[60] dealing with a lot of doping issues and arbitrating on a lot of cases concerning transfer fees in (international) soccer.[61] UEFA has recognized the power of CAS to be an arbitrator of last instance on disciplinary matters concerning UEFA and another party.[62]

10.2.3 CAS Upholds UEFA's Punishment

Feyenoord, in its submission to CAS, contended that *the club* is not to blame for the riots in Nancy.[63] It warned AS Nancy about the risks of selling tickets freely around their stadium and that a large group of potential troublemakers (whether with or without tickets) were traveling to Nancy.[64] Feyenoord further criticized the decision of the chief of police to give all supporters access to the stadium, with or without tickets.[65] Finally, Feyenoord criticized the decision to place its rogue supporters in sections of the stadium adjacent to the sections of the stadium in which the 'official' Feyenoord supporters were seated, thus giving these hooligans the opportunity to mix with the fans that had bought a ticket for the game directly from Feyenoord,[66] a perpetually volatile situation because this way it was impossible for the police and stewards to distinguish between 'good' fans and 'bad' fans.

Furthermore, Feyenoord claimed that the troublemakers were not supporters of the club under the definition given to the term supporters by UEFA.[67] These troublemakers did not buy their tickets through Feyenoord, did not travel to the stadium under the guidance of Feyenoord, could not be identified from their appearance as Feyenoord fans, and some of them even had a stadium ban in the Netherlands.[68] Feyenoord argued that nothing distinguishes these individuals as being Feyenoord fans and therefore Feyenoord cannot be held responsible for the behaviour of these individuals.[69] Finally, the team complained about the proportionality of the sanction of the UEFA Appeals Body.[70] The punishment received means that Feyenoord will miss out on a lot of income that could have been generated in the following round(s) of the UEFA Cup tournament.

---

[60] Id. at 25.

[61] Id. at 21.

[62] *Feyenoord v. UEFA*, at 7.

[63] Id. at 5.

[64] Id.

[65] Id.

[66] Id. at 6.

[67] Id.

[68] Id.

[69] Id.

[70] Id.

UEFA responded to Feyenoord's contentions, saying that it is not a question of who is at fault for the behaviour of the supporters.[71] Feyenoord is responsible for the behaviour of its supporters, irrespective of what the club may have done to either prevent or encourage this behaviour.[72] The rule is strict liability for a club regarding the behaviour of its supporters. This also means that the warnings and measures taken by Feyenoord are irrelevant to the liability question.[73]

With regard to the definition of the term supporter, UEFA stated that there is no clear definition of who is a supporter of a club. UEFA stated that the term supporter is "not linked only to race, nationality of the place of residence of the individual, nor is it linked to a contract which an individual has concluded with the national association or the club in purchasing a ticket".[74] UEFA then concluded that "there is no distinction between official and unofficial supporters of a team".[75]

CAS started its deliberations by stating it has competence to deal with this case and that the rules applicable to this dispute are the relevant UEFA rules and regulations.[76] CAS then ruled that "disciplinary law implemented in [UEFA's] regulations and directives is essentially a tool which allows UEFA to create order within the organization and to assert statutory standards of conduct through sanctions imposed by specific bodies and to ensure their appropriate execution".[77] CAS goes on to conclude that Feyenoord is subject to UEFA's rules and regulations and more specifically the ones upon which the decision by the UEFA Appeals Body is based.[78]

CAS points at Article 6 of UEFA Disciplinary Regulations, which provide that:

> Member associations and clubs are responsible for the conduct of their players, officials, members, supporters and any other persons exercising a function at a match at the request of the association or club.
>
> The host association or club is responsible for the order and security both inside and around the stadium, before, during and after the match. It is liable for incidents of any kind, and can be rendered subject to disciplinary measures and bound to observe directives.[79]

CAS pointed out that, according to this article, Feyenoord has strict liability for the behaviour of its supporters.[80] The point of contention that remained, then, was which persons can be defined as being a supporter. CAS noted that UEFA

71 Id.

72 Id.

73 Id.

74 Id.

75 Id.

76 Id. at 7.

77 Id. at 8.

78 Id.

79 Id. at 9.

80 Id.

intentionally did not define the term supporter.[81] UEFA did not specify the term supporter in terms of race, nationality, place of residence of the individual, or whether that person has a contract with a club or association by buying a ticket for a certain game.[82] Defining the term supporter would alleviate clubs of responsibilities for supporters it does not want to recognize for legal purposes.[83] The disciplinary sanctions of UEFA would in such a case apply only to supporters the club want them to apply to, while this could have never been the purpose of UEFA.[84]

CAS went on to state that by leaving the term supporter undefined, the reasonable and objective observer could determine someone is a supporter of a club.[85] Determinants that can help the reasonable and objective observer come to this conclusion are the behaviour of the individuals concerned and where they are located in the stadium and their vicinity.[86] CAS went on to point to their prior case law, in which they considered that article 6 Disciplinary Regulations was perfectly valid. CAS especially points to one case, *PSV Eindhoven v. UEFA*, CAS 2002/A/423.[87] In that case, PSV was punished for racist behaviour by its supporters directed towards players of the opponent in a match in the Champions League tournament.

In this case CAS pointed to rule 6 para 1 Disciplinary Regulations, and stated:

> According to this provision UEFA members and clubs are responsible for any breach of the UEFA Regulations committed by any of those persons. There is therefore no doubt that, under this rule, member associations and clubs bear strict responsibility for the actions of third parties, who are nonetheless specifically identified. This rule leaves absolutely no room for manoeuver as far as its application is concerned. UEFA member associations and football clubs are responsible, even if they are not at fault, for the improper conduct of their supporters…[88]

CAS further acknowledged that by penalizing the clubs, UEFA in essence aims to penalize the supporters for their conduct.[89] UEFA does not have a direct way of penalizing individual supporters and therefore focuses all measures on the one body they do have authority over-the teams. UEFA in this way tries to indirectly achieve its goal of controlling the behaviour of certain (groups of) supporters by penalizing the club these fans support. The objective of article 6, then, with regard to the behaviour of supporters is to deter and prevent violent conduct, not to

[81] Id.
[82] Id.
[83] Id.
[84] Id.
[85] Id.
[86] Id.
[87] Id.
[88] Id. at 10.
[89] Id.

penalize clubs for wrongdoings.[90] The strict liability rule makes sense in this context given that the goal is to prevent the violent acts of the supporters, so it does not matter what actions the club itself took.

CAS went on to conclude that the supporters responsible for the problems surrounding the match between AS Nancy and Feyenoord could be identified as Feyenoord supporters and therefore the strict liability rule applied.[91] The fact that Feyenoord took measures to prevent any disorder does not alter the liability of the club for the behaviour of its supporters.[92] The fact that there may have been errors in the way AS Nancy handled ticket sales, the way the French police handled the situation by giving the troublemakers access to the stadium and enabling them to mix with the 'official' Feyenoord supporters, was all held to be irrelevant for this case. Feyenoord is liable for the conduct of its fans under Article 6 para 1 Disciplinary Regulations.[93] This needs to be distinguished from the liability the home team possibly has under Article 6 para 2 of the Disciplinary Regulations as the host and the organizer of the match.

Feyenoord further appealed to CAS on the severity of the penalty.[94] However, CAS first stated that according to article 14 Disciplinary Regulations, disqualification from the UEFA Cup competition could be used as a possible penalty for violation of the Disciplinary Regulations.[95] CAS went on to assess Feyenoord's claim that disqualification would be disproportionate to the offence committed. CAS stated that according to its case law, a "sanction imposed must not be evidently and grossly disproportionate to the offence."[96] CAS came to the conclusion that UEFA was allowed to impose the heavy sanction of disqualification.[97] In reaching this conclusion it took into account that the behaviour of the fans, (e.g. breaking a wall inside the stadium to reach the supporters of the opposing team, throwing projectiles towards individuals) could have been considered as serious offences by the UEFA Appeals Body.[98] Furthermore, Feyenoord was a multiple offender with regard to supporter misconduct.[99] UEFA regards recidivism as an aggravating factor in its Disciplinary Regulations.[100] Over the past five years there have been 12 disciplinary cases against Feyenoord for supporter misconduct.[101] Finally, a disqualification

---

[90] Id.

[91] Id. at 11.

[92] Id.

[93] Id. at 12.

[94] Id.

[95] Id.

[96] Id. at 13.

[97] Id.

[98] Id.

[99] Id.

[100] Id.

[101] Id.

ensures that in the further course of the UEFA Cup season, there would not be any further incidents of supporter misconduct of Feyenoord's supporters.[102] On these grounds, CAS ruled that the sanction imposed by the UEFA Appeals Body was not disproportionate to the offences committed.

10.2.4 A Strong Signal?

In its ruling that was upheld by CAS, the UEFA Appeals Body gave a strong signal to clubs whose supporters are repeatedly involved in violence. UEFA handed down a rigorous penalty and excluded Feyenoord from further participation in the UEFA Cup tournament for the season.

Ironically, this prevented Feyenoord from playing Tottenham Hotspur in the next round of the UEFA Cup, a clash that in 1974 began the tradition of hooliganism a part of the supporters of the Rotterdam club is now known for. Even though Feyenoord tried to distance itself from these hooligans, UEFA was able to apply their rule of strict liability to them for the behaviour of their supporters. UEFA punished Feyenoord for the behaviour of a small portion of its supporters in Nancy-supporters, many of whom are not allowed inside a stadium in the Netherlands. Of course, not all Feyenoord supporters are hooligans and therefore the club's argument that these people do not belong to their club holds some merit. These hooligans do make up only a small portion of the otherwise great supporters of the Rotterdam team. And these hooligans do spoil it for all the good supporters. But the fact remains that Feyenoord is the connecting factor among these hooligans and they take the games of the Rotterdam club as an excuse to start their mayhem. No respectable club wants to be associated with such fans. This does not mean, however, that a club should not have to assume liability over the behaviour of these supporters.

Hooligans linked to Feyenoord had been involved in numerous incidents over the previous European seasons before that faithful night in Nancy and therefore the club was already on notice with UEFA.[103] There had been twelve previous disciplinary cases involving supporter misconduct in the five years before the game between Nancy and Feyenoord against the Rotterdam team, so it came as no surprise that UEFA handed down such a harsh penalty. In its reasoning with regard to the sanctions, CAS states that this punishment will have the effect of eradicating any further incidents with Feyenoord's supporters during the 2006/2007 UEFA Cup season. It is hard to argue with this, but will the outcome of this case also have the effect of preventing incidents from happening in the future?

---

102 Id.

103 Id.

From the way the question is formulated, the reader may think the answer would be a resounding no, but the answer to this question is much more complicated. Sending a strong message to a repeat offender might have a deterrent effect for the future. Next time supporters might consider that their club will be excluded from European football before they start rioting. It could help. But a strong signal in one, individual instance is not enough to 'eradicate hooliganism', as CAS stated in its award. Strong punishments will only have a noticeable effect if they are handed out consequently and in a consistent manner. It took UEFA twelve instances of supporter related misconduct to issue such a strong penalty against Feyenoord. And since Feyenoord's exclusion of the 2006/2007 UEFA Cup competition, the supporters of the club have once again been involved in violent incidents surrounding European matches against Lech Poznan from Poland[104] and against Deportivo La Coruna[105] from Spain.

Feyenoord is not the only club that is forced to deal with the problem of football hooliganism. There have been numerous problems with the fans of the English and German national teams at international games, including at the European[106] and World Championships.[107] To date, the English and German national teams have not been ruled out of any tournaments. In the Champions League, there have been large scale incidents of football hooliganism involving supporters of English side Manchester United in France (Lille)[108] as well as in Italy (Rome).[109] Manchester United has never been excluded from the Champions League or any other European tournaments. Many more examples of clubs with a record of violence can be shown, where UEFA has not handed out strong penalties.

Action taken by UEFA might have a noticeable effect in preventing further incidents, but UEFA alone cannot tackle the problem of hooliganism. In this instance, would it have made a difference if AS Nancy and Feyenoord had better regulated the sale of tickets for the game? Would it have mattered if there was a place where all Feyenoord fans could have gathered before the game, a place that had provided them with some recreation, some food and drinks? Would it have

---

104 UEFA, *Feyenoord punished for December Disturbances*, http://en.uefa.com/uefa/footballfirst/matchorganisation/disciplinary/news/newsid=802401.html

105 UEFA, *Feyenoord, Depor, Roma and Marseille fined*, http://en.uefa.com/uefa/footballfirst/matchorganisation/disciplinary/news/newsid=786431.html

106 Nick Amies, *DW-WORLD.de, The Specter of Hooliganism Returns*, http://www.dw-world.de/dw/article/0,2144,1539291, 00.html (Apr. 7, 2005).

107 Sean Ingle, *Guardian, Fan fears grow ahead of England match*, http://football.guardian.co.uk/worldcup2006/story/0,,1805689,00.html (June 25, 2006).

108 BBC Sport, *Lille and Man Utd. Fined by UEFA*, http://news.bbc.co.uk/sport2/hi/football/europe/6481931.stm (Mar. 22, 2007).

109 BBC News, *Fans in hospital after violence*, http://news.bbc.co.uk/2/hi/europe/6528049.stm (May 4, 2007).

made a difference if the so called Football Law had already entered into force and hooligans with a stadium ban would have had to report at a police station at the time of the match? All of such measures could have helped to prevent the riots in Nancy from happening. What we do know is what happened without these measures.

Does this mean that Feyenoord should not have been punished for the conduct of its supporters in Nancy? Of course not. It means that UEFA in this single instance took a strong stand against supporter violence. This must be applauded. But it also means that if UEFA wants to hand out stricter penalties for supporter misconduct, it should be consistent. After Feyenoord's exclusion, only one other team was expelled from a UEFA competition for the behaviour of their fans. In 2007, Legia Warsaw was expelled from that year's Intertoto Competition.[110] This is not enough. A zero tolerance policy will only work if clubs and supporters know beforehand what the consequences of their behaviour will be and if UEFA enforces this policy, regardless of the name or the status of the club (or country) involved.

I would propose a re-evaluation of UEFA penalties for uniformity. Deterrence is a goal that can only be achieved with a heavy hand and patience. It is crucial that UEFA is consistent and is not afraid to hand out a strong punishment, where this is warranted, regardless of the name of the team or club. If UEFA would consistently hand out similar punishments for offences, it would signal a determined shift towards zero tolerance. If, however, as seems to have been the case, penalties for similar offences are not equal or similar, the case of Feyenoord simply goes down in the books as an idiosyncrasy—an aberration. This actually frustrates the goal of preventing supporter violence.

UEFA President Michel Platini, in a reaction to the CAS ruling, said: "I am very happy with the decision of CAS to uphold the UEFA Appeals Body judgment. This sends out a strong message that acts of violence by fans within the game will be heavily dealt with and punished by the relevant authorities. Recent tragic incidents have shown that we must work together to eradicate all forms of hooliganism or violence from our game."[111] These were fierce words from the UEFA President in the immediate aftermath of the incident in Nancy. Unfortunately, it seems that the case of Feyenoord v. UEFA has not led to a zero tolerance policy that applies to *all* clubs (or national teams) whose supporters misbehave.

[110] UEFA, *Legia given suspended sentence*, http://en.uefa.com/uefa/footballfirst/matchorganisation/disciplinary/news/newsid =574658.html, (Aug. 23, 2007).

[111] UEFA, *CAS uphold UEFA Appeals Body Decision,* http://www.uefa.com/newsfiles/505338.pdf (Feb. 9, 2007).

10.3 CAS 2008/A/1688 Club Atlético de Madrid SAD v. Union des Associatons Européennes de Football (UEFA)

Juan de Dios Crespo Pérez

In the Atlético de Madrid Award the CAS had to rule on racist and discriminatory incidents which took place on 1 October 2008 during the UEFA Champions League tournament group stage match between Atlético de Madrid and Olympique de Marseille. The author analyses the CAS' ruling which reduced UEFA's sanction against Atlético de Madrid SAD to one match played behind closed doors (instead of two after the first appeal) and reduced the fine by half (EUR 75,000 instead of EUR 150,000).

10.3.1 Preamble

The racism is a plague all over the world and exists in all kind of events but in sport and particularly in football, the governing bodies have taken steps not only to avoid systematically the introduction of racist conducts in the fields and in the stadiums but also to sanction any discrimination or similar behaviour.

UEFA, as the European football governing body, is particularly conscious of this problem and its Disciplinary Regulations[112] clearly provide both the offenses and the sanctions to such comportment.

Insults to a group of persons "including on grounds of colour, race, religion or ethnic origin, shall incur a suspension for five matches or for a specified period" as for a player and "playing of one or more matches behind closed doors, a stadium closure, awarding of a match by default, deduction of points or disqualification from a competition" for a club or association.

Thus, the disciplinary measures are not a joke and have to be taken into consideration not only by players who behave directly but also by clubs that can be banned or lose matches for their crowd conduct. This, which is a problem to be discussed deeply, is known as the "objective responsibility/liability" and it has been approved by UEFA[113] when stating that:

> the host associations or clubs are responsible for order and security both inside and around the stadium before, during and after the match. They are liable for incidents of any kind, and may be rendered subject to disciplinary measures and directives.

This is not the place to discuss in length this particular objective liability even though it has been one of the arguments that Atlético de Madrid used in its statement against some of the decisions taken by UEFA.

Finally, and as for the racist topic, with the creation of FARE (Football Against Racism in Europe)[114] network, a product of a melting pot of different associations

---

[112] Article 11 bis.

[113] Article 6 of UEFA Disciplinary Regulations.

[114] www.farenet.org

throughout the continent, from the European Gay & Lesbian Sport Federation to the Progetto Ultra, the fight against racism and discrimination in sport has reach a level that has got UEFA into it with the UNITE AGAINST RACISM campaign that begun in 2003 in a conference that took place at the premises of Chelsea FC in London.

A guide has been developed by UEFA in order to give clubs that participate in European competitions the necessary weapons to tackle racism.

The guide does not include only the racist issue but also how to deal with the homophobia and sexism.

10.3.2 Introduction

The so-called "racist case of the Calderón" was widely spread on the press during quite four months (from October 2008 to February 2009) as "the case against racism" and the object of several problems not only within football but also at a legal and political level between France and Spain, and with UEFA being involved in order to let the world know that no discriminatory behaviour, particularly racism, would be tolerated in its competitions.

As we will see in this commentary, things were perhaps magnified in their initial step and the end of the history was not, at all, the one of a racist conduct.

10.3.3 Facts

On the 1st of October 2008 a match of the UEFA Champions League group stage took place at the "Calderón", the stadium where Atlético de Madrid currently plays its competition matches.

The game was against the French club Olympique de Marseille, which had an accompanying crowd of some thousand fans, who were duly situated, according to UEFA rules, to a place of their own as it is always the case in UEFA Competitions.

The UEFA Control and Disciplinary body, which is the first instance in deciding a sanction in those matters, opened a proceeding according to a complaint brought by the French club as well as to the reports submitted by the official delegate and the security officer. Those documents were supported by video footage of the incidents.

The incidents were two, divided in several actions as follows:

- *The lack of organization*, as Marseille's fans entered a banner (which should have been forbid its entrance by the stewards of Atlético Madrid) with a picture of a skull and crossbones with the word "Ultra" on it. This brought the intervention of the Spanish Police, according to the Spanish Law in which Racist behaviour is strongly prohibited and then tried to remove the banner, an action which lead to a real conflict between the policemen and the fans, with several wounded in both parties.

In the same kind of incident, UEFA says that they were insufficient measures of security in place for the journalists and representatives of the Press of French nationality to protect them from physical and verbal attacks by certain supporters of Atlético Madrid.

Finally, some disabled OM supporters were not located in an appropriate area in the stadium and then removed and halftime to another place.

- *The misbehaviour of the local supporters*, as it was said by several OM players (concretely the goalkeeper Steve Mandanda and the forward Mamadou Niang), that the crowd uttered racist chants (known as monkey noises, or UH,UH,UH) when those two blacks players got the ball.

  A black Marseille journalist gave also evidence that he was insulted by certain Atlético Madrid supporters when he shouted after the goal of the French club. Finally, a half–full bottle was thrown by Atlético's fans at a disabled supporter of OM.

10.3.3.1 UEFA Disciplinary Proceedings in First Instance

UEFA first deciding body (Control and Disciplinary) stated that, according to the Regulations[115] the home club is always responsible for "security before, during and after the match", the already mentioned *objective liability*.

Entering into the case itself, the club failed to ask UEFA first to intervene as he has the responsibility to organize and maintain the order and security at the match, including a "duty to organize cooperation with the police".

In Spain, the law against racism and discrimination permits the direct intervention of the police and thus Atletico defended itself by saying that the Spanish police action falls outside of its competence.

In fact, the police saw the skull and bones banner which is clearly mentioned in the FARE booklet distributed throughout Europe stadiums to stewards and security staff as an *"SS-Totenkopf/SS-Skull"*, a Nazi symbol used by SS groups. Olympique Marseille defended that the banner only displayed what was described as a "pirate" *(sic)*.

The Control and Disciplinary body decided that the conduct of the police (nota bene, not that of Atlético de Madrid) was "inappropriate and disproportionate" and that the incident related to a banner that "ended up not even being considered as a problem itself" produced an obvious lack of organization.

It was then clear that the club and UEFA should have been in contact together first and then should have talk to the police as they better know if the banner "breaches or not UEFA Regulations".

---

[115] 5.04 of the UEFA Champions League Regulations and 6(2) of the Disciplinary Regulations.

Just a remark before continuing, as it is evident that the national legislations have also something to say and, particularly within the Spanish Laws, the racism in sports events is not only prohibited but persecuted by the Police, as it is a matter of public order.

Here again we can sense the difficulties to disassociate the international sporting regulations from the national legislations. In this particular case, the Spanish police reacted intending to remove the banner and the behaviour of the OM fans was so tough that a battle was engaged. Then, possibly, the policemen put too much force into the ground but the images showed that OM supporters were not exactly willing to help.

But, what is clear is that something has to be improved either in the Regulations or in the meetings for security in European matches in order to have a clear step by step position for such cases.

Thus, the club was sanctioned accordingly.

As for the racism issue and the crowd misbehaviour, again the Control and Disciplinary body says that according to the rules[116] "the clubs are responsible for the behaviour of their players, officials, members and supporters, as well as any person carrying out a function at a match on their behalf".

The body says that the various reports, the statements by Olympique and the video footage were evident and that Atlético's fans uttered racist chants when the black players Niang and Mandanda got the ball.

The body stated that "there is no doubt that such behaviour insults the human dignity of a person or group of people on grounds of race".

From the very beginning, Atlético Madrid denied all the racism topic and gave video footage of the match itself and other several matches of the club where the Argentinean striker "Kun" Agüero was chanted as "KUN, KUN, KUN". And, by the way, Agüero was always near the ball when the so-called "monkey noises" seemed to appear.

But UEFA body decided also that the chants and insults exist and then sanctioned the club, as "the fight against racism is a high priority for UEFA, which has zero tolerance for racism and discrimination on the pitch and in the stands".

The Control and Disciplinary Body decided, on the 13th of October 2008, that:

1. The use of the Calderon stadium in Madrid is banned for three UEFA club competition matches. The ban for the third competition match is deferred for a probational period of five years.
2. The two following matches at home had to be played at least 300 km from Madrid.
3. A fine of 150,000 EUR is imposed too.

---

[116] Article 54.03 of the UEFA Champions League Regulations and 6(1) of the Disciplinary Regulations.

10.3.3.2 UEFA Disciplinary Proceedings On Appeal

UEFA Regulations[117] permit an appeal against the decision of the Control and Disciplinary Body and this is what Atlético Madrid did on the 16th of October 2008.

The appeal was not only made against the decision itself but also requested interim measures, such as the stay of the decision as a match had to be played quite immediately. Such stay was given by the President of the Appeal Body on the very same day of the appeal.

As for the substance of the appeal, we have to remind that normally there is a hearing which took place in the present case on the 31st of October 2008.

At the hearing, several footages of the match were displayed as well as some witnesses were heard, among them players (from both clubs), the French journalist, the UEFA Security Officer, etc....

The Appeal body decided that the club is the sole responsible for all the incidents, including those where the Spanish Police was present and overacted.

As the club has made its registration in the Champions League, he had engaged itself to fulfill all and every duties of the UEFA Regulations and that even an action by the Police is still the club's responsibility and that if the club thinks that the Police is responsible it should present a claim against it or the Spanish State.

As for the banner, the Appeal Body insists that the banner is not racist (according to the FARE booklet as the skull wears a "bandana" on it) and, what is more important in my opinion is that Atlético Madrid failed in the search of the banner when the OM fans entered the stadium. This was the main problem for the Spanish club and subsequently the club should have informed UEFA of the banner and in any case should have put the police in contact with UEFA in order to communicate with the French supporters and try to avoid the clash that finally occurred.

On the racism issue, the facts were also clear for the Appeal Body and the "KUN, KUN, KUN" chants were not evident and, on the contrary, the declarations of the players Mandanda and Niang and the French journalist were credible.

Anyhow, the UEFA representatives present at the match and at the hearing did not recognized clearly the monkey noises.

As for the disabled supporters, the duty of security was not fulfilled by Atlético Madrid and they have put them in an erroneous place in the stadium and that a bottle was thrown to them.

But, finally, the Appeal Body decided that the previous decision was excessive and then that the three matches ban of the club and to be reduced to two only, but to be disputed in the Calderon stadium instead of in a stadium situated 300 km away from Madrid. The fine remained the same of 150,000 EUR and as permitted in the appeal proceedings, Atlético was to support costs of such appeal.

---

[117] Article 48 of the Disciplinary Regulations.

Then, at least Atlético Madrid received a lesser sanction (2 instead of 3 matches), the deferred match to be for a probational period of 2 years instead of 5, and the matches to be played in Madrid (within close doors anyway) instead of 300 km away from it.

Nevertheless, the Spanish club decided to appeal before the CAS[118] which was done on the 13th of November 2008 and as the proceedings were urgent, the hearing took place on the 19th of November.

10.3.4 CAS Award

The hearing was attended by Atlético Madrid as the Appellant and UEFA as the Respondent, together with a number of witnesses, including football players of both teams, the French journalist, UEFA representatives at the match and the President of the disabled supporters association.

10.3.4.1 Atlético's Misbehaviour and Responsibility in the Spanish Police Action

The first error was that the club did not prevent the banner that started all the mess to enter and according to the UEFA Security Regulations[119] the club has the duty to search all the spectators before their entry to the stadium.

If the search had been done in a correct way, the banner would not have been permitted and, quite surely, the incidents would not have taken place:

> if the banner had a racist content, it should not have entered into the stadium.[120]

Then, and again, the UEFA Disciplinary Regulations brings a direct and objective liability to the home clubs and Atlético Madrid should have referred to UEFA responsible instead of to the police when the banner was showed and "the private security of the club tried to remove the banner with the sign of a skull".[121] This was the second error of Atlético Madrid.

If the private police was not able to remove the banner, UEFA would have intervened with the OM officials and representatives in trying to have it taken off, if the Police thought that it was racist, but the private security reported directly to the Police.

---

[118] Article 62 (edition 2007 in force then) of the UEFA Statutes.

[119] Article 33.1 and 2.

[120] Point 106 of the award.

[121] Point 86 of the award.

10.3.4.2 The Disabled Supporters

The UEFA officers said that the position of the disabled supporters "was not an ideal scenario to have away above home fans".[122]

Consequently, the club had to be responsible of the supporters behaviour as for putting the disabled supporters in a place where they could be hit, as it was quite done with a half full bottle.[123]

10.3.4.3 The Racism Issue

As for the racism, the first thing that has to be said is that the witnessing of the "French part" (players, disabled supporters and journalist) was given a higher level of credibility that those of the "Spanish part" and this was criticize by the CAS.[124]

Contrary to the reports of the "French side", the Atlético Madrid players who attend as witnesses (both black and one of them French, Sinama–Pongolle) declared that the "KUN, KUN, KUN" chant is current in the stadium and was what happened also in that match against OM.

The two UEFA representatives at the match declared that they were not sure that the monkey noises were that and not the "KUN" ones and then the Panel realized that the sanction shall be based on well established facts and on formal proofs and not on the preference of one statement instead of another.[125]

So, the racism issue was dismissed. But just for the sake of clarity, and even though the award did not mention it, the appeal body also took into consideration the insults that both players, the journalist and the President of the disabled supporters said they have heard directed to them (in the first two cases) or to black players (in the latest witnessing of the President of the disabled supporters): "puta de negra", said in Spanish.

A rough translation would end to a "black whore", but it is more subtle. What was strange is that the written statements of the players and the journalist had the same "puta de negra" and that in the hearing, all of them continued to affirm that the same insult was thrown to them, and finally the President of the disabled supporters also add his own witnessing confirming having heard such insult.

The problem, raised by Atlético Madrid at the hearing, was that such insult does not exist in Spanish as it should have been, in any case, shouted as a "puto negro", as firstly the Spanish language does not admit the "de" in between both words, "puta" and "negra"; secondly, as they were all men, it should have been said

---

[122] Point 113 of the award.

[123] Points 115 to 119 of the award.

[124] Points 125 to 127 of the award.

[125] Points 142 and 143 of the award.

"puto" (masculine) instead of "puta" (feminine); and thirdly the word "negro" (masculine) should have been said instead of "negra" (feminine).

Obviously, this was not recalled in the award but was something else to add or detract from the credibility of the witnesses in order to give more of it to the "French side" than to the "Spanish side" as the Panel finally said (see above). The racist acts alleged by UEFA could then not been established with certainty, a must in disciplinary matters.

Finally, the CAS had, again, its sanction reduce to ONE match behind closed doors (instead of two after the first appeal); the fine was reduced to half (75,000 EUR instead of 150,000 EUR) and the club was released from paying the costs of the UEFA bodies.

References

Bütler T (1986) Der Persönlichkeitsschutz des Vereinsmitgliedes, diss., Basel

Corbat C (1974) Les peines statutaires, diss. Fribourg

Heini A, Scherrer U (2006) Basler Kommentar zu Art. 60–79 ZGB. In: Honsell, H e.a.: Basler Kommentar zum Schweizerischen Privatrecht, Zivilrecht I, 3 edn., Basel/Geneva/Munich

Keller A (1979) Die Ausschliessung aus dem Verein, Zurich: Juris-verlag

Riemer HM (1990), Die Vereine, Berner Kommentar, Bern

Scherrer U (1985) Sportrecht—Fälle aus der Praxis, Münsingen

Chapter 11
Match Fixing

Jean-Samuel Leuba

Contents

Dr. Jean-Samuel Leuba—Attorney-at-Law.

J.-S. Leuba (✉)
Lausanne, Switzerland
e-mail: leuba-avocats@vtxnet.ch

A. Wild (ed.), *CAS and Football: Landmark Cases*,
ASSER International Sports Law Series, DOI: 10.1007/978-90-6704-808-8_11,

11.1 CAS 2008/A/1583 and 1584 Sport Lisboa e Benfica Futebol SAD, Vitoria Sport Clube de Guimaraes v. UEFA and FC Porto Futebol SAD

As recent scandals have shown, match-fixing is also an unfortunate reality in football. This was the motivation for the Sport Lisboa e Benfica Futebol SAD, Vitoria Sport Clube de Guimaraes v/UEFA and FC Porto Futebol SAD case being brought before the CAS. Against the background of the criminal procedure (the 'Apito Dourado') involving referee bribery a few years before, the UEFA Disciplinary Body cast doubt on FC Porto's admission to the UEFA Champions League 2008/09 season. The UEFA Appeals Body initially referred the case back, not denying admission to the UEFA Champions League 2008/2009. FC Porto's rivals SL Benfica and Vitória SC took the issue to the CAS. In the end the CAS confirmed FC Porto's admission. The author considers the right to appeal a UEFA decision, exceptions to the obligation to exhaust legal remedies prior to the appeal, the non-retroactive nature, and the independence of the federation from possible decisions of civil courts or national associations.

11.1.1 Introduction

This CAS award, issued in September 2008, deals with a number of interesting legal issues, both procedural and in relation to the merits of the case.

As far as the facts are concerned, it is clear that reference should be made to the full award. However, it is worth recalling here that the whole procedure conducted by the UEFA disciplinary bodies was concerned with whether or not FC Porto should be admitted to the UEFA Champions League for the 2008/09 season, bearing in mind the scandal and the criminal procedure known as "Apito Dourado", in which FC Porto and its president were accused of involvement in referee corruption in 2004, i.e. several years previously. In the disputed decision, the UEFA Appeals Body had decided that it did not possess all the necessary evidence and referred the case back to the UEFA Control and Disciplinary Body (first instance). The clubs SL Benfica and Vitória SC challenged this decision before the CAS, requesting that FC Porto not be admitted to the UEFA Champions League 2008/09. Their interests clearly lay in the fact that Vitória SC had finished third in the Portuguese championship, while SL Benfica had finished fourth. If FC Porto were refused admission to the Champions League, Vitória SC would have qualified for the competition without having to play in the preliminary round, while SL Benfica would have gained a place in the Champions League preliminary round rather than in the UEFA Cup. The present article looks specifically at the question of the standing to appeal the UEFA decision. To conclude, a number of other issues dealt with in the arbitral award will be briefly mentioned.

11.1.2 Standing to Appeal the UEFA Decision

Insofar as the procedure concerned the admission of FC Porto to the UEFA Champions League, it was unclear whether the other two Portuguese clubs, which appealed to the CAS, were entitled to contest the UEFA Appeals Body's decision. More generally speaking, in a procedure involving a club, do other clubs have the standing, as parties, to dispute the decision before the CAS?

Under Article 62(2) of the UEFA Statutes, "only parties directly affected by a decision may appeal to the CAS". Firstly, the Panel considered that the terms "directly affected", as mentioned in the UEFA Statutes, and "directly concerned", which appear in Article 28 of the UEFA Disciplinary Regulations, should mean exactly the same thing. In other words, the CAS held that the standing of a party is the same before the UEFA disciplinary bodies as before the CAS.

The Panel then examined the nature of the provision contained in Article 62(2) of the UEFA Statutes.

The Panel began by noting that the provision was not designed to limit the scope of the arbitration agreement by restricting the arbitrators' mandate. The Panel particularly referred to the judgement of the Swiss Federal Tribunal (BG Urteil 4P.105/2006 of 4.8.2006, No. 6.2). It then considered whether the provision of Article 62(2) of the UEFA Statutes was a condition for the admissibility of an appeal or, on the contrary, a question of justifying the request for arbitration. This is an important distinction. If the first solution is adopted, it means that the standing of the party is a condition for the admissibility of the appeal, so this must be decided first, whereas under the second interpretation, linked to the underlying right upon which standing is based, the arbitrators must consider this question at the same time as the merits of the appeal. After making various remarks on both possible solutions, the Panel left this question open as it would not have a decisive impact on the outcome of the present case.

The Panel then looked at the crucial issue of the standing of a party, i.e. how the terms "directly affected", "directly concerned" and "on whom the disciplinary measures have direct consequences" should be interpreted. None of these terms are clearly defined, since the meaning of the word "direct" is not explained. The Panel considered that the actual text of the provision did not provide an answer to this question. It therefore deemed it necessary to look at several sources to interpret the provision. As the first criterion for its interpretation, the Panel examined how it was applied in practice by the association's organs. It noted that, in the procedure in question, the UEFA disciplinary bodies (or, more specifically, the second instance body) had considered the appellants (SL Benfica and Vitória SC) as parties. This was considered that this could play a role in the Panel's interpretation of the provision. In the author's opinion, although the way in which an association's organs apply a procedural provision in practice may be useful or indeed necessary for interpreting that provision, the Panel's considerations appear unsatisfactory. Indeed, in order to analyse the practice of an association's organs, it is necessary to consider more than one case, particularly if that case is the disputed procedure itself. For in this particular procedure, the standing of a party was contested. This disputed case cannot therefore be used as a basis for deciding that the practice of an association's organs corresponds to a particular solution. It would have been necessary to examine several cases and several procedures in order to ensure that this was genuinely a practice rather than an isolated case. Unless other cases are also considered, it cannot be concluded that this is the association's practice.

This seems particularly true in the light of the practice of the UEFA disciplinary bodies, since both prior to and since the *FC Porto case*, the notion of "party" has been applied in a much more limited, restrictive manner. It should therefore be concluded that the interpretation of the notion of "party" in the *FC Porto* case is a one-off, which should not be taken as a guide in the future.

As the second criterion, the Panel examined the historical origin of Article 62 of the UEFA Statutes. The minutes of the UEFA Congress at which the provision was adopted explained very clearly that only the banned or disqualified club in question may submit an appeal to the CAS. According to the UEFA Congress minutes, other clubs had no right of appeal against a UEFA decision concerning disqualification, exclusion or the sporting consequences of disqualification. This historical interpretation of Article 62(2) clearly appears very restrictive, since only the party (the club) to which the measure is addressed has a right to appeal.

The Panel considered that the different sources for interpretation pointed in different directions. Faced with these opposing interpretations, the Panel thought that particular importance should be attached to the wording of the provision. This is clearly correct, for the application of a provision should be based primarily on the actual text of the provision. Only if the text of the provision is insufficiently clear and precise should it be interpreted with reference to sources for interpretation. Now, by definition, these sources for interpretation cannot include the text itself since, as we have seen, it is the text that is insufficiently clear and precise. Moreover, the Panel considered that "legislative materials", i.e. the historical interpretation, were less important than the wording of the provision. In the present case, the CAS's reasoning is debatable because the wording used in the provision was not inconsistent with the historical interpretation intended by the UEFA Congress. The Panel held that an association's rules and regulations should, first and foremost, be interpreted according to their objective meaning and not according to the subjective will of the association's organs responsible for adopting them. This prioritising of an objective interpretation appears questionable because Swiss association law, which applies here, gives associations a certain autonomy to organise themselves and adopt the rules they deem necessary. Depending on how the association is organised, certain organs have the power to adopt regulations. It is the meaning given to regulations by those who adopt them that appears decisive, rather than how people outside the relevant organ interpret them. Furthermore, it is hard to understand how, in relation to an imprecise provision containing indeterminate notions that require interpretation, it is possible to talk about an objective meaning, as opposed to a subjective one. If an interpretation is necessary through recourse to different sources for interpretation, it is because the provision has no identifiable, clear objective meaning.

In support if its opinion, the Panel also referred to Swiss association law (Article 75 et seq. of the Swiss Civil Code) to state that limiting the right of appeal would contravene the public policy rule under which an individual can challenge certain measures taken by an association before an outside body. In its reference to Swiss association law, the Panel did not take into account Article 72 of the Civil Code, which states that an association's statutes can sanction the expulsion of a member without disclosing the grounds for the expulsion.[1] Paragraph 2 stipulates that "in such cases, no right of action arises in regard to the grounds for the expulsion". If, under Swiss law, statutes can therefore make provision for the "extreme" measure of expulsion without disclosure of the grounds, and therefore without the possibility of challenging those grounds before a court, could the statutes not also limit the conditions under which an appeal lodged by a third party would be admissible?[2]

The Panel then had to examine the distinction between parties directly affected by the decision and parties affected indirectly. In other words, the CAS held that the distinction between "directly" and "indirectly" should be analysed in accordance with the facts of the individual case. The Panel referred to CAS case-law (CAS 2002/O/373; CAS 2006/A/1082; CAS 2007/A/1278 and 1279), in which it identified a common thread: when a third party is affected because it is a competitor of the addressee of the association's decision, it has no right of appeal, unless otherwise provided by the association's rules and regulations. In other words, unless the rules provide otherwise, effects that unfold only within the context of the competition itself are indirect consequences of the association's decision. However, if the association, in its decision, rules not only on the rights of the addressee, but also on those of a third party, the latter is directly affected, with the consequence that the third party must have a right of appeal. If the Panel's line of thinking is followed, particularly the fact that the effects of the association's decision should be considered as indirect consequences of the decision, when effects ensue only from competition, certain reservations need to be expressed with regard to the application of this principle in the present case. In the *FC Porto* case, the Panel considered that the appellants (SL Benfica and Vitória SC) were directly affected. It held that, if UEFA granted a club a place in a championship with a limited number of participants, that decision at the same time represented a negative decision about including other candidates for the available places. In the Panel's view, allocating or denying a place in the Champions League did not represent a vague hope for the club concerned. It was a decision on a right of the clubs concerned, particularly specified in the Regulations of the UEFA Champions

[1] For more detailed discussion of the scope of Article 72 of the Swiss Civil Code, and the limitations of this provision, which is particularly based on the protection of personality, see Perrin 2004, p. 149 et seq., Baddeley 1994, p. 98.

[2] The CAS has previously referred to Article 72 of the Swiss Civil Code (CAS 2002/A/423, p. 12).

League. The Panel therefore considered that, under the UEFA rules, UEFA was obliged to treat all clubs equally in terms of their participation in the competition. It particularly mentioned the provision of the Regulations of the UEFA Champions League stipulating that, if a club is not admitted, its place should be allocated to the next best placed club in the domestic league.[3] That club therefore had a right against UEFA to be admitted if it met all the requirements. In the case at hand concerning the three Portuguese clubs, the argument set out in the arbitral award raises a number of significant questions and problems.

Firstly, the principle that a decision to admit a club also represents a decision not to admit other clubs creates a situation fraught with uncertainty. This would mean that, in relation to a club's admission to a European competition, all the other clubs from the same national championship would be entitled to appeal since, by admitting one club, the others would implicitly be excluded. Clearly, such a consequence is totally excessive. The reference to the Regulations of the UEFA Champions League, particularly para 1.07, is also debatable. If this provision gives a right to the club placed directly below the club that is not admitted in the national championship, the same right should be granted to the other clubs who finish behind the second club, then the third, and so on through the whole domestic championship. In the case at hand, the club that finished directly below FC Porto was Sporting Clube de Portugal, who had finished second in the championship. Therefore, neither of the appellants, Vitória SC or SL Benfica, had finished directly below the club concerned, FC Porto. In other words, if these two clubs were considered to be directly affected, the clubs below them would also be directly affected in terms of their possible participation in the UEFA Cup. If they are recognised as parties and, in particular, granted the right to appeal to the CAS against UEFA's decision, they must also be considered as parties before the UEFA disciplinary bodies. This would mean that, in any procedure relating to the admission of a club, all the clubs below it in the championship table should also be invited to participate as parties in the procedure. Since the refusal to admit a club would, according to the competition regulations, have effects on the other clubs, this would therefore mean that these clubs were directly affected. Clearly, the CAS's reasoning here is flawed.

Otherwise, it would be necessary, before any European competition, to offer all the clubs in the national championship the chance to express their views in a procedure relating to the admission of a club from the same country. Such a consequence would be derived from the right to a fair hearing, which would need to be respected if these other clubs were considered to be directly affected parties.

It is even open to question whether the other clubs participating in the same competition should also have the right to express their views, since the admission

[3] The provision mentioned is para 1.07 of the Regulations of the UEFA Champions League 2008/09, which states: "A club which is not admitted to the competition shall be replaced by the next best placed club in the top domestic league championship of the same national association, provided it fulfills the admission criteria. In this case, the access list for the UEFA Club Competitions (Annex 1a) will be adjusted accordingly".

or non-admission of a club from a particular country can affect the designation of seeds in the competition itself. A club from one country may, for example, be directly affected if a club from another country does not participate in the European competition. Insofar as seeds are selected in accordance with UEFA rules (Article 8 of the Regulations of the UEFA Champions League 2008/09), and if the CAS's reasoning is followed, these other clubs would have to be considered as directly affected and therefore have the standing of parties. The CAS's definition of the notion of a directly affected third party in this award is clearly much too broad. Paragraph 1.07, to which the award refers, does not grant a right to the "next best placed club", but determines, by referring back to the domestic championship, the indirect consequences of a club's non-admission. The other clubs should therefore simply be considered as indirectly affected by the consequences of the decision. If they are indirectly affected, they are not considered as parties and have no standing to appeal to the CAS.

The CAS is therefore wrong to consider the appellants as directly affected parties in both the procedure before the CAS and UEFA's internal procedures.

11.1.3 Other Issues Addressed by This Award

11.1.3.1 Exception to the Obligation to Exhaust the Legal Remedies Available Prior to the Appeal (Article R47 of the Code of Sports-Related Arbitration)

In this award, the CAS also had to examine the requirement set out in Article R47 of the Code of Sports-Related Arbitration, under which the appellant must have exhausted the legal remedies available to him prior to the appeal, in accordance with the statutes or regulations of the sports-related body concerned.

Now, in the case at hand, UEFA's final instance body (Appeals Body) had lifted the first instance decision and referred the case back to the first instance body.

It could therefore be considered that the appellants, SL Benfica and Vitória SC, had not exhausted the association's internal legal remedies prior to the appeal, since further decisions were still pending.

However, the CAS considered that the requirement that all legal remedies be exhausted could not be admitted in this case, insofar as it did not appear possible, in view of the urgency of the situation and the limited time available before the start of the competition concerned, that decisions could be issued by UEFA's first, and then by its second instance body before the CAS could give its verdict in such a way as to respect the appellants' possible rights.

In other words, it can be inferred from this award that an exception to the principle that legal remedies must be exhausted prior to an appeal may be granted if acceptance of the CAS's jurisdiction is the only way of protecting the appellant's rights, bearing in mind the available procedures and, where relevant, the urgency of the situation.

11.1.3.2 Principle of Non-Retroactivity and Conditions of Admission to a Competition

During the arbitral procedure, FC Porto disputed that the specific regulations adopted by UEFA in relation to admission to the UEFA Champions League 2008/09 could take into consideration the facts of the "Apito Dourado" scandal, since these facts, which were contested anyway, were alleged to have taken place in 2004, i.e. before the regulations were adopted.

FC Porto argued that the application of subsequently adopted rules to past events represented a violation of the principle of non-retroactivity that should be applied in disciplinary, as well as criminal cases.

After referring to CAS case-law relating to the application of certain principles of criminal law and their limitations, as well as the specific nature of the relationship between federations and their athletes, the Panel clearly concluded that the principle of non-retroactivity did not apply to the rules on admission to a future competition.

To be more precise, a federation is quite clearly entitled to amend the admission criteria for any future competition without the candidates being able to rely on any previously acquired right. Candidates are obviously entitled to demand that the federation applies the rules adopted in its regulations and that it applies them in the same way to all candidates, in accordance with the principle of equality.

In addition, each candidate clearly enjoys what are called the "droits de protection" (protective rights), which particularly include the principles of equal treatment and proportionality.

11.1.3.3 Independence of the Federation From Possible Decisions of Civil Courts or National Associations

Another point examined by the arbitral award concerns the possible dependence of a federation's disciplinary bodies on procedures conducted by a country's state courts or a national association.

The Panel held very clearly that, in this case, UEFA was not bound by any decision taken by a national association against a club for match-fixing.

At the very least, the UEFA regulations gave UEFA a degree of discretion. Furthermore, UEFA should take its own decision autonomously on the basis of all the facts and circumstances available to it. To this extent, the existence of a decision taken by a national association forms only one of the elements that may be taken into consideration.

This award is interesting insofar as it confirms the autonomy of the disciplinary bodies of a federation which must simply issue a decision autonomously and independently on the basis of the elements in its possession, without automatically being bound by a procedure or decision issued at national level by an association or state court.

11.1.4 Conclusions

This Court of Arbitration for Sport award contains numerous interesting points and references to CAS case-law, even though in some respects, it is impossible to agree with the reasoning followed or the outcome of that reasoning.

Finally, it should be noted that UEFA has since amended its regulations on admission to European competitions, and in doing so has addressed many of the points raised in this award.

11.2 CAS 2009/A/1920 FK Pobeda et al. v. UEFA

In the FK Pobeda Award, for the first time the CAS imposed sanctions against a club and the club's president within the context of match-fixing. The author analyses both the merits and the procedural questions. This Award can be also called a landmark decision through its procedural matters. The main issues are the one of protecting witnesses through anonymity, the belated request of the examination of an additional witness and the alleged procedural errors on the part of the UEFA Disciplinary Body.

11.2.1 Introduction

The arbitral award issued by the Court of Arbitration for Sport on 15 April 2010 in the case FK Pobeda—Prilep, Aleksandar Zabrcanec, Nikolce Zdraveski v/UEFA (hereinafter "the award" or "the award against Pobeda") is a first in several respects, not only for UEFA but also for the CAS.

With regard to the substance first of all, it is one of the very first procedures that has led to sanctions being imposed against a club and individuals in relation to the fixing of football matches. The subject of match-fixing has attracted a great deal of media attention since the revelations made by the Bochum public prosecutor's office. However, the Pobeda case is totally unconnected to those revelations. It is the result of numerous investigative measures taken by the UEFA disciplinary bodies without the help, it should be stressed, of any state investigative or judicial authority.

This arbitral award is also a first from a procedural point of view, since the most important among numerous procedural questions that the arbitrators had to consider concerned whether or not they should accept UEFA's request that the identity of certain witnesses should be withheld and that they should therefore be examined by the CAS without their identity being made known to the appellants.

Finally, this award represents a first in terms of its outcome, since it is the first time a club and its president have been sanctioned for match-fixing in a European competition.

11.2.2 Summary of the Facts

Insofar as the present publication contains the full text of the arbitral award, there is no need to describe the facts of the case in detail, but readers are invited to examine the facts as they appear in the award.

Readers are therefore merely reminded that UEFA had opened a disciplinary investigation against FK Pobeda, a club from the Macedonian city of Prilep, on the basis of information suggesting that the home and away matches between FK Pobeda and FC Pyunik, an Armenian club, in the 2004/05 UEFA Champions League had been fixed. The UEFA Control and Disciplinary Body (first instance body), on the basis of the findings of the investigation, sanctioned FK Pobeda, its president and the team captain at the time.

Following an appeal lodged by the three parties (club, president and captain, hereinafter "the appellants"), the UEFA Appeals Body (second instance body) confirmed the first instance decision. The three appellants lodged an appeal against this UEFA Appeals Body decision with the CAS.

11.2.3 In Substance

For various reasons, particularly certain procedural reasons which are discussed later, the Panel carried out a full review of the case. The CAS confirmed the decision of the UEFA Appeals Body in relation to the sanctions imposed against the club and its president, but set aside the sanction imposed against the captain.

In the examination on the merits, the arbitral award contains some extremely important recitals.

11.2.3.1 Fundamental Principles for Sport

Firstly, while noting that the regulations applicable in 2004 did not contain any specific provisions on the sanctioning of match-fixing activities, the award states that match-fixing "touches at the very essence of the principle of loyalty, integrity and sportsmanship".

The CAS therefore considered that match-fixing and sports betting activities violated the general clause of Article 5 of the UEFA Disciplinary Regulations, which states that "member associations, clubs, as well as their players, officials and members, shall conduct themselves according to the principles of loyalty, integrity and sportsmanship." Similarly, the CAS pointed out the high social significance of football in Europe. It is therefore fundamental that the public is sure that all players (in the broad sense) act with the sole objective of beating their opponent and that all decisions are based on that objective (award, p. 14, rec. 76–78; see also CAS 98/2000/AEK Athens & SK Slavia Prague v/UEFA).

It is therefore clear that the rule prohibiting match-fixing activities is based on conduct rather than on the outcome of such activities. In other words, it is not necessary for the match to have actually been fixed. The result is not indispensable. As soon as club officials or players behave in a way which violates the principles of loyalty, integrity and sportsmanship, they may be sanctioned. This also means that any attempt and any action in breach of these principles, even if it does not result in a match being fixed, should be punished. Conduct that infringes the aforementioned principles cannot be allowed to go unpunished simply because the intended outcome did not materialise.

11.2.3.2 Reasoning of the CAS

Fixed Matches

When examining the merits, in particular the appellants' culpability, the CAS considered, firstly, whether the matches between Pobeda and Pyunik had been fixed.[4] The Panel explained very clearly its opinion that they had indeed been fixed. It mentioned various reasons for this conclusion, particularly the report of the sports betting expert, who had stated that the variations in betting patterns and odds for the first leg had clearly been extraordinary and abnormal, which proved that the match had been fixed. The appellants made no attempt to refute this.

The Panel also based its view on the testimony of the various witnesses, who reported not only that the Pobeda club was in financial difficulty, but also that the club president had mentioned his intention to fix the match against Pyunik. The witness statements on which the Panel's conclusion was based were not made by anyone who had seen money being exchanged between an intermediary and a club representative. It must therefore be concluded that, in order to establish that a match was fixed, it is not necessary to have direct proof (documentary evidence or witness statements) of every stage of the fixing of a match, particularly real evidence that money was given to a player or club representative. The witness statements contained elements confirming, sometimes indirectly, that the match had been fixed. For example, one witness stated that Pobeda players had bet on their own team losing. Reference should also be made to the recitals of the award. It is important to note that the convergence of a range of clues and evidence, even indirect, can be sufficient to justify the decision of disciplinary bodies required to rule on possible match-fixing. Finally, the Panel stated that the degree of proof required should be the same as in doping cases, i.e. "to the comfortable satisfaction of the Court having in mind the seriousness of allegation which is made" (award, rec. 85, p. 17, and CAS 2005/A/908).

[4] It should be noted that a fixed match does not necessarily have to be fixed by both teams. In the present case, there was no evidence that the Pyunik club was involved. Generally, only the team that is meant to lose or concede a certain number of goals fixes the match, while the other team, which is not involved, plays its best in order to achieve the best possible result.

It can also therefore be noted that, in order to establish that a match was fixed, technical data linked to sports betting and unusual variations in odds and/or betting patterns represent significant evidence.[5]

Involvement of the Appellants

Having concluded that the match had been fixed, the CAS considered the extent to which the appellants had been involved in the match-fixing plot. On the basis of the witness statements, the CAS decided that the president, Zabrcanec, had been actively involved in attempts to ensure that his team would lose the matches against Pyunik.

As mentioned above, the Panel considered that the witness statements were not sufficient to establish that the captain had been involved.

One interesting aspect concerns the club's involvement. The CAS firstly confirmed the application of Article 11 of the UEFA Disciplinary Regulations, which provides for the possibility to sanction member associations or clubs, particularly if "a team, player, official or member is in breach of Article 5". In other words, the club may be sanctioned for acts committed by its officials. Since the Panel was "comfortably satisfied" that the president was guilty of influencing players and the coach in order to fix the match, the club could be sanctioned on the basis of Article 11.

The award also states that, in the Panel's view, it was important to underline that there was no evidence that the president manipulated the games for personal gain.

This comment in the award raises a question. If the president had said that the match-fixing and his conduct had been exclusively dictated by a strictly personal interest and not by the interests of the club, could the club have been sanctioned in the same way? The award does not answer this question directly.

In the author's view, the answer must be yes. It is unacceptable that a club should be able to escape any sanction simply by arguing that one of its officials acted in his own personal interest and that the club should not, therefore, suffer the consequences of his actions. Such a scenario would provide too easy a way out for club officials found guilty of breaking the rules. Furthermore, by enabling the club to escape any sanction, it would go against the very objective laid down by the CAS in the same Pobeda award (see award, rec. 116, p. 25). According to the award, strong sanctions against clubs are likely to provoke reactions within the clubs when attempts are made to manipulate matches. As was pointed out in the Pobeda case, the president clearly could not have manipulated matches without the assistance of players on the pitch. This shows that it was possible, within a club, to fix a match without provoking adequate reactions. By imposing strong sanctions against the club, it is possible not only to prevent individuals from manipulating

[5] The media have recently reported on the control and monitoring measures that have been implemented, in particular by UEFA, and then by FIFA, in this area.

matches, but also to encourage other club officials, players or members to take action when they become aware of an attempt to manipulate a match. In other words, it is important that clubs or associations should be punishable when officials or players are involved in match-fixing activities. The prospect of a sanction against the club is likely to encourage the club's directors and other officials to keep a close eye on the proper running of the club and to fight against any attempt to fix matches, and even to encourage the players to refuse to participate in such activities.

Finally, it does not appear necessary to decide who will benefit from the crime. Even if the only beneficiary were a friend or acquaintance of the club president who fixed a match result with the help of certain players, it seems logical and well-founded to punish the club itself.

Sanctions

Finally, still concerning the merits, it should be noted that the CAS thought that the sanctions imposed against the club and the president were appropriate. The club was banned from all European competitions for eight years, while the president was given a life ban from all football-related activities. The fact that this sanction was considered appropriate demonstrates the gravity of the actions committed, which violated the very essence of sport and the fundamental principles of loyalty, integrity and sportsmanship.

11.2.4 Various Procedural Questions

During the appeal procedure instigated by Pobeda, the Court of Arbitration for Sport had to consider various procedural questions, some of which are examined in this chapter.

Firstly, for example, we will study UEFA's request that certain witnesses be given anonymity. Unless the author is mistaken, this is the first time the Court of Arbitration for Sport has examined witnesses whose identity has been withheld from one of the parties.

A second question concerned Article R56 of the Code of Sports-related Arbitration, in particular UEFA's request, submitted after it had lodged its response, that an additional witness be heard.

The Court of Arbitration for Sport also had to consider complaints made by the appellants concerning the procedure followed by the UEFA disciplinary bodies. On this occasion, the CAS confirmed its case-law relating to Article R57 of the Code. It should be noted that one of the questions relating to this provision was not dealt with in the award.

Finally, we will not go back over a point previously discussed: the degree of proof required by the CAS, i.e. "to the comfortable satisfaction" of the arbitrators. Reference is made to what has already been said on this subject.

11.2.4.1 Protection of Witnesses by Means of Anonymity

UEFA asked the CAS if it could examine witnesses without their identity being revealed to the appellants.

During the procedure before the UEFA disciplinary bodies, some witnesses had been heard without their identity being revealed. UEFA wanted to protect their anonymity mainly because of the risk to the lives and safety of the witnesses and their families. UEFA pointed out that, between the decisions of UEFA's first and second instance bodies, the identity of certain witnesses testifying against the club had been disclosed on the Pobeda club website, which had announced that it intended to publish photos of these witnesses. As a result, some witnesses had expressly asked for protection.

In support of its request, UEFA mentioned the practice of the Swiss state courts and the case-law of the Swiss Federal Court and the European Court of Human Rights.

The CAS decided to follow strictly the case-law of the Swiss Federal Court with regard to the protection of witnesses. It should be noted that the Swiss Federal Court itself applies the case-law of the European Court of Human Rights (Article 6 ECHR and Article 29 para 2 of the Swiss Constitution; ATF 133 I 33).

Bearing in mind all the circumstances, the Panel considered that the fears expressed by some of the witnesses could not be ignored. It therefore maintained a balance between the rights of the appellant, particularly the right to examine the witnesses, and the need to protect the witnesses.

The CAS therefore applied the case-law of the European Court of Human Rights and the Swiss Federal Tribunal. However, it should be noted that this case-law applies to criminal procedures. A disciplinary procedure within a sports organisation cannot automatically be put in the same category as a criminal procedure. It is therefore questionable whether it is really necessary to demand that all the requirements of a criminal procedure are met.

In practical terms, the appellants received copies of the minutes of the interrogations of the protected witnesses, with all clues to the witnesses' identity deleted.

In addition, the witnesses were examined by telephone. Their voices were disguised. A CAS representative was with the witnesses during this process, in order to ensure that they were answering the questions alone and, of course, to check their identity, which was known to the Panel. In this way, the appellants, who did not know the identity of certain witnesses, were able to interrogate them remotely. This procedure therefore protected the interests of the appellants as well as those of the witnesses to have their identity protected.

It is possible that, in the future, the CAS will need to use the same procedure again for hearing witnesses who need protection. Since the CAS tries to apply Article R57 of the Code in a broad way, giving the Panel full power to examine the facts and the law, it is indispensable that the examination of protected witnesses should be possible before the CAS. It should therefore be possible, where necessary, to apply practical procedures in accordance with the case-law of the Swiss Federal Tribunal and the European Court of Human Rights.[6]

11.2.4.2 Examination of an Additional Witness (Article R56)

After submitting its response, UEFA requested that an additional witness (anonymous witness Z) be examined. UEFA asked for permission to call this witness on the basis of Article R56 of the Code, particularly mentioning the existence of exceptional circumstances.

UEFA explained that it had not become aware of the testimony of witness Z until after it had filed its response. It also produced minutes of an interrogation carried out after its response had been submitted. The CAS refused to allow witness Z to be examined on the grounds that the existence of exceptional circumstances had not been established.

On reading the award, it is impossible not to imagine that the Panel refused to allow witness Z to be examined because it wanted to avoid another procedural problem. Should the fact that a party did not become aware of an additional piece of evidence until after it had submitted its written pleadings not be treated as an exceptional circumstance under Article R56? The discovery, after the submission of written pleadings, that an additional witness could provide important evidence should constitute an exceptional circumstance under Article R56.

When it filed its response, the respondent did not know what this witness might subsequently say. It therefore had no reason, at that time, to request that he be examined by the CAS.

It is logical that the CAS should have accepted that this was an exceptional circumstance in the sense of Article R56 of the Code.

When a party does not become aware of the existence of an additional piece of evidence until after the deadline fixed for the submission of its written pleadings, it should be allowed to submit that evidence to the CAS.

With regard to witness Z in the present case, the Panel probably felt uncomfortable about the issue of the minutes of the interrogation of witness Z.

---

[6] Incidentally, one of the witnesses who was meant to remain anonymous declared at the hearing that he was prepared to reveal his identity and be examined in the presence of the parties and the arbitrators. He was therefore taken to the hearing chamber and examined as an ordinary witness. This witness was a former coach of the Pobeda club, who was coaching another Macedonian team when the hearing took place. A few days after the hearing, he was sacked by his Macedonian club, particularly on the grounds that he had tarnished the image of Macedonian football. In principle, the club who sacked this coach has no links with the Pobeda club.

For UEFA requested that these minutes should not be transmitted to the appellants because their content would enable them to identify the witness. We cannot dismiss the idea that the Panel faced a two-fold problem: on the one hand, it was asked not to transmit the minutes because the safety of the witness might have been endangered, while on the other, it feared it might infringe the appellants' rights by allowing the minutes to be submitted without allowing the appellants to see them.

In the author's opinion, this problem could have been resolved either by refusing to accept the minutes of the interrogation or by asking UEFA to submit excerpts from the minutes which would not lead to the identification of the witness.

In any case, it would have been possible to examine witness Z without agreeing to the submission of the written minutes.

While it may be admitted that the aim of Article R56 of the Code is to define the parameters of the subject of arbitration and to avoid the submission of multiple written pleadings and evidence, it should not be applied in such a restrictive way that new evidence or evidence which a party did not discover until after it submitted its written pleadings is rejected.[7]

11.2.4.3 Procedural Error by the UEFA Disciplinary Bodies (Article R57)

The appellants complained, initially to the UEFA disciplinary bodies and then in their appeal pleadings to the CAS, that their procedural rights were breached by the UEFA disciplinary bodies. It may be even be suggested that the main grounds of the appeal concerned the alleged procedural errors and the violation of the appellants' rights by the UEFA disciplinary bodies.

The award does not examine these procedural complaints in detail, nor answer them. Indeed, it dismisses them with reference to the rule laid down in Article R57 of the Code, under which the Panel can hear the case de novo. Article R57 states that "The Panel shall have full power to review the facts and the law".

According to CAS case-law, any procedural errors committed by a lower instance body are cured by the fact that the Panel carried out a full review. The award also points out that CAS case-law is in line with the decisions of the ECHR. The award mentions various examples of relevant case-law (award, p. 17, rec. 87).

This CAS case-law is helpful insofar as it avoids debate surrounding possible procedural errors allegedly committed by lower instance bodies. However, it does create a number of perverse effects. For example, since it does not re-examine in detail the procedure followed by the lower instance bodies, the CAS does not decide whether a particular form of procedure is acceptable or not. In other words,

[7] The CAS applied the version of Article R56 that was in force before 1 January 2010. The amendment of this provision does not concern an element that was crucial to the question being dealt with here.

the lower instance bodies and the federations do not obtain a decision confirming that their procedure was correct or indicating what aspects of their procedure were incorrect. This creates the risk that procedural errors are perpetuated in different procedures before the federations, since the CAS does not comment on such errors.

Furthermore, the notion of hearing a case de novo, i.e. carrying out a free examination with full power to review the facts and the law, raises a problem in terms of appeal procedures against UEFA decisions.

For although the first sentence of Article 57 para 1 clearly states that "The Panel shall have full power to review the facts and the law", this provision is not in line with the UEFA Statutes.

Article 62 para 6 of the UEFA Statutes stipulates that "The CAS shall not take into account facts or evidence which the appellant could have submitted to an internal UEFA body by acting with the diligence required under the circumstances, but failed or chose not to do so".

Article 62 of the UEFA Statutes concerns the jurisdiction of the CAS as an appeals arbitration body. It is this same provision (Article 62 para 1) that recognises the jurisdiction of the CAS to hear appeals against decisions taken by a UEFA organ.

In other words, the rules laid down in Article 62 of the UEFA Statutes form part of the arbitration clause that binds the parties (UEFA and the other parties). However, as an arbitration clause, it must also bind the CAS.

The CAS and some legal writers are very restrictive and doubtful as to the possibility of limiting the powers of the CAS to review cases in an arbitration clause (see Antonio Rigozzi, "L'arbitrage international en matière de sport", p 557 ff and references to case-law). As far as we are concerned, it is hard to see why the restriction created by the UEFA Statutes should not validly limit the jurisdiction of the CAS.

Moreover, in a recent award in the "Valverde" case (CAS 2009/A/1879, p. 19), the CAS accepted the need to base its jurisdiction on the rules of the federation concerned. It wrote: "The jurisdiction of the CAS to rule de novo must be based on the rules of the federation concerned, which the CAS follows. As a private arbitration body, the jurisdiction of the CAS is limited by the jurisdiction of the arbitral procedure on which the appeal is based".[8]

The restriction imposed by Article 62 para 6 of the UEFA Statutes is extremely precise and limited. It only concerns facts or evidence which the party could have submitted to an internal UEFA body, but did not.

In other words, if a procedural error was committed by a UEFA body and resulted in the violation of a party's right to a fair hearing, such as the right to examine or submit evidence, the limitation of Article 62 para 6 would not apply in any case. For in such circumstances, the CAS would be able to conclude that the

---

[8] Unofficial translation of the following : *"La compétence du TAS à juger* de novo *doit être fondée sur les règlements de la fédération intéressée, limite à laquelle souscrit ce Tribunal. En tant qu'instance arbitrale privée, la compétence du TAS se trouve limitée par la compétence de la procédure arbitrale sur laquelle est fondé l'appel".*

party did not have the opportunity, even with the diligence required, to submit the facts or evidence concerned.

Furthermore, the examination of an alleged procedural error could lead the CAS to set aside the decision and refer the case back to the UEFA bodies.

This limitation of Article R56 of the Code by Article 62 para 6 of the UEFA Statutes did not raise any particular problem in the Pobeda procedure. However, this question could one day become a serious issue.

It is not out of the question that the failure to respect the limitation set out in Article 62 para 6 of the UEFA Statutes might be considered as a valid reason to appeal to the Swiss Federal Tribunal against the CAS award, in accordance with Article 190 para 2 of the LDIP (Swiss Federal Code on Private International Law).

In other words, such a complaint could be one of the few grounds on which an appeal to the Swiss Federal Tribunal against a CAS award is allowed under Swiss law.

Perhaps this question will be answered in the future.

11.2.5 Conclusions

As mentioned above, the CAS award in the case UEFA v/Pobeda is a first in several respects.

Quite clearly, it is extremely important because of the fact that it is the first decision connected with the fixing of football matches at European level. Unfortunately, it is unlikely to be the last.

This award also appears very significant insofar as it is sure to remain a reference point for some time as regards the evidence that is necessary and sufficient to establish the involvement of certain individuals or sports organisations and, therefore, to sanction them.

This award is also extremely important because it is the first time that CAS arbitrators have had to examine protected witnesses, i.e. witnesses whose identity was withheld from one of the parties.

Finally, as is often the case where CAS case-law is concerned, the award as a whole raises for discussion a number of interesting items related to the arbitration procedure.

References

Baddeley M (1994) L'Association sportive face au droit. Helbing & Lichtenhahn, Basel
Perrin JP (2004) Droit de l'association. Schulthess, Zurich

Chapter 12
Player Agents

Ricardo Daniel Omar Frega Navía

Contents

12.1 CAS 2007/A/1334 and 2007/A/1335, Alejandro Ruben Bouza and Alberto Cayeteno Lavalle v. Real Madrid

In recent years the CAS has handed down many decisions on disputes between clubs and agents, or between players and agents. The 'Bouza Lavalle' Award hinges on the financial risks borne by agents, particularly when verbal agreements and the players' medical checks are concerned (see Art. 30.1, 2001 FIFA Regulations on the Status and Transfer of Players). Gabriel Milito should have been transferred from Atlético Independiente to Real Madrid. However, Real Madrid refused to proceed on medical grounds, unhappy about Milito's physical condition. A few days later Milito signed a contract with Real Zaragoza (facilitated by other agents). Thus, agents Bouza and Lavalle received no payment. The CAS dismissed the appeal filed by Bouza and Lavalle. Against the background of the facts and regulations, the author believes the CAS would have done better to rule in their favour.

Dr. Ricardo Daniel Omar Frega Navía—Attorney-at-law, Estudio Jurídico Deportivo Frega Navia y Asociados.

R. D. O. Frega Navía (✉)
Buenos Aires, Argentina
e-mail: freganavia@estudiojuridicodeportivo.com

A. Wild (ed.), *CAS and Football: Landmark Cases*,
ASSER International Sports Law Series, DOI: 10.1007/978-90-6704-808-8_12,

There is no doubt that this case has given rise to much legal debate on the various issues that arise therein. Nevertheless, I must put on record my strong disagreement with the findings of this panel of the TAS, given that its Arbitration Decision contains a number of legal concepts and factual analyses which make me wonder whether the impartiality that ought to be at the heart of an arbitration existed at all, and this notwithstanding the fact that one of the parties, Real Madrid, is one of the most powerful football clubs in economic terms.

I will refrain from repeating in detail the main facts of the case, as they are contained already in the arbitral findings; therefore I will restrict myself to the said findings.

However, by way of introduction to these observations, it is worth noting that they essentially pertain to the fact that Real Madrid concluded an assignment contract with Club Atlético Independiente in relation to the footballer Gabriel Milito, who was to undergo a future medical check-up. On the basis of this check-up, the contract would be finalized.

Gabriel Milito was the captain of one of the foremost sports clubs in South America (Club Atlético Independiente), a steady player in one of the national selections with a good track record, such as Argentina, and for all these reasons the Spanish club chose to sign him up. With such a brilliant trajectory behind him, there is no doubt that Milito was in a perfect athletic condition.

Finally, to conclude the summary to the background of the case, it should be pointed out that the footballer had already agreed his conditions of employment with the Spanish club, thereby consenting to the transfer (as attested to by means of the witness statement on the part of Andrés Ducatenzeiler, who was President of Club Atlético Independiente at the time of this event, not to mention the numerous press cuttings submitted during the proceedings). He was to sign both agreements (the transfer agreement and the contract of employment) in Madrid, on completion of the match that, as a member of the Argentinean national selection, he was playing in Buenos Aires against the Uruguayan national selection. Unfortunately his performance in that match was not up to his usual standard, and it was for this reason that the Real Madrid directors changed their minds and set in train all the legal devices aimed at terminating the transfer that had been agreed. Even the Spanish media gave a full account of this appalling game.

In this context, Real Madrid stated that the decision not to proceed with the contract had been based on a medical check-up which could not possibly have been taken seriously. In that context, it should be noted that *on no occasion was the footballer officially notitied of the nature of his alleged injury, nor was this information brought forward during the proceedings before FIFA and TAS.* Both of the proceedings (FIFA and TAS) concluded with no mention at all being made of the nature of the ailment. Nor was there any mention of a medical report that may have been submitted in that respect. All we got was a mere verbal allusion from Real Madrid, which was unsupported by any medical documentation whatsoever. This shows the appalling degree of arbitrariness surrounding this club's decision not to proceed with the agreement. To further counteract the major contradictions in this club's findings, the footballer also submitted himself to a medical check-up by the Argentinean National Selection physician, and no impediment whatsoever was found therein that would affect the performance of a star footballer.

In order to conclude this brief summary of the facts of this case, it should be pointed out that within 10 days of the said transfer having been abated unilaterally by Real Madrid, the footballer was transferred to another Spanish club, Real Zaragoza, for a similar sum as had been agreed with Real Madrid, both in terms of the footballer's transfer and his contract of employment. The main difference here is that this transaction was facilitated by other agents, since the Appellants Bouza and Lavalle had only been authorized by Club Atlético Independiente to conduct business with Real Madrid, for a period of 30 days. To complete this scenario, the said club proceeded immediately to contract an English defender (to take Milito's place), notwithstanding the fact that this latter footballer was recovering from a major physical ailment and would take some time before he could return officially to the game.

Faced with this state of affairs, the agents stated that Real Madrid was in breach for non-contractual liability (Article 41 of the Swiss Code of Professional Responsibility: "Whomsoever unlawfully causes harm to another, whether intentionally, or due to negligence or imprudence, must remedy the damage thus caused"), in view of the fact that they had been prevented from receiving the commission to which they were legally entitled for having acted as intermediaries for Club Atlético Independiente, after having accomplished the task that had been assigned to them. However this entitlement had been unlawfully thwarted by Real Madrid, on the basis of a decision which gave rise to two types of legal irregularities: (a) on the one hand, under Article 30.1 of the FIFA Regulations on the Status and Transfer (as applied for the year 2001) that was applicable in this regard, which Article states that the validity of a transfer contract or an employment contract between a player and a club cannot be contingent upon a positive result of a medical examination, and on the other hand: (b) the medical cause advanced by Real Madrid was arbitrary in every meaning of the word, since no information whatsoever was provided, neither to the player, to Club Atlético Independiente, nor to the agents, regarding what future medical injury they were referring to, given that on no occasion were they informed as to the scientific basis for their decision. Let it be repeated that throughout the entire proceedings before FIFA and TAS, impossible as it may seem to be, the European club never made any reference to the type of injury that would justify its discontinuation decision. Moreover one would presume that a high-quality footballer such as Milito would be in a good physical condition, so that the party that ought to prove irrefutably that this was not the case was the party citing the alleged physical ailment (in this case, Real Madrid). There is no doubt whatsoever that it was up to the European club to prove conclusively that its decision was based on medical factors. One would presume that the player was in an optimum physical condition, and this presumption can only be negated if the other party can prove the contrary to be the case. Therefore neither the footballer, Club Atlético Independiente, nor the complainant agents were under any obligation to prove that the footballer was in prime physical condition. The onus of proof regarding a matter that has been unsupported by facts ought to be on the party making the allegation; in other words, Real Madrid should have established during these proceedings that their discontinuation decision regarding the transfer contract was warranted on the basis of a specific medical report, a report which in actual fact it failed to produce at any stage during the proceedings. Having failed to produce such a report, the legal act on which it based its unilateral decision to abate the contract becomes arbitrary, and thus unlawful.

In view of the logical brief nature of these observations, I will proceed to reflect on the various salient points of conflict raised in the issue concerning the fact that the transfer contract had not been signed by the agents and that consequently, under the Players' Agents Regulations as interpreted by FIFA and TAS, the agents would not be entitled to their remuneration unless they could prove that they had performed their task. In that regard, the witness Ducatenzeiler, in his acknowledged capacity as president of the club who assigned the agents, stated unequivocally that it was Lavalle and Bouza who had been exclusively charged with conducting business with Real Madrid. This put paid to the defensive approach taken by Real Madrid.

Before proceeding, I wish to dwell on a practical aspect of the proceedings. I refer specifically to the deliberate and non-meticulous fractionalization that the panel promoted in its findings on the statement of the said witness. This was an exhaustive statement that had been examined in-depth by the panel, yet when it proceeded to incorporate this in its findings, it was biased in its selection, completely molding it to what the arbitration tribunal wished to justify, while failing to take this statement in its entirety because it was clearly in conflict with what the arbitrators wished to uphold in their findings. In that regard, I need not mention the all but shameful attitude of the arbitrator put forward by Real Madrid, Mr Fernández-Ballesteros (also a Spanish national), who in his behavior appeared to be performing the task of the lawyer representing the other part (the Respondents), to such an extent that at the hearing, the President of the Tribunal was obliged to draw his attention to this tendentious behavior, requesting that he modify his attitude.

In doubting the impartiality of the panel, I refer to para 61 of the Arbitration Findings which contains a reasoning that is so absurd as to make us suspect that the final decision was founded on sinister motives. I refer to the argument put forward by the agents, who asked: "how could it be possible that within days of the refusal by Real Madrid to proceed on medical grounds, the same footballer passed another medical check-up without any problems, with his new employer, Real Zaragoza?" Faced with this line of questioning, the panel contended that "the fact that the footballer was signed up without delay by Real Zaragoza does not have any evidential value either because the risk tendency concerning two subjects in the same situation could be very different, and in any event there is no record in the proceedings as to whether or not the player was subject to a medical check-up by the Real Zaragoza physicians". The palpable failure of such an argument in legal terms is all too obvious. How could they presume within reason that Real Zaragoza failed to conduct an exhaustive medical check-up on the player, particularly in view of his recent failure to obtain an important transfer on medical grounds? Evidently, the said medical check-up did take place, and was obviously passed by the footballer, thus securing the contract with the Real Zaragoza club.

Another item for debate concerned the argument that even if the transfer contract had been endorsed by both clubs, it had not been signed by the footballer, given his absence from the country in which the agreement had been concluded. Notwithstanding this and having regard to the press cuttings submitted in evidence, and likewise on the basis of witness testimony, it was quite clear that the player had given his consent to the transfer contract (a matter which was not even contested by the Respondents), and to the payment conditions provided for in the contract of employment. In view of the acceptance by FIFA and TAS of the validity of players' contracts that were concluded verbally, the player's clear intention has been established in this regard and the absence of a signature would not constitute an impediment to his acceptance of the said transfer. Therefore the transfer contract was perfectly intact and had entered into effect. In that context, the contractual clause which makes the validity of the agreement subject to a condition should be voided because this is totally prohibited under the FIFA Regulations (passing of a medical check-up after signing the transfer contract).

The panel's interpretation of the provisions of Article 30.1 of the said FIFA Regulations (para 51 of the Arbitration Findings, first part) is an obvious exercise in legal science-fiction as it accords the said rule with something that it fails to establish. It invents a line of reasoning which is not contained in the Regulations at all. The text of the provision is plain and to the point and cannot be interpreted to mean the contrary. More particularly so given that in this case the footballer had given his consent and that by its unlawful act, the club prevented him from signing the agreement afterward when the footballer was in an actual position to do so (on completion of his commitment to the national selection).

On the basis of what has been argued up to this point concerning what amounts to a double unlawful act on the part of Real Madrid (on the one hand, abatement of the transfer contract on unfounded and arbitrary grounds [unsupported by any medical report], and on the other hand its setting down of a condition that was void under the said FIFA Regulations), it is clear that Real Madrid should compensate the loss and damage it caused to a third party, in this case the agents who had appropriately performed their tasks and who consequently were denied their right to receive their remuneration from Club Atlético Independiente, i.e. the club that contracted their services, and which had no hand or part in the discontinuation decision concerning the transfer; in fact it rigorously opposed the abatement decision on the part of Real Madrid (as evidenced by the witness statement from Mr. Ducatenzeiler and by the press cuttings submitted in the proceedings).

Finally, para 69 of the Arbitration Decision states that in any event a claim for loss or damage would have to be made against Club Atlético Independiente because this was the party that had a contractual obligation toward the agents. The scenario set out in the Arbitration Decision was that in not having sued Real Madrid, the Argentinean club had collapsed the causal connection, thereby obviating any causality between Real Madrid and Lavalle and Bouza.

This theory ought to be rejected because Club Atlético Independiente had no cause for action against Real Madrid in view of the fact that any damage it may have sustained had been fully remedied by the subsequent transfer to Real Zaragoza. The South American entity had been compensated, and in that context was in no position to make a claim against Real Madrid. In summary: it was not a matter of Club Atlético Independiente opting not to litigate for the breach on the part of Real Madrid, rather in the wake of the new transfer it had no opportunity to proceed against Real Madrid because the damage had been remedied with the new transfer, given the monies received, which were practically the same. Furthermore, the basis for the non-contractual liability is quite clear: the author of the unlawful act should answer for the damages caused to the third parties (i.e. the agents, with whom the author of the unlawful act had no contractual obligation).

To conclude, it should be stated that this Arbitration Decision was delivered in front of the Swiss Federal Tribunal, with no leave given to appeal, since no issues of constitutional law have arisen in this case.

Chapter 13
Players Release

Pere Lluís Mellado and Michael Gerlinger

Contents

13.1 CAS 2008/A/1622-1623-1624, FC Schalke 04, SV Werder Bremen, FC Barcelona v. FIFA

Several clubs had to release players chosen for their national teams for the Summer Olympics held in Beijing in 2008. Because the 2008 Olympic Games were not included in the international calendar, FIFA issued a Circular Letter (No.1153) 15 days ahead of the tournament. According to this letter, the clubs were obliged to release the relevant players,

Pere Lluís Mellado—Attorney-at-law, MC advocats—sport division.
Dr. Michael Gerlinger, M.A.,—Direktion Recht, Rechtsanwalt, Direktor Recht, Prokurist, FC Bayern München AG.

P. L. Mellado (✉)
Barcelona, Spain
e-mail: pere@mcadvocats.es

M. Gerlinger
Munich, Germany
e-mail: michael.gerlinger@fcb.de

A. Wild (ed.), *CAS and Football: Landmark Cases*,
ASSER International Sports Law Series, DOI: 10.1007/978-90-6704-808-8_13,

based on customary law. FC Bayern Munich, FC Barcelona, FC Schalke 04 and SV Werder Bremen refused to release their players. Ultimately the CAS ruled in favour of the clubs. Among the conclusions reached by the authors is that fast and effective proceedings, and specific knowledge of the Panel's role in sports, can resolve such issues fairly.

13.2 Introduction

The "Olympic Cases"(CAS 2008/A/1622-1623-1624) concerned a rather simple question, i.e. whether professional football clubs had a statutory obligation to release their players for the 2008 Olympic Games in Beijing or not. Nevertheless, the issue was highly disputed between clubs, federations and in the media.

In particular the fact that only shortly prior to the opening ceremony of the Olympic Games in Beijing the legal proceedings started, led to an intensive and controversial public debate on the release of players. The first match of the Olympic Men's football tournament was supposed to take place on 7 August 2008, but only on 23 July 2008, 15 days in advance, FIFA issued a Circular Letter (No. 1153) with respect to the legal basis of an obligation to release. In fact, in such Circular Letter FIFA referred to customary law as legal basis, while the respective FIFA Regulation on the Status and Transfer of Players (hereinafter "Transfer Regulations") did not provide for such obligation.

Already in January 2008, it was common understanding between many club lawyers that the Transfer Regulations explicitly declare the release for the Olympic Games as "not mandatory". Article 1 para 2 and 3 of Annex 1 to these Regulations stipulate that clubs are not obliged to release their players for matches scheduled on dates not listed in the coordinated international match calendar, with the exception of a duty to release on basis of a special decision by the FIFA Executive Committee. Since, at that time, there was clearly no special decision of the FIFA Executive Committee, neither were the Games included in the international calendar, club officials did not visualize any problems with having to release players in August.

Real problems started, when the federations that were taking part in the Olympic Men's football tournament, called their players for the Games. In the case of FC Barcelona, the Argentinian federation AFA informed the club with letter of 27 June 2008 that it requests the player Lionel Messi for the Games, while the club, having finished the league season 2007/2008 only in third place, needed to play the extremely important Champions League qualification during the Games in Beijing.

And this was precisely the heart of the problem: Since the 2008 Olympic Games were not included in the international calendar, two different competitions took place at the same time, and while AFA needed the player Lionel Messi for winning the Olympic Men's football tournament, FC Barcelona, which was obliged to continue paying the player's salary, needed to win the Champions League qualification and, of course, wanted to keep the star of the team for those matches.

13.3 Discussions Between the Clubs and Federations

Most of the federations started to call their players at the end of June/beginning of July 2008. Since the clubs were convinced that there was no legal obligation to release their players, they mostly only released players that were not part of the club's line-up and informed the federations accordingly that they would not release line-up-players.

Some federations replied immediately referring to an alleged obligation to release all players requested. Discussions started quite quickly, FIFA and the European Club Association (ECA) called on all parties to find solutions and many compromises were reached within the next weeks.

However, there were still cases that could not be solved between the clubs and the federations individually. In case of FC Barcelona and Lionel Messi, the issue was very difficult: As mentioned earlier, the team was supposed to play in the qualifying round of the UEFA Champions League for the 2008/2009 season in August (on 12/13 and 26/27 August) at the same time as the Beijing Olympics of 2008. At the time, it was essential for the club to be able to play those games with all of its players (and especially such an important one as Lionel Messi) for any setback could leave the team out of the forthcoming edition of Europe's premier club competition.

Trying to defend its interests without provoking a conflict, the first thing the club did was go to the Spanish Football Federation RFEF for advice on the issue. RFEF, in turn, approached FIFA, who, on 27 May 2008 responded in writing to RFEF to expressly state that the Beijing Olympics were not part of the international match calendar; and that the release of players aged over 23 years was not an obligation and the release of those under 23 had always been an obligation on the basis of *"customary law"*. In other words, the Olympics were not expressly included in the international calendar, but in accordance with the custom up until that point, the release of players of under 23 years was considered an obligation.

Convinced that the club was right, FC Barcelona sent AFA a letter on 11 June 2008, in which, along with the response from FIFA, it informed them that it was reserving the right not to release the player on the basis of current Transfer Regulations. AFA did not reply. Instead, on 27 June 2008, AFA sent an official call-up to the player requesting that he joins his national team on 7 July 2008.

In order to prevent any consideration that the player was refusing to join his national team, FC Barcelona wrote to AFA on 2 July 2008 saying that it was not releasing the player, duly justifying the decision on the basis of the Transfer Regulations and also basing the decision on the club's own sporting needs. At the same time, contact was initiated with AFA in order for both institutions to reach an agreement, with such proposed solutions as, for example, Lionel Messi playing the first game of the qualifying round of the UEFA Champions League and joining the Argentina team on a later date. All of these proposals were rejected by AFA.

Foreseeing that there would be no agreement, the club decided to move a step further (the Olympic Games were only a month away) and wrote to the Secretary

General of FIFA to explain the situation and requesting a clarification on the club's right not to release the player. FIFA, at first, reiterated its position of 27 May 2008 without additional arguments, which is why the club asked for a detailed position on the legal situation.

On 15 July 2008, Lionel Messi reported back to FC Barcelona after his holidays and started preseason training with the rest of the squad. A few days later, on 23 July 2008 (15 days before the start of the Olympics), FIFA issued the above mentioned Circular Letter N° 1153, in which FIFA recognised the uncertainty regarding the obligation to release players, and by means of a chronological review of the regulations and principles that FIFA had issued since 1988, indicating that the tournament was deliberately not included in the international match calendar, reiterating that the release of players was an obligation "*on the basis of customary law*".

The next day, while the player was taking part in a preseason match for FC Barcelona and the deadline was reached for him to report to the Argentinian national team, FIFA announced that it would be submitting the issue to the Single Judge of the Players' Status Committee in order to jointly resolve the requests from SV Werder Bremen, FC Schalke 04 and FC Barcelona.

In late July the events happened fast. On 28 July 2008, FC Barcelona sent its final report of arguments to the Single Judge. The decision was expected shortly after.

13.4 Decision of the FIFA Emergency Committee

A very specific element of the procedures was that during above discussions and prior to the CAS procedure, FIFA actually issued a decision on the release of players. On 29 July 2008, the FIFA Emergency Committee, which-according to Article 33 of the FIFA Statutes-is competent to decide matters requiring immediate settlement between two meetings of the FIFA Executive Committee, "confirmed" the application of customary law.

The Committee referred to a longstanding and undisputed practice and "concluded" that an obligation to release existed.

It pointed out that it was contacted to "deliberate" about such obligation, and indeed, the Single Judge deciding upon above requests of FC Barcelona, FC Schalke 04 and SV Werder Bremen explicitly referred to the conclusions of the Emergency Committee.

13.5 The CAS Procedure

The decision of the Single Judge of the FIFA Players' Status Committee, confirming an "obligation to release on basis of customary law", was then issued on 30 July 2008 and submitted to FC Barcelona, FC Schalke 04 and SV Werder

Bremen the same day. All players involved, Messi, Rafinha and Diego, were supposed to play on 7 August 2008, Rafinha and Diego with Brazil against Belgium and Messi with Argentina against Ivory Coast. This meant that only one week was left for the proceedings.

For this reason and very quickly, all parties cooperated and agreed with CAS on a schedule for an expedite procedure, a practice which CAS uses quite often for such urgent "admission cases". According to such schedule, the Appellants' submissions were submitted on Thursday 31 July 2008, FIFA's response on Monday, 4 August 2008. The hearing took place on Tuesday, 5 August 2008 and the decision was finally issued on 6 August 2008, the day before the matches.

The proceedings are a perfect example, how fast and tailored to the specific event CAS can act. The fast proceedings allowed a decision within only 6 days. Since the players, however, were already in China, the clubs needed to decide what to do with the decision they achieved. Asking the players to return would have meant additional travelling back to Europe, not knowing whether the players would be able to play for the clubs at top level after the tiring journeys.

FC Barcelona decided to find a solution, which would allow the player to stay with the Argentinian team while protecting the club's interests, in particular securing a proper insurance. For this reason, the club contacted AFA and agreed on those appropriate measures in the night of 6–7 August 2008. Messi stayed, played, scored and won the tournament with Argentina. FC Barcelona, without Messi, qualified for the Champions League, won the title as well as all other titles it could achieve in season 2008/2009. A perfect story.

But let's turn to the CAS decision itself:

13.6 The CAS Decision

In its decision, the Panel first defines the question to be answered explicitly as:

> Do/Did the Appellants 1–3 have a legal obligation to release their players Rafinha, Diego and Messi to participate in the Olympic Games 2008 with their national teams?

It then turns to the above mentioned provision in the Transfer Regulations, stipulating the two possibilities of making the release mandatory, i.e.

- The coordinated international match calendar and
- A special decision by the FIFA Executive Committee.

The coordinated international match calendar was created by FIFA in 2000 and applied as from 1 January 2002, in order to harmonize the different matches and tournaments and to prevent situations as in this case. The idea was to create a clear calendar of official matches, when no other official matches could take place. If there are dates blocked in the calendar for international matches and tournaments, no national or international club competitions can be played at the same time, so there would be no collision of matches. This principle helped a lot to avoid conflicts between club matches and national team matches and is highly appreciated in particular by the clubs.

However, the second option for a mandatory release, a special decision of the FIFA Executive Committee, would not be able to avoid such conflicts, since even if the Executive Committee decides to make the release mandatory, club competitions could take place. This is why clubs recommend elaborating the calendar further instead of taking special decisions. On the other hand, an overloaded calendar would make it impossible to play club competitions. If the period of the Olympic Games, for example, would have been included in the calendar, UEFA would have had no time to play Champions League Qualification.

The same problem of conflicts would apply, if there was a mandatory release based on customary law. Also in this case, club competitions could take place at the same time, resulting in a conflict between the national team matches and the club matches.

The Panel shortly referred to the fact that the Men Football Tournament of the Olympic Games 2008 in Beijing had not been included in the calendar. It then turned to the above decision of the FIFA Emergency Committee dated 29 July 2008. The Panel denied the existence of a special decision, since there was no urgency within the meaning of Article 33 of the FIFA Statutes, which is why the Emergency Committee would not have been competent to take such a special decision anyway.

Before assessing the application of customary law, the Panel confirms that no other written legal regulation would support an obligation to release the players, since the Transfer Regulations are exhaustive in this respect. It also clarifies that the unique character of the Olympic Games might have an impact on the application of customary law, but could not itself be a legal basis for the release of players.

The essential part of the CAS decision is the assessment and exhaustive clarification on the application of customary law in sports. There is no doubt that the general principle of customary law can also apply to the regulations of sports federations (e.g. CAS 2004/A/589 *SK Rapid Wien v FC Crvena Zvevda & FIFA*). However, there are three basic requirements that have to met for such application, i.e.

- a loophole in the law, which may be supplemented by customary law
- a constant and consistent practice (*inveterata consuetudo*) and
- a conviction of the members that the practice is binding (*opinio necessitatis*).

Without a loophole, customary law cannot apply. The Panel makes quite clear that customary law may only complement or help to interpret sports regulations. It cannot apply *contra legem*. If there is a specific rule on the legal question to be answered, customary law cannot derogate such rule. The Panel did not further investigate the existence of a loophole at this stage, since the other requirements for customary law did not apply. If it had investigated further, it would have probably come to the conclusion that already this requirement was missing. As outlined earlier, Article 1 para. 2 and 3 of Annex 1 to the Transfer Regulations clearly state that clubs are not obliged to release their players for matches scheduled on dates not listed in the coordinated international match calendar, with the exception of a duty to release on basis of a special decision by the FIFA Executive Committee. A loophole would have only existed, if the regulations did not foresee any legal consequence for matches not listed in the calendar or not subject to a special decision. Then, maybe customary law could explain the legal consequence of such fact. However, the regulations clearly say, what the legal consequence is, i.e. that "it is not compulsory to release players" for such matches. Any application of customary law, leading to a compulsory release, would be *contra legem.*

With respect to the constant and consistent practice, the Panel analyzed the Parties submissions on past Olympic Games. If there had been a consistent practice to release players, even without the clubs' will to do so and even if there was no integration in the calendar or a special decision, there could have been such practice. But the Appellants outlined that

- at least at the Olympic Games in Athens 2004, FIFA included the Olympic Football Tournament in the calendar and
- on many occasions, the Technical Reports of FIFA on the Games reported problems with clubs that didn't release their players, without FIFA sanctioning them.

The fact that many clubs released their players voluntarily to the Games could, on the other hand, only show a constant practice of *voluntary* release, while it was quite clear that a *compulsory* release was not applied, neither by the clubs, nor by FIFA. On this basis, the Panel concluded that there was no constant and consistent practice.

And also the third requirement, a conviction of the members that the practice is binding, could not be established by the Panel. A consistent practice could only lead to the existence of customary law, if the members of the respective sports organization consider such practice as mandatory. Since a FIFA regulation was concerned, the Panel examined, as far as submitted by the Parties, the conviction of FIFA's members, i.e. the national associations' and their members', the clubs'. Besides the above mentioned fact that many clubs refused to release players in the past, the Panel explicitly refers to a letter by the German Football Federation DFB of 17 July 2008, which it sent to the Brazilian Federation CBF. In such letter, DFB states that it did not see any legal basis for a mandatory release, which is why even amongst FIFA's direct members, the issue was not clear at all, which even the FIFA Emergency Committee concluded.

For this reason, the Panel also denied the existence of "*opinio necessitatis*". In fact, none of the requirements for the application of customary law was met.

13.7 Conclusion

The case is an important part of CAS jurisprudence in two aspects: It did not only clearly and exhaustively explain the application of customary law on sports regulations. It also serves as a proof for the necessity and advantage of specialized sports arbitration: The fast and effective proceedings as well as the specific knowledge of the Panel in sports helped to solve the case only shortly before the Olympic Games started. In addition, the Panel, in its "Epilogue" also tried to find a balance between the importance of the Olympic Games and the rights of the clubs and recognized the importance and spirit of the Games. In such light, it asked for cooperation between all Parties. If, for example, Messi would wish to play for Argentina, the Parties should try to find a solution. They did. They won.

Chapter 14
Stay of Execution

Stephen Sampson

Contents

14.1 CAS 2009/A/1880 and 1881 FC Sion & Essam El-Hadary v. FIFA & Al-Ahly Sporting Club CAS 2009/A/1976 and 1977 Chelsea Football Club & Gaël Kakuta v. SASP Racing Club de Lens & Association Racing Club De Lens & FIFA

Controversies between players and clubs often lead to decisions of the FIFA Dispute Resolution Chamber which include financial remedy. This can entail serious consequences both players and clubs. Banning a player or a club from participating in official

Stephen Sampson—Partner, Attorney-at-law, Squire, Sanders & Dempsey (UK) LLP.

S. Sampson (✉)
London, UK
e-mail: stephen.sampson@ssd.com

A. Wild (ed.), *CAS and Football: Landmark Cases*,
ASSER International Sports Law Series, DOI: 10.1007/978-90-6704-808-8_14,

matches/tournaments, imposing a life ban (as in the case of Ukrainian referee Oleg Oriekhov) or ordering that compensation be paid are just a few examples. The author describes how an appellant can ensure that the financial order is not enforced and the disciplinary sanction is not served pending the outcome of the appeal. With reference to the latest CAS jurisprudence—FC Sion & Essam El Hadary v FIFA & Al-Ahly Sporting Club (CAS 2009/A/1880 & 1881) and Chelsea Football Club & Gaël Kakuta v SASP Racing Club de Lens & Association Racing Club De Lens & FIFA (CAS 2009/A/1976 & 1977)—Stephen Sampson introduces significant principles to serve as guidelines for a stay of execution.

14.2 Introduction

In disputes between players and clubs decisions of the FIFA Dispute Resolution Chamber may contain a financial remedy, such as an order to pay compensation, and/or a disciplinary sanction, such as a ban on a player from participation in official matches or a ban on a club registering new players for two transfer windows. Having taken a decision to challenge the order of the FIFA DRC, it is likely to be of financial and practical importance to an appellant to ensure that the financial order is not enforced and the disciplinary sanction is not served pending the outcome of the appeal. Despite the importance of securing any necessary stay of execution, the procedure and decisions on such matters are not necessarily well known and matters are still contested that might otherwise be dealt with by consent.

The purpose of this commentary is to set out some of the relevant principles and jurisprudence, by reference to two decisions from the FIFA DRC of summer 2009 that were the subject of appeals to the CAS and resolved in 2010, *FC Sion & Essam El-Hadary v FIFA & Al-Ahly Sporting Club*[1] and *Chelsea Football Club & Gaël Kakuta v SASP Racing Club de Lens & Association Racing Club De Lens & FIFA.*[2] In both cases, in order to protect their positions the appellant clubs and players secured the necessary stays of execution of the sporting sanctions pending the outcome of the appeals.

14.3 FC Sion

In the FC Sion case it was alleged that the Swiss club FC Sion/Olympique de Alpes SA entered into an employment contract with the very successful Egyptian goalkeeper Essam El-Hadary contrary to an employment contract between the player and Al-Ahly Sporting Club from Egypt. The FIFA DRC rendered its

[1] CAS 2009/A/1880 and 1881.

[2] CAS 2009/A/1976 and 1977.

decision[3] that the player was in breach of contract without just cause during the protected period and that the new club had induced the breach of contract. Consequently, compensation of €900,000 was ordered to be paid by the new club and player jointly and severally, the player was sanctioned with a restriction of four months on participating in official matches,[4] and the new club was sanctioned with a restriction on registering any new players for the next two entire registration periods.[5] On 18 June 2009 both the player and the club filed their Statements of Appeal with the CAS and requested an interim stay of the FIFA DRC Decision. On 7 July 2009, before the CAS arbitration panel was constituted, the Deputy President of the Appeals Arbitration Division of the CAS granted both applications for stays of the FIFA DRC. Finally, by decision of 1 June 2010, the CAS determined that the appeal filed purportedly on behalf of FC Sion was inadmissible and the player's appeal as to liability failed, thus the stays on the imposition of the disciplinary sanctions were lifted.

14.4 RC Lens

In the RC Lens case it was alleged that Chelsea entered into an employment contract with the French player Gaël Kakuta while he was under contract with RC Lens. The FIFA DRC rendered its decision[6] that the player was in breach of contract without just cause during the protected period and that the new club had induced the breach of contract. Consequently compensation was ordered to be paid by the new club and the player jointly and severally, the player was sanctioned with a restriction of four months on participating in official matches, and the new club was sanctioned with a restriction on registering any new players for the next two entire registration periods. On 16 October 2009 both the club and the player filed their Statements of Appeal with the CAS and requested an interim stay of the disciplinary sanctions imposed by the FIFA DRC. By order of 5 November 2009 the President of the Appeals Division of the CAS granted both applications for stays of the FIFA DRC Decision. Finally by Award by Consent of 4 February 2010 the sanctions were overturned following the acknowledgment by RC Lens that the alleged contract between the player and the club was not valid, thus there had been not contract to breach and no liability for inducing a breach.

[3] Decision of 16 April 2009.

[4] In accordance with Article 17.3 of the FIFA Regulations on the Status and Transfer of Players (the "FIFA Regulations").

[5] In accordance with Article 17.4 of the FIFA Regulations.

[6] Decision of 27 August 2009.

14.5 Relevant CAS Procedural Rules

The rules relevant to an application for a stay of execution are those set out in R48 and R37 of the CAS Code of Sports Related Arbitration (the "CAS Code").[7]

R48 of the CAS Code sets out the requirements for the content of the appellant's Statement of Appeal. It provides that, among other things, the statement should include "if applicable, an application to stay the execution of the decision appealed against, together with reasons".

The CAS jurisprudence provides that such an application for a stay is treated as a request for provisional and conservatory measures, pursuant to R37 of the CAS Code. R37 provides, in part

> The President of the relevant Division, prior to the transfer of the file to the Panel, or thereafter the Panel may, upon application by one of the parties, make an order for provisional or conservatory measures. In agreeing to submit to these Procedural Rules any dispute subject to appeal arbitration proceedings, the parties expressly waive their rights to request such measures from state authorities. If an application for provisional measures is filed, the President of the relevant Division or the Panel invites the opponent to express his position within ten days or within a shorter time limit if circumstances so require. The President of the relevant Division or the Panel shall issue an order within a short time. In case of utmost urgency, the President of the relevant Division, prior to the transfer of the file to the Panel, or thereafter the President of the Panel, may issue an order upon mere presentation of the application provided that the opponent is heard subsequently.

Several points arise by way of further comment: Firstly, whether the terms of R48 to file the application for a stay in the Statement of Appeal is a mandatory requirement or whether an appellant who fails to do so may nevertheless secure an order for provisional measures at some other time can be the subject of dispute. R37 does not contain any requirement specifying the time at which an application is to be filed; consequently the authorities support the view that to fail to apply for a stay in the Statement of Appeal is not fatal to a later application. In *Ortega v Fenerbahçe & FIFA* the Panel commented "[i]t appears to the Panel that an appellate body which was denied the ability in appropriate circumstances to make an interim order would run the risk of its final decision being in vain. Such conclusion ought not readily to be reached."[8]

Secondly, in all but the most urgent cases, the application for a stay will be dealt with *inter partes* rather than *ex parte*. Given that transfer windows are fixed and cover only a limited period of each year and the practice of the FIFA DRC to provide for bans on registrations to cover the two next entire windows, it seems

---

[7] The Code is accessible at http://www.tas-cas.org/rules.

[8] CAS 2003/O/482, Preliminary Decision issued on 19 August 2003, para 8.4. See also *AS Roma v FIFA*, CAS 2005/A/916, Order of Provisional Measures issued on 23 August 2005, para 11, *"les mesures provisionnelles....doivent pouvoir être déposées en tout temps, au vu de l'urgence et pour prévenir d'un dommage irréparable".*

unlikely that a club would be faced with the need to apply on *ex parte*. The situation of a player may be more difficult, given that official matches may be played during the majority of a year.

Thirdly, the appellant may consider whether it would prefer the application for a stay to be dealt with by the President of the Division prior to the appointment of the Panel or by the Panel once it is constituted. In that regard, a time consuming challenge to the appointment of an arbitrator that would require a decision from the ICAS, may take such a decision from the hands of the appellant.

Finally it is noteworthy that, contrary to the waiver set out in R37, in the *FC Sion* case the player applied to the District Court of Zurich, contesting the FIFA DRC Decision and requesting its annulment, applying for *ex parte* interim relief, which application was rejected.

Order for the payment of compensation: no need to apply for a stay of execution.

When an appellant receives an order from the FIFA DRC providing for the payment of compensation, it will not want to have to pay the money over pending the outcome of an appeal. The CAS jurisprudence supports the appellant in this position. It provides that, so long as an admissible appeal is filed before the CAS,[9] it is unnecessary for a party to apply for a stay of execution of the compensation award element of a decision as such award is incapable of enforcement pending the outcome of the appeal.[10]

The explanation of this principle is set out in the *Fulham* case, at para 13.

> To execute and enforce such a decision [of the FIFA DRC] [the receiving club] would need the assistance of the competent state authorities. However, because of the present pending ordinary arbitration, [the receiving club] is not legally in a position to enforce the Decision. The Panel relies upon and adopts the reasoning of the CAS in its decision dated 16 June 2003 (CAS 2003/O/460, 5.3): 'The Panel has concluded that it need not make any ruling on this application. The Decision is one made by a Swiss Private association, and as such it cannot be legally enforced, if it is challenged, either before the ordinary courts, pursuant to Article 75 of the Swiss Civil Code, or, as in the present case, before an arbitral tribunal, such as the CAS (see Margareta Baddeley, L'Association sportitve face au droit—Les limites de son autonomie, Basel 1994, pp. 224–226 and pp. 309–312; Jean-Francois PERRIN, Droit de l'association (Article 60–79) CC), Fribourg 1990, pp. 141–142)'

No doubt the need not to pay out money where the liability to do so is contested will be of some relief to the appellant. However, the sporting sanction is likely to be of greater significance to both a player and a club given the impact such a sanction will have on their season and beyond.

[9] Or some other challenge to the decision is commenced before a court.

[10] See *Fulham FC v Olympique Lyonnais* CAS 2003/O/486 and *Christian Maicon Henning v Prudentipolis Esporte Club & FIFA* CAS 2004/A/780.

14.6 Disciplinary Sanction: Issues to be Assessed in Making an Application

The established case law of the CAS provides that there are three cumulative conditions that must be satisfied for a stay of execution of a disciplinary sanction to be granted[11]:

(a) the measure must be useful to protect the application from irreparable harm;
(b) there must be at least a plausible case that the facts relied upon by the applicant and the rights that it seeks to enforce exist and that the material conditions for the legal cause of action are fulfilled; and
(c) the interest of the applicant must not be outweighed by those of the other parties.[12]

14.6.1 First Condition: Irreparable Harm

Harm is irreparable if it cannot be compensated for if the appeal is subsequently successful but the sanction is served in full or in part in the intervening period. It seems likely, therefore, that an appellant player or club subject to a significant sporting sanction is able to show irreparable harm.

Where a player is concerned, if he is wrongly banned from playing he is prevented from exercising his profession which prevention cannot be undone. In *FC Sion*, the player was not to be banned until the beginning of the forthcoming season, leaving open the possibility, but not the likelihood, that the case could be resolved within the summer months. Further, while it seems likely that a player would be entitled to the contractual remuneration from his club during the period of any ban, it is conceivable that the club could challenge the entitlement during the period of any ban or that the level of remuneration could be determined according to the player's ability to participate in matches or achieve certain performance targets during matches.

Where a club is concerned, firstly it would lose the playing services of the player which loss could not be undone. Secondly, it would not be possible to undo the loss of the opportunity for registering new players for a transfer window. Thirdly the club would suffer reputational harm. Fourthly, irreparable harm would be caused to innocent third party players who, but for the ban, would have joined the club or who might wish to leave the club (but who would not be capable of being replaced).

---

[11] The author acknowledges the article produced by Tom Hickman and available at http://www.blackstonechambers.com/news/newsletters/sports_law_focus_articles/stays_of_execution.html.

[12] See e.g. Henning para 5.8 and CAS 2006/A/1141 *M.P. v FIFA & PFC Krilja Sovetov* Order of 31 August 2006, para 16.

That harm of this nature was irreparable was recognised by the CAS in *AEK Athens v Slavia Prague & UEFA*[13] when addressing the question of whether there would be irreparable harm if the club was kept out of a UEFA competition pending the determination of the case. The CAS stated: "the Court is of the opinion that such risk is self evident. In part at least, that harm is difficult to quantify or not quantifiable at all and thus qualifies as irreparable. This is so in any event for the loss or reputation and of opportunity may also partly apply to lost revenue."[14]

Further, if the harm was in fact considered the sort of harm that could be reparable, and compensated by a payment of money, it is unclear who would be liable to make such payment.

Finally, while CAS proceedings will be resolved promptly, there is a real possibility that the case could take longer to resolve than a four month period of a ban, or at least the period covering one transfer window, in which case the appeal would be rendered academic and undermine the right of the parties to appeal to the CAS.

14.6.2 Second Condition: Arguable Case

This condition is self explanatory. The only other relevant comment is that the jurisprudence provides that a party's chances of success on appeal must be prima facie reasonable and "cannot definitely be discounted".[15] The reasoning advanced by the appellant will obviously be determined by the facts of the case. Plainly in both the *FC Sion* and *RC Lens* cases, this threshold was satisfied.

14.6.3 Third Condition: Balance of Interests

The question for the CAS to determine is "whether it would do greater harm to grant the preliminary relief than to deny it."[16]

While previously a sports governing body such as FIFA will no doubt have sought to object to the grant of a stay of execution in order to preserve the integrity of its tribunal and their orders, given the recent jurisprudence from the CAS it seems likely that to oppose the grant of a stay would be the exception rather than the rule. It seems to be hard argument for a sport's governing body to win to say that the sanction must be imposed and served immediately or in accordance with its tribunal's order rather than following the determination of an admissible appeal, unless perhaps the sanction was imposed at participation in a particular event.

---

13 Procedural Order, 17 July 1998.

14 Ibid para 43.

15 Henning, para 5.10.

16 AEK para 70, Henning para 12.

The sanction is imposed to act as a deterrent rather than to compensate or otherwise benefit the wronged party and in both *FC Sion* and *RC Lens* it does not appear that the sanction was time specific in any sense. Consequently if it was later found, as in the *FC Sion* case, that the sanction should be imposed, it would lose none of its force; the player was still to be banned from playing for four months and the club would suffer the transfer ban. Conversely if, as in the *RC Lens* case, the CAS agreed that the sanctions should not have been imposed such a decision does not undermine the deterrent effect and to have permitted the sanction to have been served in full or in part in the intervening period would have been unjust.

This position was summarised by the CAS in *Henning*,[17] when it states: "FIFA assumes that the Appellant is in breach and merited the sanction, but that is the very matter that the Panel to be appointed will have to determine. Likewise, the deterrent effect of the sanction will not be undermined if its imposition is merely postponed and not cancelled. The risks incurred by the Appellant in the event of immediate execution of the decision seem thus to outweigh the disadvantages for FIFA in being deprived from such execution."

14.7 Conclusion

The decision of the FIFA DRC commonly marks only a staging post in a claim for compensation and/or the imposition of disciplinary sanctions. *FC Sion* and *RC Lens* illustrate that the order to pay compensation is unenforceable and an appellant club or player has a good prospect of securing a stay of execution of a disciplinary sanction pending the outcome of the appeal. That must be the right and just position in the majority of cases and respondents may find it appropriate to invest their resources in dealing with other aspects of the appeal rather than the issue of a stay. Thankfully matters before the CAS always proceed promptly and so the period of the postponement of the order to pay compensation or the imposition of the disciplinary sanction will not be excessive; alternatively the orders will be overturned in which case to have served any part of a sanction or paid over money not due and owing would have been unjust.

[17] Para 5.12.

Chapter 15
Young Football Players: Protection of Minors

Alexander Wild

Contents

15.1 CAS 2008/A/1485 FC Midtjylland A/S v. Féderation Internationale de Football Association

In the Midtjylland case the CAS considered the transfer of young minors coming from poorer countries. In 2006 and 2007 the Danish Football Club Midtjylland A/S transferred young Nigerians to Denmark. Against this background FIFPro contacted FIFA and pressed charges against FCM for having systematically transferred minor Nigerians in violation of Art. 19 par. 1 of the FIFA Regulations for the Status and Transfer of Players. According to this, '[i]nternational transfers are only permitted if the player is over the age of 18'. The FIFA Players' Status Committee issued a strong warning against FCM and DBU—a

Alexander Wild—Attorney-at-law, Dr. Falkenstein & Partner.

A. Wild (✉)
Stuttgart, Germany
e-mail: wild@falkenstein-partner.de

A. Wild (ed.), *CAS and Football: Landmark Cases*,
ASSER International Sports Law Series, DOI: 10.1007/978-90-6704-808-8_15,

decision ultimately confirmed by CAS. The author analyses the scope of Art.19 RSTP and its telos—the protection of minors and guaranteeing their education. Great store is set on the analysis of EC Law, particularly the Cotonou Agreement.

15.2 Facts

In the past few years FC Midtjylland A/S (FCM), a Danish Premier League Club and FC Ebedei, a Nigerian Club, established a cooperation concerning the transfer of young Nigerian talents to FCM. In the course of this agreement, FCM registered three minor Nigerian players in June 2006. In accordance with the Amateur Regulations in the relevant version of the Danish Football Association (DBU), the DBU registered these players as amateurs (however according to Article 3 para 4 Annex 3 of FIFA's Regulations for the Status and Transfer of Players (RSTP) on a provisional basis, since there was no reply from the Nigeria Football Association concerning the relevant International Transfer Certificate request).[1] When FCM applied for the registration of three other Nigerian players of FC Ebedei in February 2007, the Danish Football Association declined to issue amateur player licenses pending resolution of an ongoing case before the Players' Status Committee concerning potential violation of Article 19 RSTP.

All the players took part in the youth teams of FCM. The younger players attended in 10th grade—at the age of 16—the Ikast Youth Centre—a public council school. The schedule at Ikast Youth Centre consisted of 10 lessons of 1 h and 20 min, in total 13.3 h a week. At the age of 17 they were taught at Idrætshøjskolen Ikast (Ikast Sports School), a school that is also open to everyone. The older players attended the public upper secondary school (Ikast Sports School) right from their arrival. The players under the age of 18 received room and board as well as a little allowance. According to the statement of FCM the minor Nigerians received not more than DKK 24,000 per year[2] that draws the line for the determination of the status as amateur in the sense of the DBU's Amateur Regulations.

At the age of 17 the players became enrolled under FCM's football academy. The Danish Immigration Service granted the needed residence permits excluding the right to work and limited to a short-term stay as students. In February 2007, the Fédération Internationale des Associations de Footballeurs Professionels (FIFPro) got in touch with FIFA and pressed charges against FCM for having systematically transferred minor Nigerians in violation of Article 19 para 1 of the RSTP that says that "International transfers are only permitted if the player is over the age of 18". On 25 October 2007, the Players' Status Committee of FIFA issued a strong

[1] As the Players' Status Committee of FIFA noted, FIFA had received no request—neither from DBU nor from FCM - for authorization to register these Nigerian minors.

[2] € 3.219.

warning against FCM and DBU.[3] This decision was served on FCM on 25 January 2008. On 14 February 2008, FCM brought an appeal against this decision before the Court of Arbitration for Sport (CAS).

15.3 Submissions Made by the Parties

FCM considered amateur players being outside of the scope of Article 19 para 1 RSTP. Since the players would meet the criteria of the amateur status according to the DBU's Amateur Regulations, the transfers at issue would thus not violate Article 19 para1 RSTP.

Yet acting on the assumption that the minor Nigerians were professionals in the sense of Article 2 RSTP there would have been no violation of Article 19 para 1 RSTP. This would result from the application of the Cotonou Agreement, a Partnership Agreement between the European Community and the ACP Group of States.[4] These provisions would be subject existing EU legislation and also binding upon FIFA. The Nigerian minors, legally residing in Denmark, would have the right to be treated equally to Danish citizens. Therefore the application of Article 19 para 1 RSTP made by the Players' Status Committee would mark a discrimination based on nationality since it would prevent minors, coming from a non-EU or non-European Economic Area, from the participation in playing football in an organized Danish Football club. Thus the exceptions in Article 19 para 2 b RSTP should be also applied to the Nigerians since being professional players, they would also have the status of workers. Otherwise there would be an unjustified discrimination in the context of working conditions. This would violate Article 13 para 3 Cotonou Agreement that could be invoked by the players. In that respect FCM stressed the *Simutènkov* award rendered by the Court of Justice of the European Union, the CJEU.[5]

The application of Article 19 RSTP should be limited purely to minors, whose intention for gaining a residence permit is solely motivated by sporting reasons.

---

[3] The warning of the DBU was based on the violation of Article 19 para 4 RSTP that says that "Each association shall ensure the respect of this provision by its clubs." The Committee issued its warning with regard to the transfers in June 2006 and the pending application of the above mentioned three more Nigerian minors. The persistence of registering minor players in violation of Article 19 para 1 RSTP would have "severe consequences" both to FCM and DBU.

[4] The ACP Group of States-African, Caribbean and Pacific Group of States-consists of 79 countries. They all (also Nigeria) signed the Cotonou Agreement on 23 June 2000 in Cotonou (Benin) with the exception of Cuba. In contrast to Denmark, Switzerland is not a party of this agreement. The Cotonou Agreement involves about 683 million people.

[5] C-265/03, *Simutènkov* [2005] ECR I-2579. In this award the CJEU ascertained the direct effect of the partnership agreement between the European Communities and the Russian Federation. The CJEU ruled that the provisions set by the RFEF—containing a non-European clause—would break European Law as regards the partnership agreement. Thus Russian players have to be treated equal to European Union players.

Another application would result in an obviation of the spirit of Article 19 RSTP. In the present case there would not be any exploitation and abuse. The Nigerians would have been merely registered for the purpose of participating in youth tournaments within the DBU regime during their leisure time that means for the sake of playing football on an amateur level. Thus football would only amend the players' studies. This in turn, would enable a personal, social, cultural and educational development.

The interpretation of Article 19 RSTP made by the Players' Status Committee of FIFA would contravene the human rights, namely Article 12 Charter of Fundamental Rights, the freedom of assembly and association and Article 21 Charter of Fundamental Rights, the protection against discrimination caused by nationality.

Furthermore the strong warning would mark an unequal treatment since FIFA had not imposed any sanctions on another club who handled a comparable transfer.[6]

FIFA in turn was of the opinion that Article 19 RSTP would be applicable to professional and amateur players. Article 13.3 Cotonou Agreement as well as the exceptions of Article 19 para 2 RSTP would not be given since the Nigerian would not be workers in the sense of the European Law, but students. With reference to the case law of the CAS, FIFA submitted, that Article 19 RSTP would not violate mandatory principles of public policy and Swiss law, insofar as the Regulations intend a legitimate objective, e.g. the protection of young players from international transfers which could disrupt their lives (*cf. Cádiz & Acuña* CAS 2005/A/955 & 956).

Solely based on the parties' written submissions,[7] on 6 March 2009 the Panel concluded,

> ... that the Appellant has breached Art. 19 of the RSTP and that it was justified to impose a sanction for the registration of the Players. Furthermore, the Panel is of the opinion that the nature and the level of sanction imposed on the Appellant is totally appropriate.

In detail the relevant ruling of the Panel can be summarized as follows[8]:

1. "The Panel [...] considers that Article 19 of the Regulations applies equally to amateur and professional minor players."
2. "[...] the status of "Professional" or "Amateur" as defined by the RSTP is not to be confused with any other status, which is not specific to the RSTP or to the activity of playing football, such as the status of "Worker" or "Student"."
3. "[...] the list of exceptions Article 19 para 2 is not exhaustive and that this provision has been construed as allowing other exceptions, concerning students."

---

[6] FC Bayern Munich transferred a South-American minor.

[7] A hearing was not held as according to Article R 57 of the Code both parties deemed this not to be necessary.

[8] According to Article R 57 of the Code the remarks given by the Panel concerning the RSTP were based on the RSTP 2005, since this version was not disputed between the parties.

These unwritten exceptions need to be applied in a restrictive sense. An international transfer is therefore only legal if the transfer is driven by reasons of better education or if the clubs provide that strict conditions e.g. academic guarantees, limited period of time because of a development program between the association of origin and the new club, are given. These exceptions are not given in the present case. In the instant case the transfers were motivated primarily by sporting reasons.

4. EC Law is basically not binding upon the CAS as regards FIFA Regulations, unless the parties have chosen the direct application of EC Law provisions.

Both parties accepted Article 60 para 2 FIFA Statutes, within the RSTP and additionally Swiss Law. E contrario the direct application of the EC Law provisions was excluded by the parties since a decision regarding these provisions was not made by the parties. However the Panel asserts, that

> … an Arbitral Tribunal, having its seat in Switzerland, has to a certain extent to take into consideration the application of mandatory foreign laws where this is justified by a sufficient interest (Jean-François Poudret/Sébastian Besson, Comparitive Law of International Arbitration, 2nd edition, London 2007, N.707 c, page 615). In order to claim that a specific provision of EC Law is to be applied in cases involving FIFA Regulations and submitted to Art. 60 par. 2 of the FIFA Statutes, one has to establish that the relevant EC provisions are of a mandatory nature according to Swiss law, which is the law of the seat of arbitration.

5. Article 19 RSTP does not contradict any provision, principle or rule of EC Law, of mandatory nature or not.
   a. Article 13 para 1 and 2 Cotonou Agreement is not directly applicable in contrast to Article 13 para 3 Cotonou Agreement. The players do not have employment contracts and are not employed in Denmark. According to the Danish immigration legislation the players are students. Thus the players are not workers and not inside of the scope of Article 13 para 3 Cotonou Agreement.
   b. Since the players are either workers nor legally employed, the *Simutènkov* case is not applicable to the present case.
   c. "[…]the registration with a football club is not protected by the right of freedom of assembly and of association, Article 12 of the Charter" of Fundamental Rights of the European Union. Beyond that generally spoken there is also possibility to justify limitations (see Cádiz & Acuña CAS 2005/A/955 & 956 and CAS 2002/A/256[9]).

6. There is no equality in illicit situations. This principle (*nemini dolus alienus prodesse debe)* is recognized by Swiss Law and the case law of the Swiss Supreme Court referring to the prohibition of discrimination (see Auer/Malinverny/Hottelier,

[9] According to the CAS the protection of young players builds a legitimate objective that justifies the contested FIFA Rules limiting the international transfers of minors.

Droit constitutional Suisse, vol. II. 2ème edition, Berne 2006, pp. 501 et suivantes). The only exception of this principle marks a constant illegal practice. However evidence has not been adduced. According to Article 60 Swiss Civil Code FCM or DBU could invoke a claim against FIFA.

15.4 Analysis

The decision made by the CAS is in the outcome correct and strengthens FIFA and FIFPro in the combat against the exploitation of minor players.

(I) With the CAS one has to admit that all in all the better arguments are striking for an interpretation of Article 19 RSTP that beholds both professional and amateur minors inside of the scope of that provision. The Panel therefore correctly failed to determine whether the Nigerian minors fulfill the status of amateur or professional players.

Of course it is quite easy to understand that FCM tried to advance the wording of Article 19 para 2 b ii RSTP, that could indeed *prima facie* speak in the favor of the exclusion of amateur minors by the scope of Article 19 para 2 b ii RSTP. For a better understanding of the debate we should turn our attention to the wording of Article 19 par. 2 b ii RSTP, which is the following:

> It shall guarantee the player an academic and/or school and/or vocational education and/or training, in addition to his football education and/or training, which will allow the player to pursue a career other than football should he cease playing professional football.

While reading only the simple wording of this paragraph one might get the impression that Article 19 para 2 b ii RSTP would expressly state the exclusion of amateur minors. However as we set our sight both on the spirit and purpose—the *telos*—and the systematic of Article 19 RSTP, it becomes clear that CAS made the only correct decision. It is to assert (how the Panel did) that the titles of Chapter V of the RSTP and Article 19 RSTP purely name "minors". There is no determination made between professional and amateur minors. On the contrary, the title of Chapter IV names explicit the "professionals". It shall also be noted that the wording of Article 19 RSTP as a whole does not terminologically differentiate between amateurs and professionals, while this happens e.g. in Article 10 para 1, 15, 17 para 2 RSTP (just to call some of the numerous provisions that contain such a differentiation). This shows that the legislator was aware of the different terms while creating his provisions. He knew well in which cases he wanted to rule situations concerning either amateurs or professionals or both together. One can assume that the legislator would have named solely the professionals if he had intended to rule only the transfers of professional minors. In this case the legislator would not have used the words "the player" (see Article 19 para 2 b ii RSTP), but "professional", like he did in Article 10 para 1, 15, etc.

Furthermore the systematic and the spirit and purpose of Article 19 RSTP are important tools of a provisions' interpretation and shall be therefore also applied:

Article 19 RSTP is titled "International Transfers involving Minors". With the Panel it is to assume that this title cannot be understood without reflecting the system of the provisions of the RSTP. Thus the term "Transfer" is to be linked with the notion of "Registration". According to Article 5 para 1 RSTP this procedure concerns professionals *and* amateurs.

Article 19 RSTP was enacted before the background of the human trafficking, particularly of minors coming from poorer countries like South America and Africa. It has occurred and unfortunately still happens that mostly socially deprived minors were unscrupulously exploited by agents or clubs who wanted to make big money. Especially the home-grown initiative bears the risk of child trafficking as some clubs could transfer children below the age of 16. Starting as amateurs, the minors build cheap investments. Thus a transfer marks only a low financial risk for the clubs and agents linked with the perspective of earning a high transfer fee in the future or getting cheap labor forces earning important money for the club by a good performance on the pitch. In the perspective of the transferred minor players the situation is completely different. The risk to fail is often totally out of scale. The minors are asked to leave their home countries and to settle down in countries the culture and the way of living are completely different to what they are used to. If they do not live up to expectations they are abandoned, not knowing how to survive in a foreign country without an education and mostly without any relations to people they know.

In March 2001 the European Commission, FIFA and UEFA concluded an agreement setting *inter alia* the goal to protect the minors in an efficient way. As a consequence of this agreement FIFA enacted Article 19 RSTP. Thus the intention of Article 19 RSTP is on the one hand to protect minors from becoming victims of the said transfers and on the other hand to secure the education of minors. This education is important to enable the players to make their careers outside the professional football and provide them with a social guarantee. The Players' Status Committee mentioned in its decision on 25 October 2007, "that solely an interdiction allowing only very limited exceptions under specific circumstances could bring a halt to such a situation and protect minor players from their rights being infringed upon".[10]

Considering the wording of Article 19 para 2 b ii RSTP once more, one should consider the term "should he cease professional football" in the context as outlined above. This being said it is clear that the status as amateur player must be seen as included in the wording of Article 19 para 2 b ii RSTP as a consubstantial minus of the professional players' status. Another interpretation of Article 19 RSTP would mark a legal loophole in favor of the clubs and agents but stacked against the minors. Clubs would be able to take minors from all over the world pretending to let them play football only in their leisure time without providing

[10] Decision of the Players' Status Committee dated 25 October 2007, para 13.

them with a written contract and not paying more than the expenses the players effectively incur (*cf.* definition of a professional according to Article 2 para 2 RSTP). Such an application would completely contravene the intention of the legislator—the protection of minors—by adding Article 19 RSTP. FIFA itself insists on the strict application of the rules on the protection of minors and averred this by its Circular Letter no. 801, dated 28 March 2002. However such a strict ruling could lead in individual cases to undue hardships for the clubs and even for the minors. Thus the legislator introduced the exceptions named in Article 19 para 2 RSTP. Furthermore the Panel rightly accepts several unwritten exceptions—concerning students—as compensation for this strict ruling. Marking a further "minor protection barrier" it is for the club to prove that the minors are transferred not for sporting but educational reasons or that a development program that fulfills strict conditions is given between the association of the country of origin and the new club. No one of these written and non-written exceptions is met in the instant case, even not Article 19 para 2 b RSTP. A possible benefit of this provision by the Nigerians however is to be issued in the context of EC Law, particularly the Cotonou Agreement.

(II) After having examined the scope of Article 19 RSTP we should now turn our attention to the statements of the Panel concerning the contradiction of any mandatory provision of public or any other provision of EC Law by Article 19 RSTP.

The Panel put its scope of the examination on the question whether Article 19 RSTP contradicts "EC Law" that means "The Cotonou Agreement", "The *Simutènkov* case" and the "Freedom of assembly and of association" in the Sense of the Fundamental Rights.

Even if the parties did not declare the direct application of EC Law, the Panel is right in its assertion that it has "to a certain extent, to take into consideration the application of mandatory foreign laws where this is justified by a sufficient interest" (see also Jean-François Poudret/Sébastian Besson, Comparative Law of International Arbitration, 2nd edition, London 2007, N.707 c, p. 615).

Yet the Panel left the question unanswered whether the relevant EC Law is mandatory. For the Panels purposes this was correct, since it came to the result that Article 19 RSTP does not contradict any provision or principle of EC Law; albeit a statement would have been interesting as regards future cases concerning the Cotonou Agreement. Thus reference is made at this point to the CAS 98/201 *Celtic Plc/UEFA* award of 7 January 2000.[11] Here the CAS made statements regarding Article 19 of the Swiss Federal Act on Private International Law ("LDIP") and the determination of mandatory foreign laws, especially Article 39 EC.[12]

[11] CAS 98/201 *Celtic Plc UEFA*, p. 6.

[12] The statements in the context of the EC Treaty are based on the valid version before the Lisbon Treaty became operative. The valid provisions are named in the footnotes. Article 39 EC corresponds now to Article 45 TFEU.

15.4.1 Cotonou Agreement

The Panel examined whether Article 19 RSTP would contradict the Cotonou Agreement. At this juncture the Panel failed to broach the issue of the direct effect on the signatory States of that agreement and of the legal binding to FIFA—the so-called horizontal effect. The Panel just asserted that Article 13 para 3 Cotonou Agreement "could have a direct effect on the signatory States". This approach made by the Panel dues to the fact that the Panel firstly found its final result—the nonexistence of a contradiction of Article 13 para 3 Cotonou Agreement—and subsequently took—fully correct and appropriate to the practice related needs—the shortest way to constitute this result. From a more dogmatic perspective however it would have been preferable to broach the issues named above. This shall be done in the following.

15.4.2 Direct Effect of the Cotonou Agreement

Regarding Article 9, 13 para 1 and 13 para 2 Cotonou Agreement a direct effect is to negate. With the CJEU it is to be said that "in regard to well-established case-law, a provision in an agreement concluded by the Communities with a non-member country must be regarded as being directly applicable when, regard being had to its wording and to the purpose and nature of the agreement, the provision contains a clear and precise obligation which is not subject, in its implementation or effects, to the adoption of any subsequent measure (judgments in Case C-63/99 *Gloszczuk* [2001] ECR I-6369, paragraph 30, and in Case C-171/01 *Wählergruppe Gemeinsam* [2003] ECR I-4301, para 54)".[13] These requirements are not fulfilled by Article 9, 13 para 1 and 13 para 2 Cotonou Agreement. The terms of these Articles do not contain a clear and precise obligation.

Up to now the CJEU has not ruled about the direct application of Article 13 para 3 Cotonou Agreement. As FCM stated there is a ruling of the CJEU about the direct effect in the *Simutènkov* case. In this case the CJEU ruled that the Partnership Agreement between the European Communities and Russia would only be of a direct nature if the non-EU national was already a lawful resident of a Member State, owning a work permit for that respective Member State and where a national regulation bared the aggrieved party to enjoy the same settings of employment as were granted to EU nationals in a comparable way.

Before dwelling on the direct effect of Article 13 para 3 Cotonou Agreement it is important to read the wording of the relevant provisions:

Article 23 para 1 Agreement between the European Communities and the Russian Federation, signed in Corfu on 24 June 1994

[13] C-265/03, *Simutènkov* [2005] ECR I-2579, para 21.

> Subject to the laws, conditions and procedures applicable in each Member State, the Community and its Member States shall ensure that the treatment accorded to Russian nationals, legally employed in the territory of a Member State shall be free from any discrimination based on nationality, as regards working conditions, remuneration or dismissal, as compared to its own nationals.

Article 13 para 3 Cotonou Agreement

> The treatment accorded by each Member State to workers of ACP countries legally employed in its territory, shall be free from any discrimination based on nationality, as regards working conditions, remuneration and dismissal, related to its own nationals. Further in this regard, each ACP State shall accord comparable non discriminatory treatment to workers who are national of a Member State.

When drawing a comparison between the wording of Article 13 para 3 Cotonou Agreement and Article 23 para 1 Communities Russian Agreement one can find a small, maybe important difference. ACP workers are granted a treatment "free from any discrimination based on nationality" while according to Communities Russian Agreement the "Member States shall ensure that the treatment accorded [...] shall be free from any discrimination based on nationality". Just focusing on the wording, one could get the impression that the Communities Russian Agreement intends to emphasize stronger the obligation of Member States ensuring a non-discriminatory treatment. This perspective however seems to be too narrow minded. Article 3 of the Cotonou Agreement states that "The Parties shall, each as far as it is concerned in the framework of this Agreement, take all appropriate measures, whether general or particular, to ensure the fulfillment of the obligations arising from this Agreement [...]". Therefore Article 13 para 3 Cotonou Agreement is to be considered as having a direct effect. This interpretation may implicate far reaching consequences for the EU, however this becomes qualified by the double criterion of lawfully employment and working in the EU.

15.4.3 FIFA and the Cotonou Agreement

The agreements made by the Communities are basically addressed just to the signatory States. In the *Simutènkov* case however the CJEU laid down, that the doctrines of *Bosman*[14] and of *Kolpak,*[15] led to a horizontal effect in regard to Article 23 para 1 Communities-Russia Agreement, binding the Royal Spanish Football Association. Both the text and the intention of Article 13 para 3 Cotonou Agreement is very similar to the wording and the intention of the relevant provisions in the doctrine of *Kolpak* and *Simutènkov* and to the wording and intention of Article 39 para 2 EC[16] in which context the CJEU stated a horizontal effect.

[14] C-415/93 *Bosman* [1995] ECR I-4921.

[15] C-438/00 *Kolpak* [2003] ECR I-4135.

[16] Article 45 para 2 TFEU.

Even if the obligation to equal treatment in Article 39 EC outreach the one of Article 13 para 3 Cotonou Agreement as regards the access to a market, both provisions have the prohibition of discrimination in the working conditions in common. In the *Walrave and Koch* case[17] the CJEU pointed out that for the purpose of an effective and consistent EC Law, the EC Law "does not only apply to the action of public authorities but extends likewise to rules of any other nature aimed at regulating in a collective manner gainful employment and the provision of services".[18] For these reasons and for the sake of the *effet utile* it is to expect that the CJEU would answer the question of the horizontal effect of Article 13 para 3 Cotonou Agreement in the affirmative. However, one should consider the following.

In the *Walrave and Koch* case the CJEU stated that the application of EC Law was limited to rules that were not of pure sporting interest, but had something to do with economic activities, the fundamental idea of the EC Treaty fixed in Article 2 EC.[19] In its *Bosman* ruling the CJEU also stated: "Having regard to the objectives of the Community, sport is subject to Community law in so far as it constitutes an economic activity within the meaning of Article 2 of the Treaty, as in the case of the activities of professional or semi-professional footballers, where they are in gainful employment or provide a remunerated service".[20] One could therefore raise the question, whether the application of Article 13 para 3 Cotonou Agreement also requires an economic activity[21] and if so, whether the players at hand fulfilled this requirement. This would be an interesting topic in case the players had to be considered as amateurs. Unfortunately the Panel did not mention this issue at all. It should be seriously questioned whether the Panel has realized this issue or whether the Panel just wanted to avoid this delicate matter.

Yet the answer to this question would be too far reaching at this place. It would be worth being the topic of an own comment.

15.4.4 Application of Article 13.3 Cotonou Agreement

According to the wording of Article 13 para 3 Cotonou Agreement only "workers of ACP countries legally employed in its territory" are inside of the scope.

With the Panel it is to assert that Article 13 para 3 Cotonou Agreement is only applicable to workers who are already standing inside the labor market that means workers who have already taken the hurdle of access to employment. The term

[17] C-36/74 *Walrave and Koch* [1974] ECR I-1405.

[18] C-36/74 *Walrave and Koch* [1974] ECR I-1405, para 17.

[19] C-36/74 *Walrave and Koch* [1974] ECR I-1405, para 4. See Article 3 TEU.

[20] C-415/93 *Bosman* [1995] ECR I-4921.

[21] This could be said if Article 13 para 3 Cotonou Agreement is considered to be the corresponding rule to Article 39 para 2 EC.

"its" is to be read in connection to "each Member State". It is therefore irrelevant whether the players were legally employed in their home countries. The Panel rightly noted that according to the submissions of FCM the players either had employment contracts, nor were employed in Denmark. Furthermore, their visa excluded the right to work and were limited to a short-term stay as students. Thus the players did not fulfill the requirements of Article 13 para 3 Cotonou Agreement as they were not "legally employed" and not inside of the scope.

With respect to the question whether the players fulfilled the status of workers (that was negated by the CAS), basically there is to refer to the CJEUs' doctrine of Lawrie Blum[22] that legally defines the EU worker term. However precaution is demanded. According to the CJEU the similar wordings of the association agreement and comparable provisions of the EC Treaty do not justify the transfer of the interpretation made by the CJEU in the context of Article 39 EC, to the interpretation of the association agreement.[23] Both the association agreement and the Treaty have to be interpreted in the context of their spirit and intentions.[24] The terms "working conditions, remuneration or dismissal" *in* Article 13 para 3 Cotonou Agreement however argue for an interpretation in the sense of the interpretation in the context of Article 39 EC.

15.4.5 Simutènkov Case

The Panel based its examination on the assumption whether "the case law of the European Court of Justice especially the *Simutènkov* case would support the point of view that the Players have a legal claim to be treated equally to citizens of the European Union or of the European Economic Area, that is to say, to benefit from the exception of Article 19 para 2 b of the RSTP". However the Panel failed to make clear, that at hand, case law can only be linked to a special provision, here Article 13 para 3 Cotonou Agreement. This dues to the fact that the Simutènkov ruling was based on an agreement between the EU and Russia. According to Article 310[25] and 300 para 7 EC,[26] such an agreement takes only effect *inter partes* that means between the signatory States. Therefore it is not possible to apply the ruling about such an agreement as general principle to cases in which parties are involved who are not members of the agreement. Each case has to be solved individually.

It is therefore to be mentioned that the *Simutènkov* ruling with all its facts and in particular Article 23 para 1 of the Communities-Russia Agreement can only be examined from the perspective of a transfer to Article 13 para 3 Cotonou

[22] C-66/85 *Lawrie Blum* [1986] ECR I-2121.

[23] C-162/00 *Pokrzeptowicz-Meyer* [2002] ECR I-1049, para 32.

[24] C-162/00 *Pokrzeptowicz-Meyer* [2002] ECR I-1049, para 33.

[25] Article 217 TFEU.

[26] Article 216 para 2 TFEU.

Agreement. Thus the correct question begged to be asked was, whether the principles of the Simutènkov ruling in the determination of the direct effect could be applied to the question of the direct effect of Article 13 para 3 of the Cotonou Agreement. This is to be answered in the affirmative as addressed above. The Panels' determination of its scope of examination however bears the risk to be misunderstood. Without bringing home the relation to the Cotonou Agreement, it is not traceable for the reader—who is not well versed in the European Law—that the application of the *Simutènkov* decision is closely linked to the issue of the Cotonou Agreement and the benefit from the exception of Article 19 para 2 b RSTP.

15.4.6 Fundamental Rights

The Panel was right in stating that the Charter of Fundamental Rights is not a legal document having binding effect. Furthermore the players are outside of the scope both personally—as they cannot invoke an equal treatment with citizens from the EU or the non-European Economic Area—and objectively. Additionally it has to be mentioned that on 1 December 2009 the Lisbon Treaty came into force. Since this date the Charter of Fundamental Rights is legally binding according to Article 6 para 1 TEU (Lisbon).[27] It can be let unanswered in the instant case whether there is also a binding effect for FIFA and whether this provision is mandatory according to Swiss Law.

15.5 View

With its ruling the CAS braced FIFA in its fight against the exploitation of minors. The application of Article 19 RSTP for amateurs is of particular importance. This will be of great effect for the clubs also in the context of the home-grown initiation,[28] predominantly however for the protection of the minor players.

---

[27] However there are several exceptions caused to the opting out clauses: Great Britain, Poland and Czech Republic (the latter will be ratified with the next contract amendment) are not bound to the Charter.

[28] The English Premier League for example introduced a home-grown player rule that requires all teams to have 8 home-grown players out of a squad of 25 and came into force with the beginning of the 2010/2011 campaign. A home-grown player is hereby a player that is trained for three years under the age of 21 inside the English or Welsh club (see http://news.bbc.co.uk/sport2/hi/football/eng_prem/8255784.stm).

The UEFA's definition of home-grown players differs minimal. Thus home-grown players are players who, regardless of their nationality or age, have been trained by their club or by another club in the national association for at least three years between the age of 15 and 21. It shall be applied to clubs participating in UEFA's competitions (see http://en.archive.uefa.com/uefa/keytopics/kind=65536/index.html).

Referring to the Cotonou Agreement it is to state that this agreement does not provide for the employment market access. Thus it is still up to the Member States whether employment market access, residence or work permit is granted. However it has to be noticed that the players—coming from one of the ACP states and being legally employed as workers in the Member States (that is very controvertible for amateur players)—can invoke their right of non-discrimination resulting from the Cotonou Agreement, but not regarding the access to the labor market.

Intending to avoid the protection of minors and to guarantee at this an equal treatment, FIFA established a special sub-committee appointed by the Players' Status Committee that started on 1 October 2009 and supervises all international transfers of minors. This was announced by FIFA with its Circular letter no. 1190 dated 20 May 2009. According to the new Article 19 para 4 RSTP—that came into force on 1 October 2009—this sub-committee is in charge of the examination and possible approval of each transfer of every minor and each first registration of a minor, who has never previously been registered with a club and is not a national of the country in which he wishes to be registered for the first time. Each violation (both to the future and the former association (!)) of this Article is to be sanctioned by the Disciplinary Committee in accordance with the FIFA Disciplinary Code.

The sub-committees' approval is obligatory for each of these transfers or first registrations and must be obtained prior to any request from an association for an International Transfer Certificate and/or first registration. According to the new Article 19 bis RSTP all clubs that operate an academy with legal, financial or de facto links to the club are obliged to report all minor players to the association upon whose territory the academy operates. In addition, each association is bound to ensure that all players who are attending an academy that is not linked to a club in the aforementioned sense are reported to the association. However under special circumstances an exemption of the approval by the sub-committee can be done according to the Annex 2 that came into force with the new RSTP. These exemptions can only be granted, if minor amateur players intend to be registered with purely amateur clubs. However Article 19 and 19 bis RSTP have to be respected. The amateur club registering the amateur player is only entitled to possible future training compensations or solidarity contributions when the association concerned is enabled to prove that the provisions protecting the minors are respected. Article 19 and Article 19 bis RSTP are now on the list of Articles that are binding at national level and must be included without amendment in association regulations.

The official website of FC Midtylland still[29] contains details describing the cooperation between FC Midtjylland and FC Ebedei. However, contrary to the old version, the current website does not contain any longer information about the transfer of players below the age of 18.

We will see what the future might hold.

[29] Dated 20 November 2010.

Chapter 16
Young Football Players: Training Policies

Sophie Dion and Cédric Aguet

Contents

16.1 CAS 2003/0/530 AJ Auxerre v. Valencia and M. Sissoko

Sophie Dion

Mohammed Sissoko was trained by AJ Auxerre. According to French regulations, such youngsters have to sign their first contract with the training club, provided such a contract is offered by the club. Finally AJ Auxerre offered the player conversion of the trainee contract into a professional 'intern player' contract. However, Sissoko signed a

Sophie Dion—Special Advisor for Sport to French President Nicolas Sarkozy.
Cédric Aguet—att., LL.M., Partner, Attorney-at-law, Bonnard Lawson.

S. Dion (✉)
Morzine, France
e-mail: sophie.dion74@gmail.com

C. Aguet
Lausanne, Switzerland
e-mail: ca@ilf.ch

A. Wild (ed.), *CAS and Football: Landmark Cases*,
ASSER International Sports Law Series, DOI: 10.1007/978-90-6704-808-8_16,

professional contract with FC Valencia. AJ Auxerre thus filed a CAS case, and the ruling was eventually decided in their favour. For the first time in CAS' history the training club received financial compensation which exceeded the basic training indemnities. This compensation covered both transfer and youth team costs. The author analyses these regulations and explains the result of this decision: strengthening the principle of the free movement of young players, and establishing the training club's right to receive fair financial compensation.

16.1.1 Introduction

The *Sissoko* award rendered by the Court of Arbitration of Sport (CAS) on 27 August 2004 is an award of the utmost importance: it defends the protection of the young football players' training.

In fact, the *Sissoko* award constitutes a crucial decision for the French football and its training system since it offers new legal means to insure its durability.

The facts of the case are the followings: Mohammed Sissoko and the French Club "AJ Auxerre" signed a 3-years "aspirant" contract on 16 February 2000. Before the end of his "aspirant contract" (officially 30 June 2003) and according to the Professional Football Charter, which is considered as a collective labour agreement in France, the Auxerre Club offered M. Sissoko to sign a new professional "intern player" contract (*joueur stagiaire*). M. Sissoko declined to sign it.

Mohammed Sissoko signed a new 5 seasons labour contract as a professional player with FC Valence on 1 July 2003. The FIFA authorised the Spanish Royal Federation of Football to qualify M. Sissoko on a temporary basis for evolving in FC Valence. The FIFA Dispute Resolution Chamber (DRC) confirmed this authorisation and invited AJ Auxerre to ask FC Valence for training indemnities. In this decision, the DRC refused the implementation of the French Professional Football Charter. The DRC considered that an international transfer must exclusively be governed by the FIFA rules according to which, a player is free to get hired by the club of his own choice as long as his former contract is expired.

Before examining the contribution of the *Sissoko* award on the player status (II), one needs to briefly analyse the major point here at stake: training policies for young sportsmen and -women (I).

16.1.2 Training Policy for Young Football Players in Question

The training of the young football players has been one of the most important concerns of the French (B) and European (A) sport authorities.

16.1.2.1 An European Issue

The Presidency conclusions of the Nice European Council Meeting on 7, 8, 9 November 2000 says that "training policies for young sportsmen and -women are the life blood of sport, national teams and top-level involvement in sport and must be encouraged". The other European institutions have also recognised the importance of training policies. With the famous case *Bosman,*[1] the European Court of Justice (ECJ) states the fundamental objectives that justify a breach of the principle of freedom of movement (point 106—*Bosman*). Article 165 of the Treaty on the Functioning of the European Union (TFEU) inserts for the first time "sport" within the founding treaties. Article 165 TFEU also insists on the social and educational functions of sport. It also stresses the importance to protect, physically and morally, young sportsmen and -women.

Pursuing the same logic, the European Commission in its White Paper on Sport (2007) states that "investment in and promotion of training of young talented sportsmen and sportswomen in proper conditions is crucial for a sustainable development of sport at all levels". In order to ensure the reintegration of professional sportspersons into the labour market at the end of their sporting careers, the Commission also emphasises "the importance of taking into account at an early stage the need to provide "dual career" training for young sportsmen and sportswomen and to provide high quality local training centres to safeguard their moral, educational and professional interests."

Finally, the Presidency conclusions of the French Presidency of the European Union (December 2008), underlines the social and educational functions of the sport, especially related to the "dual career" of the sportsmen.

The necessity to protect young sportsmen and -women with high standard training policies that associate education and sport has become an European question. This question was, originally, a French concern.

16.1.2.2 A French Concern

In order to have a good understanding of the legal issues of the Sissoko case, one needs to explain the contractual aspects of the French training policy for young football players.

In France, the training policy for young football players is characterised by a training cycle that is completed by the player between his 16th and his 21st years. Section L.211-5 of the French "Code du Sport" requires the player and the football club to sign a "Convention de formation" (agreement for training).

Section R. 211-91 (*sqq.*) of the "Code du Sport" specifies which stipulations must be included within the "Convention de formation".

Thus, in France, a football player for his training can sign two types of contracts simultaneously but pursuing different goals:

- the "*Convention de formation*" establishes reciprocal rights and obligations of the player and of the Club

[1] ECJ, 15 December 2005, *Bosman*, C-415/93.

- the "*Contrat de joueur en formation*" (Apprentice, Aspirant, Trainee or Elite) determines the conditions of employment—payment... Such contracts are considered as labour contracts.

In other words, the training player is linked to his club by a "convention de formation" to which can be added a "*contrat de joueur en formation*".

As a result, all training player must sign a "*convention de formation*" with their training club.

This obligation is stated by the Professional Football Charter. In France, contrary to other countries, a collective labour agreement in the football field (the Charter mentioned above) exists and is applicable. This collective labour agreement was negotiated and signed by all, even by the football players.

With the *Sissoko* case, debates in front of the Court of Arbitration of Sport were mainly related to the scope of the French Charter.

16.1.3 The Recognition of the Importance of Training Policies for Young Football Players

The *Sissoko* case constitutes an outstanding award within the CAS case-law (A). This award was confirmed in 2005 by a very similar case N'Zogbia. This confirmation of the *Sissoko* award expresses clearly the CAS' position on the question of training policies regarding young football players (B).

16.1.3.1 The Contribution of the Sissoko Award

In the *Sissoko* case, the award rendered by the CAS is threefold.

First of all, in order to respect fundamental freedoms, it is not possible to reintegrate M. Sissoko in his former French club. Secondly, M. Sissoko had refused to sign a trainee-contract (*contrat de stagiaire*) with his training club and signed a professional contract with FC Valence. Due to these facts, M. Sissoko has violated the Professional Football Charter and thus, his contractual obligations. Thirdly, AJ Auxerre should get financial compensations for damages superior to the simple training indemnities. In other words, with the *Sissoko* award, the CAS admits the principle of free movement of football players but, for the first time, it establishes the right for the training club to get a fair financial compensation.

In this Award, the CAS concluded that M. Sissoko had violated his contractual obligations (1). Thus, the CAS developed the right of the training club to get a fair financial compensation for damages (2).

Violation of Contractual Obligations

The Court confirmed that Sissoko could stay in Spain. It could not have decided in a different way: according to the principles of contractual freedom implemented in the French "Code civil" and "Code du travail" it was not possible to force M. Sissoko to reintegrate his former French club.

After having acknowledged the existence of a contract between M. Sissoko and AJ Auxerre and its binding effect, the CAS has recognized the violation of these contractual obligations.

> 47. Il est évident que les règles de la Charte sont de portée nationale et ne sauraient prétendre déployer leurs effets dans un autre Etat. La Chambre se devait toutefois d'examiner, au regard des "arrangements" nationaux français, les conséquences d'une violation, par S., de certaines de ses obligations contractuelles à l'égard de l'AJ Auxerre. Cet examen constitue la "prise en compte" instaurée à l'Article 43 du Règlement FIFA; il doit porter non seulement sur le comportement du joueur et ses conséquences, mais aussi sur celles de l'attitude de Valence CF, dont il paraît évident qu'il était en pourparlers avec S. alors que ce dernier était encore sous contrat avec la demanderesse.

Thus, the CAS consecrates the provisions of a national collective labour agreement.

On a general basis, according to the FIFA rules, the CAS considers that the FIFA is responsible for all international transfers and that the FIFA must take into account national provisions in order to guarantee legal security.

> 49. De manière générale, il est de la responsabilité de la FIFA, dans chaque cas de transfert international, et en tenant compte, le cas échéant, des "arrangements" d'ordre national par le jeu de l'article 43 du Règlement FIFA, d'examiner les engagements pris par toutes les parties impliquées et den tirer alors les conclusions pertinentes, dans un souci de garantie de la sécurité juridique des intervenants notamment.

Compensation for Damages

According to the CAS, the damages allocated to the training club have to be higher than the arithmetical calculation of the training indemnities planned by the FIFA rules.

For the first time, the CAS allocates to the training club damages in order to compensate the loss of a player.

The Right of the Training Club to get a Fair Compensation

The FIFA rules related to training indemnities create an infringement of the principle of free movement if general interest is at stake here: the training policies for young football players. The CAS also considers that the FIFA DRC must obtain from FC Valence a training indemnity for AJ Auxerre. In bill n°826 of 31 October 2002, the FIFA plans that "in specific circumstances, the amount of the training indemnity should be adjusted in order to take into account specificities of the case in question" (point 53). The CAS also underlines the possibility for the French football club to ask for damages, a sum higher than the training indemnity, if some evidence shows that the club is a victim of a disloyal headhunting.

The Exception: Training Indemnities can be Revised if Exceptional Circumstances Happened

Based on the FIFA rules, the CAS has determined some specific circumstances that prove the existence of a damage suffered by AJ Auxerre. It is related to the violation by the player of his contractual obligations towards his training club and the bad faith of FC Valence.

The Court deduces the right for AJ Auxerre to ask for financial compensations higher than the simple sum for training indemnity calculated in compliance with the FIFA rules (point 54).

Beyond the refund of the amount invested in training and educating the player, the French club must get an additional indemnity in order to compensate the damage that was caused by the departure of the player.

It remains to evaluate such damage. The question was not asked to the CAS. It sends the question back to the DRC:

> 54. Il n'échoit pas à la Formation d'examiner plus en détail les prétentions que la demanderesse peut faire valoir à l'encontre de Valence FC ou de M. Sissoko. En effet, elle n'a pas pris de conclusions, même subsidiaires, tendant au paiement d'indemnités en sa faveur. La Formation ne saurait dès lors statuer ultra petita et, dans ces circonstances, elle ne peut que renvoyer l'AJ Auxerre à faire valoir ses prétentions devant les organes compétents de la FIFA, auxquels il appartiendra de se prononcer dans le sens des considérants de la présente sentence.

After months of negotiations, the two clubs agreed on a transactional indemnity.

The Confirmation of the Sissoko Award

In 2007 the CAS confirmed the *Sissoko* award with the *N'Zogbia* award.[2]

This case opposed the French football club Le Havre to M. N'Zogbia who was just transferred to Newcastle Club. M. N'Zogbia had refused to sign a "*contrat de stagiaire*" offered by his training club Le Havre and preferred to be transferred to Newcastle. This transfer was contradictory to French law.

In this particular case, contrary to *Sissoko*, a "convention de formation" existed between the French Club and the player. The goal of this convention was to determine the practical details of his education and professional training. The same question that was asked in the *Sissoko* case was raised in the *N'Zogbia* case. The question was to know if the player had to sign his first professional contract at the end of his training with the club that trained him.

The arbitrators in this case gave the same answer that they did it in the *Sissoko* award. The TAS confirmed one more time the need to protect the training policies

---

[2] CAS, 28 October 2005 and CAS, 17 July 2007, *Le Havre AC c. FIFA, New Castle, Charles N'Zogbia.*

for young football players. After the CAS has rendered this award, the *N'Zogbia* case came in front of the Federal Swiss Court which rejected the appeal.

16.2 CAS 2004/A/791 N'Zogbia

Cédric Aguet

With the N'Zogbia Award the CAS confirmed its ruling established in the Sissoko Award. The dispute arose when N'Zogbia moved from his training club Le Havre to Newcastle Club. In breach of French regulations N'Zogbia refused to sign a 'contrat de stagiaire' with Le Havre. In contrast to 'Sissoko,' N'Zogbia and Le Havre had set up a 'convention de formation' covering N'Zogbia's education and professional training. As already demonstrated in the Sissoko Award, the CAS upheld the validity of the regulations obliging the player to sign his first professional contract with the training club at the end of his training. However, contrary to the Sissoko Award, N'Zogbia was required to pay Le Havre compensation of € 545,812. The author regards this compensation as a 'deterrent to contractual freedom.'

16.2.1 The Dispute

The undersigned defended Charles N'Zogbia in an attempt to annul the second award rendered by the CAS, appeal which was rejected for the Swiss Supreme Court considered that the decision to appeal should have been the partial award.

In March 2003, Charles N'Zognia, a player born in May 1986—thus aged 16 and 10 months at the time—, signed three agreements with the French club Le Havre, the first being named "convention de formation" (training agreement), a mandatory agreement imposed by the French football league allowing young players not only to be formed on-field but also to receive a proper professional education, the second "*contrat de joueur aspirant*" (aspirant player agreement) and the third "*dispositions particulières*" (special clauses) according to which the club was supposed to offer to the player a trainee agreement in April 2004 and to propose him a professional agreement in April 2006, should the player's results be sufficient. The first agreement was valid from July 2003 until June 2006, the second for one year and the third did not have any specified duration.

The training agreement between the player and Le Havre stated that in case the player would terminate the agreement without cause, he could be condemned to a training compensation should he play in any other French club. This agreement also contained a mandatory choice of forum clause whereby any dispute between the training club and a player would need to be brought before the French professional league—and then to the administrative judicial bodies in France.

In July 2004, the player did not return to practise in Le Havre; he was then hired by Newcastle in early August 2004. This club requested from the FA that it requests the international transfer certificate from the FFF, which the FFF refused.

Le Havre then seized the FIFA of a claim against the sole Newcastle, procedure to which the player was not a party; by this claim, Le Havre requested that the player be obliged to come back and to sign a professional agreement with Le Havre and, subsidiarily, that Newcastle be condemned to pay a compensation.

On 26 November 2004, FIFA's dispute resolution chamber decided that it was not competent to decide upon a training agreement between a minor and a French club, that since the player had not entered into any employment contract with Le Havre, he was free to go to Newcastle and that the latter had to pay to Le Havre a training compensation of EUR 300'000.

On 17 December 2004, Le Havre seised the CAS of an appeal directed against *the sole FIFA*. By this appeal, Le Havre sought (a) the annulment of FIFA's decision, (b) a declaration that the player was contractually bound to Le Havre, (c) that the player be condemned to sign a trainee agreement with Le Havre, (d) the suspension of the player until he would reintegrate Le Havre and (d) that all persons or entities having encouraged the breach of the training agreement with the player be condemned to any and all sports and financial sanctions foreseen by the FIFA regulations.

Both the player and Newcastle requested to intervene and thus became parties.

On 27 October 2005, the CAS rendered a partial award.

16.2.2 Partial Award

In that decision, the CAS considered, among other things, that FIFA had been wrong in deciding that it was incompetent to decide upon the club's and the player's rights and obligations pursuant to the training agreement. In addition, the CAS considered that the player had breached his "contractual obligations" towards the club and stated that the parties would be invited to file a written statement "on the issue of possible additional compensation due to Le Havre, in accordance with the grounds of this partial award".

According to para 91 of the partial award, these grounds are that "since the training agreement unilaterally terminated by the player and the employment agreement he signed with Newcastle must be taken into consideration, the Panel must determine whether the special sanctions foreseen by the training agreement and/or the ones applicable in terms of maintenance of contractual stability in football according to the FIFA regulations must be applied and to what extent".

On 17 February 2006, *without filing any evidence* to support this claim, Le Havre requested that the player and Newcastle be condemned to pay it between EUR 3,700,000 and 4,260,000.

On 7 June 2006, the player rose that such plea was inadmissible since (a) the CAS did not have jurisdiction to condemn him for breach of the training agreement and (b) Le Havre never sought any payment from him, be it before the FIFA or in its declaration and statement of appeal before the CAS.

16.2.3 Final Award

More than a year later, on 17 July 2007, the CAS decided that the player had to be condemned to pay EUR 545,812 to Le Havre.

This indemnity was segregated in two, EUR 195,812 for the so-called harm caused to Le Havre for the lack of possibility to use the player on-field for two seasons, calculated according to the player's future salary as a trainee (EUR 19,812 in total) plus EUR 88,000 per year of costs to train him—which means that a prejudice was calculated by adding *non-incurred* expenses. Second, the CAS considered that an additional sum of EUR 350,000 was due as loss of chance (*perte d'une chance*) to negotiate a future transfer for that player, amount fixed *ex aequo et bono*, by *reference* to Article 42 para 2 and 43 para 1 of the Swiss code of obligations, plus interest at 5% per year as of 1st August 2004.

16.2.4 Commentary

Both awards rendered by the CAS in the *N'Zogbia* case are perfect examples of what should not be done, from a procedural point of view, on the merits and in terms of opportunity.

From a procedural point of view, Le Havre did not seise the CAS of a case against the player or Newcastle. The appeal was directed against FIFA, period. Sure, the player (and Newcastle) intervened in the arbitral proceedings but though this intervention made them defendants, it did not have as a result to change Le Havre's pleas requesting the annulment of FIFA's decision, a declaration that the player had breached his training agreement and a claim based on tort against the ones who had incited him to breach said agreement—and certainly not a claim based on contract against the player.

In addition, the CAS had no jurisdiction to decide upon the enforcement of a training agreement between a junior player and a French club, containing a clause designating the French football league as the sole competent jurisdiction in case of dispute.

On the merits, one has difficulties in understanding how on earth it can be possible to:

- consider that a young player can be condemned to pay compensation to its French training club whereas (a) the foreign club which obtained the player's services already paid a training compensation and (b) the agreement binding both parties only foresees the possibility to condemn the player when he leaves his training club for another French club, in other words only when the player competes against the club which trained him;
- whatever the applicable law (in such case French law), decide that a prejudice can be made of non-incurred expenses, which is a total heresy;

- decide upon an indemnity *ex aequo et bono* by reference to provisions of the Swiss code of obligations whereas the training agreement was subject to French law;
- use equity to fix an indemnity to cover the absence of demonstration of the prejudice.

Last, in terms of opportunity, it is a shame that the CAS considers that training agreements between juniors and clubs cannot be terminated by the player, the condemnation to pay EUR 600,000 plus interest being a definitive deterrent to contractual freedom. A junior should have the choice of the place where he wants to learn how to play football—and to learn in general—and clubs should be able to keep promising players only if they provide them with sufficient support and a future.

MIX
Papier aus verantwortungsvollen Quellen
Paper from responsible sources
FSC® C105338

If you have any concerns about our products,
you can contact us on
ProductSafety@springernature.com

In case Publisher is established outside the EU,
the EU authorized representative is:
Springer Nature Customer Service Center GmbH
Europaplatz 3, 69115 Heidelberg, Germany

Printed by Libri Plureos GmbH
in Hamburg, Germany